EMBATTLED CONFEDERATES

Embattled

BONANZA BOOKS

NEW YORK

An Illustrated History

Confederates

TEXT BY BELL IRVIN WILEY

ILLUSTRATIONS COMPILED

BY HIRST D. MILHOLLEN

of Southerners at War

LIBRARY OF CONGRESS CATALOG CARD NUMBER: 64–18069

This edition published by Bonanza Books, a division of Crown Publishers, Inc., by arrangement with Harper & Row, Publishers, Incorporated.

H

Contents

Foreword   ix

I   The Parting of Ways   1

II   Harassed Politicians   13

III   The High Brass   43

IV   Officers and Enlisted Men   69

V   Armament and Industry   97

VI   Life in Town and Country   112

VII   Transportation and Communication   128

VIII   A Navy from Nothing   144

IX   Confederate Women: The Staunchest Rebels   163

X   Religion and Morals   185

XI   Journalism and Literature   200

XII   Education   220

XIII   Negroes   231

XIV   The Collapse of the Confederacy   245

APPENDICES

A   Confederate Cabinet   257

B   Confederate Congress   258

C   State Governors   274

D   Generals   275

E   A Representative Infantry Company: Company A, Eighth Alabama Volunteers   279

Picture Credits   281

Index   283

Foreword

As the title suggests, this is primarily a book about people. Through a combination of words and pictures the authors have attempted to portray Southerners and their activities during the period when they were striving for independence. This was a period of light and shadow, of goodness and evil, of excitement and boredom, of gayety and sorrow, of staunchness and weakness, of heroism and cowardice and of high hopes and bitter frustration. These extremes we have attempted to depict, along with the less dramatic emotions and experiences that lay in between.

With the exception of some Crimean photographs taken by Roger Fenton in 1855, the Civil War was the first conflict to be recorded by the camera. Confederates had no Mathew Brady, and the South's beleaguered and impoverished condition restricted photographic activities. Nor were Southern newspapers and magazines able to employ talented artists, like the Wauds and Edwin Forbes, to sketch pictures of soldiers, camps and battlefields. But the South had some first-rate photographers, including George S. Cook and Julian Vannerson; and scores of local cameramen, whose names are lost to history, set up shop in towns and camps to make likenesses of Johnny Rebs and their loved ones. A few amateur artists sketched their impressions of persons and scenes observed behind the lines and along the battle fronts. For many years Hirst Milhollen has been collecting these photographs and drawings from libraries, museums, antique shops and private homes. In this volume, for the first time, is expertly reproduced a substantial and representative sampling of photographs and sketches depicting Southerners at war.

This is not—nor is it intended to be—a complete history of the Confederacy. No attempt is made to portray military campaigns. That phase of the story has been told many times, and well. Even if it were told again, there would be no good pictures to illustrate it because combat photography and sketching were virtually unknown until recent times. But we have tried to represent faithfully and in some detail, in both words and pictures, the people who fought the battles and the folk who stayed at home.

Both the author of the narrative and the compiler of the pictures have become indebted to many individuals and institutions in executing their respective assignments. The former gratefully acknowledges grants from the Guggenheim Foundation, Emory University and the Henry E. Huntington Library, which enabled him to take leave of his classroom duties for itinerant research. For information and inspiration he owes a debt of gratitude to many librarians and archivists throughout the country, to fellow historians of the Confederacy and to graduate students at Emory University. He is especially indebted to Ezra J. Warner, author of *Generals in Gray*, for material on the Confederacy's "High Brass"; Professor Willard E. Wight of the Georgia Institute of Technology for information on religion drawn from an unpublished dissertation at Emory University on "Churches in the Confederacy"; Professor May S. Ringold of Clemson College for material on state legislatures obtained from her unpublished dissertation on that subject at Emory University; and

Betty Lou Curry for use of her master's thesis at Emory University on the early history of Wesleyan College. For the typing of notes and drafts abundant thanks are given to Lucy Fisher, Martha Simms, Bernice Steele, Jeannette Scholes and especially to Anna Hallman, who prepared the manuscript in its final form.

The compiler of the pictures acknowledges with deep appreciation the kindly assistance of the following: Mrs. Contee Adams, Hamilton, Virginia; Mrs. Carl Black, Jr., Librarian, Department of Archives and History, Jackson, Mississippi; Peter Brannon, Director, Alabama Department of Archives and History, Montgomery, Alabama; V. Jordan Brown, Asheville, North Carolina; Mrs. Mary Bryan and Mrs. Ruby F. Thomas, Georgia State Department of Archives and History, Atlanta, Georgia; Mrs. Peel Cannon, Holly Springs, Mississippi; Miss Josephine Cobb, specialist in Civil War Iconography, Elmer O. Parker and Miss Virginia S. Wheeler, National Archives, Washington, D.C.; Confederate Museum, Charleston, South Carolina; Mrs. Ralph Caterall, (former) Librarian, Valentine Museum, Richmond, Virginia; Alexander McCook Craighead, Dayton, Ohio; Dr. Llerena B. Friend, Librarian, University of Texas, Austin, Texas; Craddock Goins, Jr., and John Rawls, Smithsonian Institution, Washington, D.C.; Fred Goff, Rare Book Room, Donald Holmes, Chief of the Photoduplication Service, William E. Davis and Elmer King, Library of Congress, Washington, D.C.; Mrs. Walter B. Hill, Clarksville, Georgia; Mrs. Mabel Huckaby, Confederate Museum, Austin, Texas; John Howells, Houston, Texas; William A. Jackson, Harvard College Library, Cambridge, Massachusetts; Jay Johns, Director, Stonewall Jackson House, Lexington, Virginia; V. C. Jones, Centreville, Virginia; Mrs. McCook Knox, Washington, D.C.; Richard E. Kuehne, West Point Museum, United States Military Academy, West Point, New York; Mrs. Richard J. Lake, Philomont, Virginia; Mrs. J. S. Land, Curator, Confederate Relic Room, State Capitol, Columbia, South Carolina; Charles J. Long, Witte Memorial Museum, San Antonio, Texas; Manassas National Battlefield Park, Manassas, Virginia; Dr. Isidore S. Meyer, Librarian, American Jewish Historical Society, New York, New York; John Hunt Morgan House, Lexington, Kentucky; James W. Patton, Director, Southern Historical Collection, and William S. Powell, Librarian, University of North Carolina, Chapel Hill, North Carolina; John R. Peacock, High Point, North Carolina; Colonel Paul A. Rockwell, Asheville, North Carolina; Mrs. Carter Smith, Historic Mobile Preservation Society, Mobile, Alabama; Mrs. Julia W. Smith, Virginia Military Institute Museum, Lexington, Virginia; Mrs. Alice E. Starner, Associate Director, Historical Society of York County, York, Pennsylvania; Miss India Thomas, (former) Regent, and Miss Eleanor Brockenbrough, Assistant House Regent, Confederate Museum, Richmond, Virginia; William H. Townsend, Lexington, Kentucky; Treasure Room, Emory University, Atlanta, Georgia; Kenneth T. Urquhart, Director, and Henry Clay Watson, Curator, Confederate Memorial Hall, New Orleans, Louisiana; Mrs. Hendrik B. van Rensselaer, Summit, New Jersey; Mrs. Bertha Waldrop, Alexandria, Virginia; Lee Wallace, Arlington, Virginia; Washington and Lee University, Lexington, Virginia; Western Reserve Historical Society, Cleveland, Ohio; Mrs. Alice Williams Whitley, Round Hill, Virginia.

Both partners in the collaboration have benefited immeasurably from the advice, assistance and encouragement of Cass Canfield, M. S. Wyeth, Jr., and their associates of Harper & Row, a firm whose history reaches back beyond the times and events here recorded.

BELL IRVIN WILEY
HIRST D. MILHOLLEN

I. The Parting of Ways

Lincoln's election to the Presidency in November, 1860, brought to a climax a long and bitter quarrel between Southerners and Northerners and precipitated secession. South Carolina severed her ties with the Union on December 20, 1860, and within six weeks the other six states of the lower South followed her example. Early in February representatives of these states met at Montgomery, organized a new government patterned on the one recently abandoned, chose a president and vice-president and settled down to making laws adapted to the needs of the infant republic.

The speed with which disunion was accomplished and the Confederacy created did not mean that Southerners were in full agreement concerning the action taken. The movement for separation gained strength and momentum after the triumph of the Republicans, but it continued to meet considerable resistance, even in the deep South, until the outbreak of hostilities at Fort Sumter. Opposition to secession was strongest among yeomen of the mountains, hills and piney wood sections and among planters of Whig background. Spokesmen for the antisecessionists included Benjamin F. Perry of South Carolina; Alexander Stephens, Benjamin Hill and Herschel V. Johnson of Georgia; Robert Jemison and William R. Smith of Alabama; William L. Sharkey and B. L. C. Wailes of Mississippi; and Sam Houston of Texas. These leaders generally took the position that Lincoln's election was not sufficient reason for dissolution of the Union and that the South was likely to lose far more than it would gain by severing its ties with the Federal government. Some of them denied the legality of secession and asserted that the only basis for withdrawing from the Union was the time-honored right of revolution which, they believed, should be exercised only as a last resort and with the states acting in concert.

Benjamin F. Perry, upcountry South Carolina journalist, wrote the editor of the Charleston *Courier* shortly before Lincoln's election, pointing up the blessings of Union and warning against "the horrors of civil war, and the dangers of revolution to liberty and civil government." Should the Republicans win the Presidency, he added, Lincoln would be powerless to do any great injury to the South and slavery, because a majority of the Senate would be opposed to the new administration.

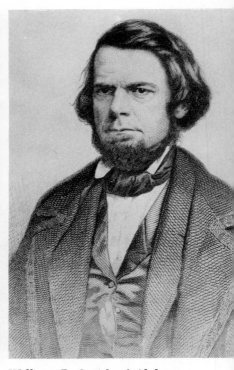

Herschel V. Johnson of Georgia   *Benjamin H. Hill of Georgia*   *William R. Smith of Alabama*

Governor Sam Houston of Texas

EMBATTLED
CONFEDERATES

Very likely Lincoln would seek to appease the South by a rigid adherence to the Constitution. "The election of President, in conformity with the Federal Constitution," he added, "is no ground whatever for breaking up the Republic, no matter how bitterly opposed to him we may be. We must wait and decide on his acts and measures; nothing less will justify us in the eyes of the world, or in the opinions of our people." Perry continued to denounce secession as "madness and folly," but when his state left the Union, he accepted the majority verdict, remarking as he did: "You are all now going to the devil and I will go with you."

Benjamin H. Hill, a long-time Whig and a supporter in 1860 of Bell and Everett, the Constitutional Union party nominees for the nation's highest offices, wrote on December 26, in accepting election to the Georgia convention: "The dissolution of this Union may be a necessity . . . but . . . I cannot regard such an event as an occasion for rejoicing. . . . I shall dissolve this Union as I would bury a benefactor—in sorrow of heart. For, after all, the Union is not the author of our grievances. Bad, extreme men, in both sections, insult each other, and then both fight the Union, which never harmed or insulted either. . . . For myself, I shall never ask for more true liberty and real happiness under any government than I have enjoyed as a citizen of this great American Union. May they who would destroy this Union *in a frolic* have wisdom to furnish to our children a better."

On November 30, 1860, Herschel V. Johnson, running mate of Douglas in the recent Presidential campaign, wrote his fellow Georgian,

Alexander Stephens: "I feel a deep interest in the fate of the Union; for in its perpetuity I think all that is valuable to me and my children and the coming generation is involved. Hence, whatever I can do, I will do to avert impending calamities, to preserve our government and consequently liberty and its blessings." Like Hill and Johnson, Stephens advised giving the Lincoln administration a trial and trying to obtain new guarantees of Southern rights within the Union. But, also like them, he bowed to the will of the majority when the Georgia convention voted overwhelmingly for secession.

The anguish suffered by Unionists hopelessly engulfed in a flood of opposing sentiment was vividly reflected in the letters that William R. Smith wrote to his wife while participating in the Alabama secession convention. On January 10 he wrote: "Before this reaches you Alabama will be a *Sovereign State*. The people will be overwhelmed with trouble —but there will be a day of reckoning for the wicked." When, despite Smith's earnest opposition, the convention on January 11 passed the ordinance by a vote of 61 to 39, he made a speech pledging his continuing loyalty to his state. "But this is all very sad," he wrote his wife shortly afterward. "The sternest men have been weeping like children." Smith served for a time in the Southern army and then was elected to the Confederate Congress. But like many other old Whigs he was never fully reconciled to the fact of disunion.

In the crisis of 1850–1851, Stephens, Johnson, Perry and other moderates had been able to prevail over secessionist "fire-eaters" such as Robert Barnwell Rhett and William L. Yancey and keep the South in the Union. In 1860–1861 circumstances favored the fire-eaters, and these zealots made the most of their advantage. Ten years of intersectional controversy had intensified distrust, deepened hatred, and aroused emotions to a high pitch. Northern gains in population, industry and wealth had enhanced the South's uneasiness about its influence and security in the Union. Many of the lower South's most powerful politicians, including Robert Toombs and Howell Cobb, who in 1850 had taken the lead for compromise and Union, were now ardent champions of secession. By 1861 the secessionists had won control of the political machinery and gained the active support of most of the newspapers throughout the deep South. They also had on their side a majority of ministers and educators.

Advocates of secession marshaled an impressive array of arguments to support their position. The legality of secession was beyond question, they asserted, because of the character of the Federal Union. The Union was a compact of sovereign states. When the states entered the compact they delegated specific powers to their agent, the central government. But they reserved the right to resume the delegated powers at the discretion of their people, acting through the instrumentality of conventions.

Secessionists claimed that dissolution of the Union was an economic

Robert Barnwell Rhett, Sr., of South Carolina, before hostilities an ardent secessionist and during the war a severe critic of President Jefferson Davis

Robert Toombs of Georgia, an ardent champion of secession, later the first Secretary of State

THE PARTING
OF WAYS

3

necessity. The South, the nation's great producing area, they said, was exploited, plundered and drained of its wealth by merchants, bankers and shippers of the North. Southerners sold their produce in a free market and bought in a protected market, paying annually in tariffs millions of dollars of tribute to Northern manufacturers. If the South were to pull out of the Union and form a separate government, wrote a Vicksburg editor in 1860, "the enormous wealth she is now pouring into

Howell Cobb of Georgia, president of the Provisional Congress, February 4, 1861– February 17, 1862. Later a major general in the Confederate army

Mass meeting at Institute Hall, Charleston, South Carolina, November 12, 1860, to endorse the call of the legislature for a secession convention

EMBATTLED
4   CONFEDERATES

the lap of the North would at once be withdrawn and become tributary to Southern prosperity and Southern power."

The threat to slavery, the South's peculiar institution, was the argument used most frequently and with greatest effect in advocating secession. Southerners were deeply attached to slavery—as an economic investment valued by some at four billion dollars; as a dependable and necessary source of labor; and most important, particularly to the

Baptist Church, Columbia, South Carolina, where Secession Convention was first held, December 17, 1860

nonslaveholders who comprised three-fourths of the Southern white population, as an effective means of maintaining white supremacy. Fire-eaters in Congress, in the legislative halls, at local rallies, in the pulpit and in the newspapers proclaimed in impassioned phrase that Republican victory in the election of 1860 spelled the doom of slavery. Northern antipathy to slavery had been on the increase for several decades, they asserted. Northern states, in defiance of sacred rights of property and a Supreme Court decision, had passed laws obstructing the recovery of fugitive slaves. Prominent citizens of the North had financed John Brown in his attempt to incite slave insurrection and when the murderer was executed for his foul crime they had hailed him as a martyr. Now the election of 1860 had placed the national government under the control of a party and a leader avowedly hostile to slavery and bent on its ultimate extinction. The Republicans had already flouted

EMBATTLED
CONFEDERATES

the Constitution by denying Southerners the right to carry their slave property into Federal territory. It was only a matter of time until they would attack slavery in the states and destroy it altogether. Destruction of the South's peculiar institution would reduce the region to political impotence, economic ruin and social chaos. Honor, security and self-preservation all demanded that the South dissolve partnership with a people so unreasonable and so evil and establish a government of its own, where the states would be sovereign, slavery would be secure and the people prosperous and happy.

The fire-eaters denounced as submissionists and traitors those who counseled delay or compromise. "When a [secessionist] scheme is put on foot," wrote a nationally minded Mississippian in 1860, "the *Mississippian* roars and all the little country papers yelp, the cross road and bar room politicians take it up and so it goes, and if anyone opposes them they raise the cry of Abolitionist and traitor, two words of awful import in this country. Any modest or peaceable man [had] rather let the rascals rip than to incur the odium of opposing them."

Proponents of disunion scorned the idea that secession would lead to war. Senator James Chesnut of South Carolina stated in November, 1860, that "the man most averse to blood might safely drink every drop shed" in establishing a Southern confederacy. Secession leaders declared that Yankees were too deeply absorbed in making money to give much thought to the Union and that some of the states of the upper Mississippi Valley felt greater kinship with the South than with the North. If war should come, they said, the South need have no fears, for Southerners were a braver, hardier people than Northerners and on the field of battle one "brave Southron" would put to rout a whole squad of "Yankee mud-sills." "The army that invades the South to subjugate her," declared William Barksdale, a Mississippi congressman who in less than three years was to die at Gettysburg, "will never return; their bodies will enrich Southern soil."

The secessionists also had a ready answer for those who pointed to the North's superiority in factories, mines, ships and other material resources. The South had always possessed enormous industrial potential, they said; freed from its economic vassalage to the North, the South would rapidly develop this potential and establish a balanced and thriving economy. Moreover, in a contest with the North, Southerners would not be alone, for Europe had to have cotton and, to obtain cotton, England and other industrial nations would espouse the cause of the secessionists, break the Northern blockade and pour the abundance of their factories into Southern harbors in exchange for precious lint. "Would any sane nation make war on cotton?" asked James H. Hammond of South Carolina in the United States Senate in March, 1858. "Without firing a gun," he added, "without drawing a sword, when they make war on us we can bring the whole world to our feet. . . . If no cotton was furnished for three years . . . old England would topple

Interior of Secession Hall, Charleston, South Carolina

Senator James Chesnut, Jr., of South Carolina, husband of Mary Boykin Chesnut

Ex-President of the United States John Tyler, President of the Peace Convention in Washington, D.C., February 4, 1861, later a member of the Provisional Congress

Peace Convention in Concert Hall, attached to Willard's Hotel, Washington, D.C., February 4, 1861

headlong and carry the whole civilized world with her. . . . No sir, you dare not make war on cotton. Cotton is king."

Hammond's boast was repeated many times throughout the deep South as intersectional tensions increased. Secessionist leaders of the various states kept in touch with each other through interchange of commissioners and personal correspondence. They also maintained close cooperation with Southern delegations in Congress, whose members in some instances were deeply resentful of their diminishing influence in

Senator John J. Crittendon of Kentucky, Southern moderate whose efforts to head off secession were defeated

national affairs. One of the fire-eaters' greatest fears was that secession would be delayed and their efforts thwarted by compromise proposals introduced in Congress in December, 1860, and referred to the "Committee of Thirty-three" of the House and the "Committee of Thirteen" of the Senate. But these committees had hardly started functioning when on December 13 about half of the cotton states' representatives and senators issued an address to their constituents stating that "all hope of relief in the Union through the agencies of committees, Congressional

An Ordinance,

To dissolve the Union between the State of South Carolina and other States united with her under the compact entitled, "The Constitution of the United States of America."

We, the People of the State of South Carolina, in Convention assembled, do declare and ordain, and it is hereby declared and ordained,

That the Ordinance adopted by us in Convention, on the twenty-third day of May, in the year of our Lord one thousand seven hundred and eighty-eight, whereby the Constitution of the United States of America was ratified, and also, all Acts and parts of Acts of the General Assembly of this State, ratifying amendments of the said Constitution, are hereby repealed; and that the union now subsisting between South Carolina and other States, under the name of "The United States of America," is hereby dissolved.

EVANS & COGSWELL, PRINTERS, CHARLESTON.

Review of Volunteer troops in Fort Moultrie, Charleston Harbor, South Carolina, in the

legislation or constitutional amendment is extinguished, and we trust that the South will not be deceived by appearances or the pretense of new guarantees." This address, widely publicized in the press, virtually eliminated any remaining likelihood of compromise and gave a great boost to the cause of disunion.

Despite the earnest argument and tremendous pressure of secessionists, upper South moderates were able to hold their states in the Union through the critical early months of 1861. In response to an invitation from the Virginia legislature, delegates from twenty-one Northern and Southern states met early in February in one last effort to compromise sectional differences. This peace convention, held in Washington and presided over by former President John Tyler, drew up

EMBATTLED
CONFEDERATES

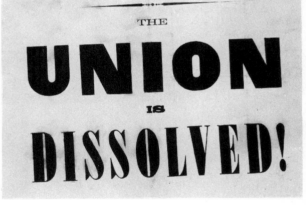

presence of the wife and daughter of Governor
Francis W. Pickens

a plan incorporating proposals previously made in the Senate by John J. Crittenden of Kentucky. This plan called for constitutional amendments extending the Missouri Compromise line to the Pacific, protecting slavery in all territories south of that line, and providing further guarantees to slavery in the states. Extremists in both North and South were opposed to the plan and its submission to Congress in March proved a futile gesture.

Moderates in the upper South were weakened by the failure of compromise but they still were able to stay the tide of disunion. Some went over to the secessionists after reading Lincoln's inaugural but most remained firm in the belief that the South's best hopes lay with the Union. Few, however, were willing to admit the authority of the

THE PARTING
OF WAYS

national government to maintain the Union by force of arms. When Lincoln's attempt to reprovision Fort Sumter on April 12 led to an outbreak of hostilities and a call of the President for militia to crush resistance and enforce Federal law in the states that had seceded, the cause of moderation collapsed. The states of the upper South quickly aligned themselves with the Confederacy. Virginia seceded on April 17; Arkansas, May 6; Tennessee, May 7; and North Carolina, May 20.

The secession ordinances were ratified by popular vote in Texas on February 23; in Virginia, May 23; and in Tennessee, June 8. In the other eight states of the Confederacy, the people had no opportunity to vote directly on secession, but there is no reason to believe that a popular referendum would have changed the result in any instance.

Quill pen used by Colonel Henry W. Garlington to sign the ordinance of secession

II. Harassed Politicians

The Confederate government was headed throughout its history by Jefferson Davis of Mississippi. Chosen first on a provisional basis on February 9, 1861, by forty-three delegates from six states of the lower South, Davis in November, 1861, was elected by popular vote and without opposition for a single six-year term beginning February 18, 1862.

Davis seemed to be an excellent choice for the Presidency. He was a respected member of the "cotton aristocracy" and had won renown both as a soldier and a statesman. Following graduation from West Point in 1828 he served seven years at various frontier posts before quitting the army. In 1845 he was elected to Congress but he resigned the next year to command a regiment in the Mexican War. After brief but brilliant service in Mexico he came home a wounded hero and was sent to the United States Senate where he was chairman of the committee on military affairs. He left the Senate in 1851, but re-entered public life two years later as Secretary of War under President Pierce. He displayed exceptional initiative and imagination in administering the War Department. In 1857 he went back to the Senate and before he left that body in January, 1861, he was recognized by both friends and foes as "the foremost man of the South."

Davis' political and military distinction must have carried greatest weight with those who selected him to head the Southern government. But he had other notable assets. He was an excellent speaker, with a clear and pleasing voice, and people who listened to him were as favorably impressed by what he had to say as by the persuasive manner in which he spoke. He was attractive in appearance. His sharply chiseled features, his erect figure, his neat attire and his dignified bearing caused him to stand out in a crowd. He was reserved but courteous in his demeanor. He had a sense of humor, and was by no means devoid of sentiment. But he rarely revealed the lighter and warmer side of his nature outside the family circle.

He was an honest, moral man, of "unfeigned reverence for his Creator," though he manifested little interest in religion until he became a communicant of the Episcopal Church in 1862. One of his most outstanding virtues was a lofty sense of duty which manifested itself in earnest application to the toils of public office. He was also a person of strong convictions. His belief in the rightness of the Southern position increased during the war until it became an obsession. He gave his full measure of devotion to the cause that he led and lost.

Davis also had some outstanding weaknesses, though these were not apparent to the men who selected him to head the Confederacy. It was only in the crisis of war, under the stress of new and staggering burdens, intensified by swelling criticism and dwindling prospects of success, that the man's shortcomings were clearly revealed. First, he lacked the prime essential of efficient administration, the willingness to delegate authority. Instead of surrounding himself with a corps of able assistants and entrusting administrative routine to them, he wasted precious time and energy on minutiae. Another notable defect was his inability to get along with people. He was impatient of opposition and he tended to dislike those who disagreed with him. He was also lacking in tact. When crossed, he was inclined to flare up and fight back. He had neither the disposition nor the wisdom to meet vehemence with softness, to concede a minor point in order to gain a major objective, to cajole, to humor or to flatter. He had little time for small talk. In most of his relationships he was formal and unbending. His ineptness in human relations did incalculable harm to the cause which he headed. For among the many who became hostile to him were some of the Confederacy's ablest and most influential leaders.

Davis lacked popular appeal. He had none of the common touch of Andrew Jackson or Abraham Lincoln. His dealings with Congress, state leaders and the press left much to be desired. He had no systematic mode of handling public relations and he made some costly errors in treating major issues and personalities. He did not prepare the people for such revolutionary and uncongenial measures as conscription, impressment and the suspension of the writ of habeas corpus, by telling them ahead of time why these measures were necessary and how they would operate. Hence many found it easy to believe the charge made by his enemies that he was trying to establish a dictatorship.

His deficiencies as President were due in part to poor health. In 1858 he had a severe attack of glaucoma which blinded him in one eye. During the war he suffered much from eyestrain, neuralgia, nervous indigestion and various other illnesses. These curtailed his labors, restricted his social intercourse and made him impatient and irritable. In view of the nature of his maladies, and particularly in view of the fact that he enjoyed excellent health in his later years, it seems reasonable to conclude that his troubles were largely psychosomatic. He did not want to be President; the duties of his office were uncongenial and burdensome; he was extremely sensitive to criticism; and he had no relaxing diversions to give him relief from his cares. So he worried himself sick and illness in turn made him less able to cope with the problems which prostrated him. He was a thoroughly discredited chief-

President Jefferson Davis   15

The White House of the Confederacy, Richmond, Virginia

tain when he fled from Richmond in the spring of 1865. Not until after the Federals imprisoned him and made him the martyr of the Lost Cause did he regain the esteem which he had enjoyed at the beginning of the war.

With all his limitations, Jefferson Davis was a tower of strength and a peak of perfection in comparison with the Confederate Vice-President. Alexander H. Stephens was a successful lawyer, a shrewd parliamentarian, a brilliant constitutional theorist, a formidable debater, a great orator, and a distinguished legislator with sixteen years' experience in the Federal Congress. He was a gracious host, a friend to the needy and a kindly master to his slaves. But he was also erratic, inconsistent, hypersensitive and unrealistic. He had piercing eyes and an engaging countenance but he was sickly and slight and never weighed a hundred pounds. He suffered from a nervous malady and his behavior suggests that he needed the constant approval and frequent praise of his associates to compensate for his dwarfed body and chronic debility. He was often petulant in attitude and partisan in tactics but he always claimed, and perhaps sincerely believed, that he was motivated by lofty principles. He repeatedly avowed disinterest in high office and public acclaim, yet few men worked harder than he to achieve both.

Stephens was an effective campaigner in an era when politics was a rough and dangerous business. In a joint debate in the congressional campaign of 1843, Judge Walter T. Colquitt contemptuously remarked

EMBATTLED
CONFEDERATES

that Stephens was so small that he "could swallow him whole and never know the difference." "Little Ellick," as he was known by his friends, immediately retorted: "Yes, and if you did there would be more brains in your belly than there will ever be in your head."

Unfortunately for the Confederacy, Stephens' brilliant intellect, moving eloquence and enormous prestige were not utilized to sustain the Southern cause, but rather to undermine it. After a brief period of active cooperation in launching the Confederate government, Stephens soured in his attitude toward Davis and virtually abandoned his position as Vice-President. In the latter part of the war Stephens allied himself with an extreme state rights, antiadministration group which included his brother, Linton Stephens, Governor Joseph Brown of Georgia and Robert Toombs. In March, 1864, the anguished and imperiled Confederacy was treated to the incredible spectacle of its Vice-President castigating the President and his policies in a three-hour speech before the Georgia legislature.

Stephens' strange shift from enthusiastic support of the Davis administration to active opposition was due in large part to his blind and stubborn adherence to state rights. He regarded each state as a nation unto itself and he was unwilling for it to yield sovereignty, even temporarily, until the South could achieve independence. In 1862 he declared: "The citizen of the State owes no allegiance to the Confederate States Government . . . and can owe no 'military service' to it except as required by his own state. His allegiance is due to his State." In his speech to the Georgia legislature in 1864 he said: "Tell me not to put confidence in the President. . . . The most ill-timed, delusive and dangerous words that can be uttered are 'can you not trust the President?'"

If Stephens had resigned the Vice-Presidency early in the war, his stringent opposition to the Confederate administration could be understood, if not condoned. But for him to denounce and obstruct the team of which he was a leading member cannot be justified on any reasonable grounds. His ill-considered conduct impaired Southern morale, gave aid and comfort to the North and did immeasurable injury to the Confederate cause. But his people quickly forgot and forgave, elected him United States senator in 1866, congressman in 1872 and governor in 1883. And today he is regarded by many as one of the greatest Southern leaders of all time.

In administering the executive branch of the Confederate government Davis and Stephens were assisted by a cabinet, the organization of which was the same as that of the Federal government except for the absence of an interior department. Turnover in the Davis cabinet was great, the six offices having a total of seventeen heads, three of whom were ad interim appointees.*

All fourteen of the bona fide members of the cabinet had college

Alexander H. Stephens, Vice-President of the Confederacy

* A list of cabinet members and other governmental information will be found on pages 257–274.

*Inauguration of Jefferson
Davis at Montgomery,
Alabama, Monday,
February 18, 1861*

degrees or the equivalent. All were trained in law except George A. Trenholm and he was an affluent banker. All at one time or another owned plantations and slaves. All were politically experienced. Five had served in the House of Representatives and six in the United States Senate. John C. Breckinridge had been Vice-President; Robert M. T. Hunter, Speaker of the House; and Thomas Bragg, governor of North Carolina. Several of them were of Whig background and some joined the secession ranks with much reluctance and misgiving. Four of them began their lives in humble circumstances. John H. Reagan, the son of a poor farmer and tanner of east Tennessee, was a Mississippi overseer before moving to Texas. Stephen R. Mallory, born in Trinidad, of a Connecticut father and an Irish mother, had to leave school when he was fifteen to help his widowed mother run a boardinghouse at Key West, Florida. Judah P. Benjamin, a native of St. Croix in the Virgin Islands, spent most of his childhood in North and South Carolina, where his father eked out a meager living as a clerk and merchant. Christopher G. Memminger, who was born in the German duchy of Württemberg and who lost both parents before he was five, lived in a Charleston orphanage for seven years before moving to the home of a local lawyer.

On the whole, the heads of the Confederacy's executive departments were well-meaning, honorable men with creditable records in public and private life. If their government had enjoyed the peaceful career which many expected at its inauguration, they would probably have given a good account of themselves in their new positions. Unfortunately, few of them had either the temperament or the talent for meeting the exceptional responsibilities created by war.

The ablest member of the cabinet, and the most brilliant man in the Confederate government, was Judah P. Benjamin. Despite the impecuniousness of his parents, Benjamin obtained an excellent education, including two years at Yale. In 1828, when he was seventeen, he went to New Orleans where he soon achieved outstanding success as a lawyer. He joined the Whig party, rose rapidly in politics and in 1853 entered the United States Senate where he remained until 1861. He was one of the most articulate exponents of Southern rights.

Davis was not intimately acquainted with Benjamin during their Washington sojourn and a misunderstanding between them on the floor of the Senate almost led to a duel. But the affair was patched up and they came to regard each other with esteem and respect. When William L. Yancey turned down the opportunity to become first Adjutant General of the Confederacy, Davis gave the position to "the little man from Louisiana." Benjamin quickly organized his office in such a way as to relieve himself of routine. He devoted his surplus time so effectively to greeting visitors, counseling office-seekers and performing other duties which otherwise would have fallen on the President, that the hard-pressed Davis turned increasingly to him for assistance and advice. Benjamin's quiet efficiency and enormous capacity for work made him a very useful helper; and his loyalty, his unfailing cheerfulness, his irrepressible optimism and his consummate skill in dealing with the President endeared him personally to Davis. The absence of Benjamin's wife, who established a separate residence in Paris in 1843, left him free to spend many evenings at the Confederate White House. Mrs. Davis was charmed by his urbane manner and sparkling talk and this helped ingratiate him with the President. Within a few months Benjamin became Davis' closest associate and most trusted counselor. He was one of the few persons prominent in the Confederate government who never quarreled with the President. He did not always agree with his superior but he had the rare ability to dissent without giving offense; and when overruled he bowed to the President's authority readily and without rancor.

When the sickly and inept Leroy P. Walker resigned from the War Department in September, 1861, Davis named Benjamin as his successor. Benjamin took over the difficult job with characteristic zeal; in a short time he had cleared up the debris of unfinished business and made the War Department a model of efficient administration. His initial efforts elicited much favorable comment. But after a few weeks, sentiment

Judah P. Benjamin, first Attorney General, second Secretary of War, and fourth Secretary of State

Leroy P. Walker, first Secretary of War

HARASSED
POLITICIANS   19

Robert M. T. Hunter,
second Secretary of State

Thomas Bragg of North
Carolina, second Attorney
General

Thomas H. Watts of
Alabama, third Attorney
General

EMBATTLED
CONFEDERATES

began to turn against him. By March, 1862, he was one of the most unpopular men in Richmond.

Benjamin was blamed for the military setbacks suffered early in 1862 at Fort Henry, Fort Donelson and Roanoke Island. Actually he could have done little if anything to prevent these disasters, but this was not known at the time. His unpopularity was due in some measure to anti-Semitism and to jealousy of his position as the confidant and favorite of Jefferson Davis. But the Secretary of War played into the hands of his critics by the ill-considered manner in which he dealt with some of the generals. He violated military usages by issuing furloughs, making details and giving orders to field commanders without regard to the chain of command.

Davis intended to continue Benjamin as Secretary of War under the permanent government inaugurated on February 18, 1862. But the President soon realized that the Senate would not approve Benjamin's reappointment. Reluctantly, Davis nominated George W. Randolph in Benjamin's stead, and made Benjamin Secretary of State. The Senate approved the change as a compromise but some legislators in both houses deeply resented retention of Benjamin in the cabinet in any capacity.

Benjamin conducted the Department of State with the same efficiency that had characterized his administration of the Justice and War Departments. But he faced insuperable obstacles in achieving his primary objective—recognition and intervention by England and France. As a last resort he sent Duncan F. Kenner to England to offer emancipation as an inducement to recognition, but this proved a futile gesture.

As the South's fortunes declined, there was an increasing tendency to point to Benjamin as the Confederacy's evil genius. Denunciation of him reached a new peak in February, 1865, when he publicly advocated making soldiers of the slaves and freeing those who volunteered for Confederate service. On February 11 Louis Wigfall introduced in the Senate a resolution expressing lack of confidence in the Secretary of State, but it was defeated by a tie vote. Benjamin wrote Davis on February 21 offering his resignation, but the President, never of a disposition to heed criticism directed at his friends, became more attached than ever to his trusted adviser. The two remained intimate until the collapse of the Confederacy compelled them to follow separate courses.

Benjamin was a highly efficient administrator, a loyal adviser and a conscientious public servant. He had less of wisdom than of shrewdness, and this was his principal weakness. Of his superior ability there can be no doubt, and if any proof of it were needed it could be found in his post-Confederate career. Uprooted and exiled in his fifty-fourth year, he went to England. There he quickly rose from bencher to barrister, published a *Treatise on the Law of Sale of Personal Property* and in a few years was pleading cases before the Privy Council. He eventually became one of the foremost members of the English bar with an annual

*Stephen R. Mallory, Secretary
of the Navy*

*John H. Reagan, second
Postmaster General*

income exceeding $75,000. He died on May 6, 1884, in the apartment of his reconciled wife, full of years and of honor.

Two men shared with Benjamin the distinction of remaining in the cabinet for the duration of the Confederacy. They were John H. Reagan, the Postmaster General, and Stephen R. Mallory, Secretary of the Navy. Reagan, who took office only after Henry T. Ellet had declined the appointment, was a self-made man of superior ability who had worked his way up the political ladder in Texas from state legislator to congressman. After the war he returned to Washington, first as a member of the House and then as senator, and was co-author and sponsor of the Interstate Commerce Act of 1887. Reagan was an admirer and loyal supporter of the President and this was one of the reasons that he held his office throughout the war. Another reason was the efficiency with which he did his job. His position was a relatively minor one, but he encountered and overcame many formidable difficulties and achieved the remarkable feat of making his department self-sustaining.

The problems of Reagan were trivial in comparison with those of his good friend and colleague, the head of the Navy Department. Mallory had to build a fleet from virtually nothing and to operate and maintain it under the most unfavorable conditions. Mallory was not brilliant but he had exceptional ability and considerable capacity for growth. When measured in terms of what he accomplished, in the face of appalling obstacles, he must be rated as one of the ablest members of the Confederate cabinet.

Mallory displayed exceptional imagination and initiative in developing modern equipment peculiarly adapted to the Confederacy's resources and needs. He was responsible for raising the *Merrimack* and converting it into the ironclad *Virginia* which wrought much destruction at Hampton Roads before she was thwarted by the *Monitor*. From the beginning to the end of his administration he urged the importance of developing iron-armored ships, for he realized that the day of the wooden navy had passed. He was also a pioneer in the use of submarines, torpedoes, mines and other modern instruments of naval war. To him belongs much of the credit for the Confederacy's winning the distinction of sending to the bottom the first warship ever to be sunk by a submarine. This was on the night of February 17, 1864, near Charleston, South Carolina, when the *H. L. Hunley* sank the *U. S. S. Housatonic*.

Three weeks after Appomattox, Jefferson Davis summarized thus his estimate of Mallory's work: "Your minute knowledge of naval affairs . . . has been to the Administration a most valuable support. For the zeal, ability and integrity with which you have constantly labored, permit one who has the opportunity to judge to offer testimonial and in the name of our country and its sacred cause, to return thanks."

The person ranking next to Benjamin, Mallory and Reagan in length of service in the cabinet was Christopher G. Memminger, Secretary of the Treasury from February, 1861, to July, 1864. Before the war Memminger had been a successful lawyer in Charleston and a pioneer in public education. He possessed a superior intellect and was one of the most conscientious and industrious members of the Southern cabinet. But he lacked warmth and color and offended many people by his reclusiveness, abruptness and seeming hauteur. He got along well with Davis, but their harmonious relationship was based more on mutual respect than on intimate association.

Memminger tried to put Confederate finances on a sound basis by a combined program of loans obtained through the sale of bonds and taxation sufficiently heavy to meet payments of principal and interest and to combat inflation. But he was unable to sell bonds in anything like the quantity required to meet the country's enormous needs and Congress and the public resisted heavy taxation. He was compelled to resort increasingly to paper money and as the notes poured in ever growing volume from the Treasury's presses, their value depreciated and prices soared to fantastic heights. In July, 1864, Memminger bowed before a storm of public and congressional criticism and returned to private life. His record was by no means brilliant. But, in view of the South's inherent economic weaknesses and the deep-seated aversion of the people to taxes, it is extremely doubtful if anyone else could have done any better. Certainly George A. Trenholm, the personable, wealthy and successful Charleston merchant who took over the Treasury Department in July, 1864, proved no more successful than the studious and dedicated little financier who preceded him.

Christopher G. Memminger, first Secretary of the Treasury

George A. Trenholm, second Secretary of the Treasury

One of the most promising members of the cabinet was George W. Randolph, grandson of Thomas Jefferson, who on March 18, 1862, succeeded Benjamin as Secretary of War. Randolph brought to the war office splendid personal qualities and valuable military experience including youthful service as a midshipman and solid success as an artillery officer in the early campaigns of the Civil War. But in Richmond he was handicapped by poor health and was annoyed by the President's tendency to bypass his office and regard him as a mere clerk. Randolph was a high-minded, honorable and conscientious public servant. What he might have done if the President had given him authority commensurate with his position must remain a matter of speculation. His tenure was brought to an abrupt end in November, 1862, when he made the mistake of issuing an order, without consulting the President, authorizing General Theophilus Holmes to move from Arkansas to Mississippi and take over the defense of Vicksburg. When the President objected, Randolph modified the order but the Secretary was offended by the President's rebuke and shortly afterward sent in his resignation. Ten days later he wrote his brother: "My resignation was not caused by any quarrel with the President but by difference of opinion as to the discretion which should be vested in the Secretary. He wished to impose restrictions which in my judgement were derogatory to the office and hurtful to the public service and to which I could not submit without sacrificing my self respect and the public interest."

Gustavus Woodson Smith, acting Secretary of War, November, 1862

Capitol Building, Richmond, Virginia

George W. Randolph, third Secretary of War   *James A. Seddon, fourth Secretary of War*

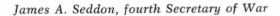

Randolph's successor, James A. Seddon, did not appear to be physically able to fill a position of great responsibility. A. T. Bledsoe, Assistant Secretary of War under Benjamin, urged Davis not to take Seddon into the cabinet. "A man of fine parts, a most estimable character, an accomplished gentleman, and as true a patriot as ever lived," Bledsoe wrote the President in November, 1862, "his *physique* is too feeble. The labor of the office would kill him in one month. Especially as he is, neither by nature nor habit, a worker." But Seddon was not as frail as he looked. Like Randolph, he came from an aristocratic Virginia family. His home, Sabot Hill, graciously presided over by his gay and charming wife, Sally Bruce, was a beautiful country place twenty miles from Richmond. In the prewar years the best of Virginia society frequently was entertained at Sabot Hill. Seddon served for two terms in Congress but voluntarily withdrew from public affairs in 1851 to follow the more congenial life of scholar and gentleman. He served in the Confederate Provisional Congress from July, 1861, to February, 1862, when he again retired to his plantation. He remained there until Davis appointed him to the cabinet.

Authorities disagree concerning Seddon's influence and efficiency as Secretary of War. Robert G. H. Kean, who may have been prejudiced by his friendship for Randolph, wrote in his journal on December 22, 1862: "There have accumulated on Mr. Seddon's table since he came in some 1500 papers, *all* touching appointments to officers. He does not look at them because on the terms on which impliedly he took office he cannot act on them. They are for the President." Kean came to like Seddon personally but he never changed his mind about the Secretary's subserviency to Davis. Shortly before Seddon's resignation in 1865, Kean wrote: "Submission to dictation has lost him much respect."

It seems reasonable to conclude on the basis of available evidence that during his first months in the cabinet Seddon tackled the problems confronting him with vigor, enjoyed the confidence of Davis and had considerable authority. It also appears that his influence and prestige began to wane in 1863; that he became discouraged by his inability to carry any real weight in the President's councils; and that instead of fighting for more recognition and authority he accepted the inevitable and devoted himself increasingly to routine administration.

Within the limits of the authority allowed to him, Seddon worked diligently to promote the military fortunes of the Confederacy. He pushed conscription, kept a close eye on exemptions, sought earnestly to apprehend deserters and exerted himself unstintedly to see that the armies were adequately supplied. But his task was a hopeless one and his efforts yielded less and less return. As the military situation deteriorated he became the object of a mounting tide of criticism. This he bore with commendable fortitude. But when, in January, 1865, the Virginia delegation, in a move aimed primarily at Davis, asked the President to reconstruct the cabinet, Seddon immediately sent in his resignation. Davis tried to persuade him to reconsider, but the harassed Secretary was convinced that his usefulness had ended. He continued in office until John C. Breckinridge took over as his successor on February 6. He then withdrew to the serenity of Sabot Hill.

Of the remaining cabinet members Robert Toombs was the most colorful. Aptly characterized by one historian as the Confederacy's Falstaff, he had many attractive qualities. Tall and powerfully built, with a quick mind, a ready wit and an enormous capacity for good fellowship, he was highly esteemed by his friends and greatly admired by his Georgia constituents. He was an accomplished student of finance and a powerful orator. He was forthright in his dealing, salty in his talk and lavish in his hospitality. But he also had some notable faults. He was stubborn, impetuous, prone to excess in drinking, sometimes extreme in his judgments and often reckless and intemperate in his remarks. He was as bitter and implacable toward his enemies as he was warm and generous toward his friends.

Toombs accepted the Secretaryship of State with reluctance and was restive under the inactivity inherent in the position. It was with genuine relief that he gave up the office in July, 1861, to become a brigadier general. But he was not suited either by background or disposition for

John C. Breckinridge, fifth Secretary of War

military command. He chafed at the defensive policy pursued by his superiors and was irked by their insistence on ceremony and regimentation. Longstreet placed him under arrest for disobeying an order in August, 1862, but released him just before Second Manassas and praised him for his gallantry in that fight. Toombs also proved his bravery at Antietam. But neither his immediate superiors nor Davis thought him deserving of promotion to major general and Toombs left the army in March, 1863. He returned to Georgia where for the remainder of the war he devoted himself largely to growing cotton and denouncing Jefferson Davis.

Legislative functions of the Confederate government were exercised by successive groups, known as the Provisional Congress, the First Congress and the Second Congress. The Provisional Congress, a unicameral body which served both as a constitutional convention and a legislature, held five sessions between its first meeting on February 4, 1861, and final adjournment on February 17, 1862. The First Congress met in four sessions from February 18, 1862, to February 17, 1864; and the Second Congress held two sessions between May 2, 1864, and March 18, 1865. In the First and Second Congresses, which were bicameral, each state had two senators and the same number of representatives that it had had when it left the Union. Senators were chosen by the legislatures and representatives by popular vote. The first two sessions of the Provisional Congress were held in the Alabama Capitol at Montgomery; after the government moved to Richmond, Congress met in the Virginia State Capitol.

The 267 men who at one time or another sat in Congress varied greatly in background and ability.* More than one-third of them had been members of the Federal Congress and some others had served in state legislatures.

The Provisional Congress was in general a more distinguished group than its successors. An analysis by Charles Robert Lee of the fifty men who drew up the permanent Constitution shows fifteen lawyers, twenty-seven lawyer-planters, five planters, one doctor, one college professor and one cotton factor. Nine of them had served in the United States Senate and eighteen in the House. Two had been in the national cabinet and one had been a Federal judge. One had been governor, two had been state chief justices and forty-five had been state legislators. Forty-two of the fifty were college trained. Most of them were well-to-do, and some, including Harrison, Sparrow, Toombs, Perkins and Kenner, were very wealthy. Seventeen had belonged to the Whig party.

One of the most illustrious members of the Provisional Congress was the presiding officer, Howell Cobb of Georgia. Cobb had a long and distinguished career in the Federal House of Representatives climaxed

* A list of congressmen will be found on pages 258–273.

by one term as speaker. He was governor of Georgia from 1851 to 1853, and Secretary of the Treasury under Buchanan. Of aristocratic background, he was amiable, well-balanced, tactful and honorable. He was considered for the Presidency of the Confederacy in February, 1861, and in view of his administrative talents, his admirable personal qualities and especially his ability to get along with people, he might have made a better Chief Executive than Jefferson Davis. Certainly he was an outstanding success as president of the Provisional Congress. Cobb did not seek election to the First Congress but after February 18, 1862, devoted full time to the military duties that he had assumed on a part-time basis in the summer of 1861. He was promoted to brigadier general on February 12, 1862, and to major general on September 9, 1863. He was handicapped by lack of military experience and achieved only limited success as a combat commander. His most outstanding service was as commanding officer of the District of Georgia, where his responsibilities were primarily administrative.

Thirty-one of the fifty delegates who launched the Confederate government eventually entered the army and five of them were killed. After inauguration of the permanent government, congressmen who accepted military commissions had to vacate their seats and officers elected to Congress were required to resign their commissions.

After Fort Sumter, membership of the Provisional Congress increased to twice its former size. The Arkansas delegation and part of that from Virginia arrived in May, causing a change of the meeting place from the Alabama Senate chamber to the hall of the lower house. The remainder of the Virginia delegates took their seats when the Congress first assembled in Richmond in July. North Carolina members were also admitted at that time. Tennessee's delegates arrived in mid-August and Missouri's and Kentucky's in December and January. Granville H. Oury was recognized as the delegate from the Arizona Territory on January 24, 1862, but he was replaced by Malcolm H. MacWillie on March 11. The Cherokee Nation had no delegate until Elias C. Boudinot took his seat in the House of Representatives on October 9, 1862. The delegates were allowed to introduce measures pertaining to their territories but were not permitted to vote.

Virginia's delegation of sixteen was the largest in the Provisional Congress. It was also one of the most distinguished. One of the members was a former President, the venerable John Tyler, who died on January 18, 1862.

The roster of the Provisional Congress after the admission of all the delegations contained 106 names. But all members were not in attendance at any one time.

The most important achievements of the Provisional Congress were the drawing up of the permanent Constitution, the establishment of the executive department, the setting up of the judicial system and the enactment of the numerous laws necessary for mobilizing, equipping and

Major Elias C. Boudinot, Second Cherokee Mounted Rifles, and Cherokee delegate to the First and Second Confederate Congress

maintaining the Confederacy's land and sea forces. The record of the Congress was by no means perfect. There was much wrangling over inconsequential matters, and business sometimes proceeded so slowly as thoroughly to disgust the members and their constituents. But on the basis of what it accomplished, under circumstances which frequently were baffling and discouraging, this body deserves creditable rating.

The membership of the First and Second Congresses was considerably less distinguished than that of the Provisional Congress. Many able men were diverted from legislative service by the attractions of military duty. Others had responsibilities at home which made it impracticable for them to be in Richmond for several weeks at a time over a period of two years. Then, congressional service had increasingly less glamour and appeal, and more and more of hardship and frustration as the war continued, public morale declined and prospects of victory diminished.

Disillusionment of both the congressmen and their constituents was reflected in the enormous turnover of personnel which occurred during the four years of the Confederacy. Only seven senators and twenty representatives remained in Congress all the way through. More than one-third of the men who took their seats in the Second Congress, which assembled in May, 1864, had not been members of the preceding Congress. Many of the newcomers were former Whigs who had been lukewarm toward secession if not downright opposed to it. Their election, in the autumn of 1863, not long after the great reverses at Gettysburg and Vicksburg, was a protest against the secessionists who had urged disunion on the ground that it could be peaceably consummated or that if war came it would result in a quick and easy victory. Some of the newcomers to Congress in 1864 were men of superior abilities, but as a group they did not measure up to the men whom they replaced.

The First and Second Congresses were concerned mainly with recruiting and supplying the armies, combating inflation, balancing military with civilian needs, restraining disloyalty and meeting the many problems created by invasion and blockade. As a general rule Congress enacted the major legislation requested by the administration, and the legislators deserve more credit than they have commonly been given. On April 16, 1862, they passed the first national conscription act in American history, making all white males between eighteen and thirty-five, not legally exempt, subject to the call of the President. On September 26, Congress extended the upper age limit to forty-five; and on February 16, 1864, another extension took in seventeen-year-old boys, and men between forty-five and fifty. On March 26, 1863, Congress took another revolutionary step by passing a law authorizing impressment for military use, at prices fixed by Confederate and state commissioners, of provisions required by the armed forces. This law also authorized the impressment of slaves for labor on fortifications. Still another unusual power granted to the central government at the President's request, though with increasing reluctance, was suspension of the writ of habeas corpus. The President was authorized to suspend the writ in emergency situations and areas for three specific periods: February 27 to October 13, 1862; October 13, 1862, to February 13, 1863; and February 15 to August 1, 1864. An attempt on the part of Davis' supporters to obtain further suspension was narrowly defeated after a bitter fight in both houses. Still another important achievement of Congress was the passage on April 24, 1863, of a comprehensive revenue measure providing a license tax on business, occupations and trades, a 10 percent tax on profits resulting from the purchase and sale of enumerated items most commonly dealt in by speculators, a graduated income tax, and a tax-in-kind which required farmers to contribute to the government one-tenth of their wheat, corn, cotton, sugar, tobacco and other specified products. Congress was tardy in passing the law, and the measure fell short of the need. But when judged according to the ideas of the time, the tax act of April 24, 1863, was a far-reaching and drastic piece of legislation.

Congress conducted most of its important business in secret. Journalists were much annoyed by exclusion from the legislative halls, and there can be no doubt that the policy of secrecy resulted in unfavorable publicity and helped to create a lasting impression that Congress was a weak and ineffectual body. Some of the congressmen condemned secrecy as an ill-considered and injurious practice. Henry C. Chambers of Mississippi said in the House on November 10, 1864: "It is a great mistake to suppose our people cannot bear the whole truth on any and every question . . . and from our enemies there is no longer anything to be concealed." But the protest was of no avail.

Sessions occasionally were marred by abusive language and physical violence. In a heated discussion over the proposal to establish a supreme court, Senator William L. Yancey of Alabama accused his Georgia colleague, Benjamin H. Hill, of telling a falsehood. Hill retaliated by throwing an inkstand at Yancey, which cut the Alabamian's face and caused blood and ink to run down his cheek. Hill then rushed at Yancey with a chair, but friends intervened to stop the fight. In the House, Henry S. Foote of Tennessee became so incensed in a debate with E. S. Dargan of Alabama that he called his adversary a damned rascal. Dargan assailed Foote with a bowie knife but several colleagues restrained him before he could drive the weapon home. After Dargan was safely pinned down and disarmed, Foote struck a bold pose and declared, "I defy the steel of the assassin." The brash and tempestuous Foote had few friends in or out of Congress. The editor of the Arkansas *Weekly Gazette* wrote in 1862: "Foote has gabbed on all sides of all questions. Politically he has turned backside foremost, inside out and topside down. In one thing he has been consistent—that is his hatred of President Davis; and now he appears in the selfishly unpatriotic attitude of a man ready and anxious to sacrifice principle, country and all to the gratification of his egotistic personal hatred."

Early in 1865 Foote vacated his seat in Congress and left the

William L. Yancey of Alabama, member of the Confederate Senate

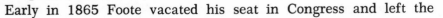

HARASSED
POLITICIANS   29

Confederacy. On February 27, 1865, the House by a two-thirds vote of the members adopted a resolution expelling him from membership. After a brief confinement by the Federals, Foote was permitted to sail for Europe. He later returned to the South where he devoted himself mainly to reminiscent and historical writing. He died in Nashville in 1880.

Another blustery and colorful figure in Congress was Senator Louis T. Wigfall, sometimes referred to as the Confederate Mirabeau. A South Carolinian by birth, Wigfall migrated to Texas in the 1840's, after a turbulent career in law and politics during which he killed one of his political enemies. In 1859 he entered the United States Senate. He was a strong proponent of slavery and state rights and an early advocate of secession. He left the Federal Senate on March 23, 1861, and went to Charleston where he played a bizarre role in the Fort Sumter crisis. After a short career as Confederate brigadier, during which he also served as a member of the Provisional Congress, he resigned his commission on February 18, 1862, to enter the Senate. Because of his intelligence, forthrightness, persistence and articulateness, Wigfall became a power in the upper house. He effectively supported conscription and impressment and other measures to strengthen the Southern armies. In the purely military realm he was a strong advocate of concentration of forces and unity of command. He and the President were on cordial terms in the early part of the war but after a few months they were estranged. It was rumored in Richmond and elsewhere that the break resulted from Wigfall's drunkenness. Whatever the origin of the antagonism, it was intensified by disagreement concerning high command and military policy. Wigfall deeply resented what he regarded as Davis' mistreatment of General Joseph E. Johnston and Quartermaster General A. C. Myers, and he castigated the President for preferring Bragg, Northrop, Pemberton and other "pets" over leaders whom Wigfall considered far more deserving.

Some of the most significant work in both houses was done by committees. Of these, the most important were those on military affairs. The Senate Military Affairs Committee was headed by Edward Sparrow of Louisiana, who was one of the few members of the upper house to serve in the legislative branch for the duration of the Confederacy. Sparrow was characterized by a South Carolina lawyer-planter who visited Richmond in 1864 as a "working, sensible man but not much above mediocrity," and this seems to be a fair evaluation. Much abler and more influential was his counterpart, William Porcher Miles, chairman of the House Military Affairs Committee. In the 1850's Miles served successively as mayor of Charleston and a member of Congress. He entered the Confederate Congress in February, 1861, and served for the remainder of the war. Though often at odds with Jefferson Davis, whom he considered "opinionated, self-willed and obstinate," Miles kept in close touch with high-ranking military leaders and worked diligently to sustain the armies and increase their effectiveness. After the war he served for

*Louis Trezevant Wigfall, active
at Fort Sumter and a member
of the Confederate Congress*

*William Porcher Miles of South
Carolina, Chairman of the House
Committee on Military Affairs*

two years as president of the University of South Carolina and then in
1882 moved to Louisiana to run the sugar plantation of his father-in-law.
He died on May 11, 1899.

The Senate Finance Committee was headed by another distinguished South Carolinian, Robert W. Barnwell. After graduating from
Harvard with highest honors in 1821, Barnwell served in both houses
of the national Congress and from 1835 to 1841 was president of the
University of South Carolina. He actively supported the secession of
South Carolina though he was not considered a fire-eater. He was a
member of the Provisional Congress and played a key role in the election
of Davis to the presidency. Davis offered him the position of Secretary
of State but he declined. He entered the Confederate Senate in February,
1862, and served in that body until the end of the war. His staunch and
consistent support of the administration caused one of his anti-Davis
constituents to complain in 1864 that "he has no policy but to sustain
the President."

The President had another staunch supporter in Benjamin H. Hill
of Georgia, chairman of the Senate Judiciary Committee. Davis referred
to this distinguished Georgian as "Hill the faithful"; and in a tribute

delivered in Atlanta when the Hill monument was unveiled in 1882, Davis stated: "From the beginning to the end . . . he was one on whose shoulder I could place my hand and feel that its foundation was as firm as marble." Hill's strong support of the President was the more remarkable in view of the fact that he had been a Whig and had earnestly fought secession to the last.

Another former Whig who served with distinction in the Confederate Senate was William A. Graham of North Carolina. After graduating from the University of North Carolina with high honors, Graham practiced law, with notable success. He was a United States senator, 1840–1843; governor of North Carolina, 1845–1859; and Secretary of the Navy under Fillmore, 1850–1853. In all of these positions he displayed exceptional statesmanship. During the secession crisis he worked diligently for the preservation of the Union, but when war came he promptly espoused the cause of the South and contributed five sons to the Confederate army. In May, 1864, he entered the Confederate Senate. His maturity, experience, gentility and wisdom gave him great prestige among his colleagues, and he was often consulted by President Davis. He worked to counteract the extreme state rights leaning of Governor Zebulon Vance of North Carolina, but he strongly opposed suspension of the writ of habeas corpus and some other measures designed to increase Presidential authority. His opposition to Davis was political rather than personal, although he thought the President lacking in statesmanship. By mid-February, 1865, if not before, Graham reached the conclusion that the Confederacy was doomed. But he remained at his post until Congress adjourned on March 18. In 1866 he was elected to the United States Senate but was not permitted to take his seat. He died in 1875.

Graham deserves to be rated as one of the ablest and most admirable members of the Confederate Senate. Among those who sat in the lower house, one who compared favorably with him in ability and character was J. L. M. Curry of Alabama. Curry, twenty-one years younger than Graham, was a Calhoun Democrat. Even so, the two had much in common. They were both of the planter class, tolerant, cultured, and strong advocates of public education. After graduating from the University of Georgia and the Harvard Law School, Curry served for several years in the Alabama legislature and was completing his second term in the United States House of Representatives when Alabama seceded. In the Confederate Congress he was a consistent supporter of the administration, although he once complained that "Mr. Davis gave to Congress very little information." He often presided over the House when Speaker Thomas S. Bocock was absent, and his colleagues were so impressed by his demeanor that some of them wanted to run him as Bocock's successor. The Richmond *Whig* described him as "a ripe scholar —a polished gentleman—a pious, exemplary Christian . . . a gifted orator—not only brilliant but solid . . . indefatigable as a practical working man, in committees and elsewhere." One of Curry's most no-

Jabez L. M. Curry of Alabama, member of the House

EMBATTLED
CONFEDERATES

table achievements was the preparation for a joint congressional committee of an "Address to the People of the Confederate States." This paper, enthusiastically approved by Congress in February, 1864, was printed in pamphlet form and widely circulated among soldiers and civilians. It reviewed the struggle between North and South, urged the people to support their leaders and sustain the armies, and predicted ultimate triumph of the Southern cause.

Largely because of his identification as a "Davis man" Curry was not elected to the Second Congress. In 1864 he became a lieutenant colonel in the Confederate cavalry and served as aide to Joseph E. Johnston and Joseph Wheeler. After the war he had a long and distinguished career in Southern education, serving as president of Howard College, agent of the Peabody and Slater Funds and supervising director of the Southern Education Board.

The majority of Confederate congressmen were men of much less ability than Curry, Graham and Barnwell, noticeably less colorful than Wigfall and considerably more stable than Foote. Some were time-servers, interested mainly in drawing their pay. Others were the eager sort who felt constrained to speak their views on every subject and who bored their associates with long-winded discourses. A few were more regular in their attendance at theaters and bars than in legislative halls and committee rooms. Most of them were neither geniuses nor dullards, saints nor knaves, spellbinders nor bores. Rather they were politicians of average ability and attainment who worked hard at their jobs and who represented reasonably well the interests of their constituents. They were criticized for shortsightedness, slowness, inefficiency and lack of courage in opposing the administration; and much of the censure was unquestionably deserved. But they were not as worthless and ineffectual as they were reputed to be. Many, such as W. S. Oldham and Herschel V. Johnson, supported administrative measures that ran counter to their views, on the ground that their opposition might do the country more harm than the laws to which they objected. Some of the problems which they were condemned for not solving, such as inflation and defeatism, were by their very nature impossible of solution. Their shortcomings were due in large part to inherent weaknesses in the system of representative government. Lawmaking bodies in a truly democratic government are generally slow, talkative and prone to the adoption of compromises which represent the desires of no one. The Confederate Congress appeared in a worse light than most legislative bodies because it represented a "nation with nothing," involved in a great modern war with a country whose resources were practically unlimited. In the light of the enormous difficulties with which it had to contend, its accomplishments appear more impressive than its shortcomings.

Congressmen usually worked in close collaboration with the governors of the states that they represented. All in all, thirty men served as governors of the thirteen Confederate states.* The governors of Missouri and Kentucky were exiles during most of their terms, though they attempted to keep in touch with constituents by correspondence, advised President Davis and other Confederate officials concerning political and military affairs affecting their states and maintained a semblance of executive authority. Governors in other invaded states, including those of Tennessee, Arkansas, Louisiana, Mississippi, Georgia and South Carolina, had to flee when the Federals approached. For some of them the removal was only temporary, but for a few it was for the duration of the war. Governor Isham G. Harris was one of those who had to abandon his capital early in the war. He was never able to resume his gubernatorial functions in Nashville owing to permanent occupation of the city by the Federals. Governor Harris commandeered a special train to take him and his entourage from the Tennessee capital when the invaders approached in February, 1862, and some of the civilians thought his exit inglorious. A McMinnville woman wrote in her diary in March: "Oh! Isham! Gallant, chivalrous, courageous and swift in the run Isham. We are yours in haste." And one of her neighbors, when asked, "Where *is* Harris?" replied: "We haven't been able to get a train swift enough to catch up with him and find out where he is." These aspersions on the Governor's courage were unfair, for he showed a special fondness for the battlefield. He was a volunteer aide of Albert Sidney Johnston and was with that general when he died. He later served on the staffs of Braxton Bragg and Joseph E. Johnston and was in nearly every major battle in which the Army of Tennessee participated.

The situation of Harris and other executives in exile, trying as it was, in many respects was less difficult than the plight of those who stayed on the job and wrestled with the problems that beset them. Because the Confederate government at first lacked administrative machinery and funds, the governors had to take the initiative in raising, organizing and equipping the South's fighting forces. And even after the central government was fully established, the governors were impelled by traditional views of state sovereignty to insist on playing a major role in the organization and control of Confederate troops raised within their boundaries. Disagreement between central and state authorities as to the areas of their jurisdiction produced vehement controversy and did much to impair the South's military effectiveness.

The governors also bore major responsibility for equipping and administering forces for local defense, preserving order, maintaining roads, providing relief for needy families and devising means for obtaining scarce commodities. All of these activities required money, and one of the major problems faced by all of the governors was that of raising the funds necessary for financing the expanded state services incident to war.

Governor Isham Green Harris of Tennessee

EMBATTLED
CONFEDERATES

* A list of governors will be found on page 274.

With the exception of Harris, whose executive functions after February, 1862, were nominal, the only governor whose incumbency extended throughout the Confederate period was Joseph E. Brown of Georgia, and Brown was without doubt the most turbulent and controversial of the Southern executives. Reared in the mountainous country of north Georgia, Brown worked as a farm laborer until he was nineteen. He then studied and taught for a while before entering the Yale Law School in 1845. After graduation he settled in Canton, Georgia, where for several years he devoted himself to law and politics. In 1849 he was elected to the state senate and eight years later he became governor. He was re-elected in 1859, 1861 and 1863.

Governor Joseph Emerson Brown of Georgia

Some of Brown's political foes regarded him as an unprincipled novice. But he proved to be a shrewd, rugged-minded politician, acutely sensitive to the public will. He endeared himself to the masses by his support of free schools and his ability to identify himself with popular needs and aspirations. He had boundless energy and was a forceful speaker.

He was an early and consistent advocate of secession and his devotion to state rights bordered on fanaticism. He displayed great initiative and zeal in raising troops and providing for them and their families. But he tended to think primarily in terms of Georgia's interests and his own prerogative, and he found it impossible to work harmoniously with the central government for the common good of the Confederate states. He doubtless thought that what was good for Georgia was good for the Confederacy, but his narrowness, combativeness, stubbornness and ambition brought him frequently into conflict with Confederate authorities and lessened the South's ability to cope with its foes.

Georgia's Chief Executive struck at conscription through a Confederate law which exempted civil officials whom the governors declared essential to the operation of the state governments. Brown concluded that practically all civil functionaries, including notary publics, tax collectors, clerks and militia officers were indispensable. He created new positions and gave blanket commissions to militiamen to increase the number of exemptions. Jefferson Davis claimed that 15,000 Georgians of conscript age were exempted as state officials while the Superintendent of Conscription estimated the total number of Georgians drafted into Confederate service from the beginning to February, 1865, at only 8,992.

Brown vehemently denounced impressment, martial law, suspension of the writ of habeas corpus, compulsory reduction of the currency and the arming of the slaves. On one occasion he wrote to Alexander Stephens: "I fear we have more to apprehend from military despotism than from subjugation by the enemy." His angry protests and his chronic obstructionism were a sore trial to President Davis and the Confederate cabinet, and many Georgians, including Howell Cobb, deeply deplored his resistance to the Confederate administration.

Governor Zebulon Baird Vance of North Carolina

But he seemed always able to command staunch support from the masses and was laying plans to stand for re-election when Lee surrendered at Appomattox. After the war he switched to the Republican party and became Chief Justice of the Georgia Supreme Court. When the Republicans lost out in Georgia, he became a Democrat again, entered actively into corporate business and amassed a large fortune. In the closing years of his life he served eleven years in the United States Senate.

Another governor who often came in conflict with the Confederate government was Zebulon Vance of North Carolina. Vance's background was similar to Brown's. He was the son of a farmer-merchant of western North Carolina, and his education was interrupted when he was only fourteen by his father's death. He eventually studied law at the University of North Carolina, practiced for a while and then entered politics as a Whig. He served two terms in Congress just before the outbreak of hostilities and staunchly opposed disunion. After Fort Sumter he became a strong advocate of secession. In May, 1861, he organized a volunteer company and three months later was elected colonel of the Twenty-sixth North Carolina Regiment. He proved a gallant and popular combat commander.

In June, 1862, the Conservative party of North Carolina, made up largely of old Whigs, chose Vance to run for governor against an original secessionist. Owing largely to popular dissatisfaction with the Democratic "ultras" who had taken the lead in secession, Vance won a decisive victory. His triumph was represented by his opponents as a setback to the Confederacy, but in his inaugural in September Vance pledged his administration to a vigorous prosecution of the war. He was an honest man and a loyal Confederate, and he lived up to his promise. But he had a deep concern for state rights and he shared the belief of many of his fellow North Carolinians that Confederate affairs were poorly managed.

The situation confronting Davis and Vance from the latter's election to the end of the war was one calling for mutual understanding and tolerance and a high order of statesmanship. Unfortunately neither executive measured up to the needs of the times. Vance tended to think too much in terms of state sovereignty and the interests of North Carolina. Davis, on the other hand, failed to take full cognizance of Vance's problems in combating dissident elements centering around W. W. Holden, peace-minded editor of the *North Carolina Standard* in Raleigh, and in sustaining enthusiasm for the Confederate cause.

Vance quarreled with the President over impressment, the suspension of the writ of habeas corpus and the administration of conscription. In claiming exemption for state officers he outdid the Governor of Georgia. He even declared the employees of cotton mills having state contracts to be state officials and hence beyond the reach of the draft. In the latter part of the war 15,000 to 20,000 men escaped military service as a result of Vance's exemption. Even more damaging to the Confederate cause perhaps was his insistence on importing supplies for the exclusive use of North Carolinians and devoting the military output of the state's forty cotton mills (one-third of all those in the South) to North Carolina troops alone. According to Professor Frank Owsley, "Governor Vance boasted that at the end of the war he had every one of his soldiers well clothed and had on hand in warehouses 92,000 uniforms, thousands of blankets, shoes and tents. But at the same time Lee's men in Virginia were barefooted, almost without blankets, tents, and clothing. Vance had enough uniforms to give every man in Lee's army two apiece."

It was exaggerated state consciousness and state pride more than anything else that caused Governor Vance to hoard this abundance and oppose Confederate policies. He took enormous pride in the fact that his state furnished about 125,000 troops for Confederate service. In the spring of 1864, when the peace movement in North Carolina reached threatening proportions, Vance toured the camps of Lee's army to inspirit Tarheel soldiers, and with notable results. General Lee rated the Governor's speeches as worth a reinforcement of 50,000 men. Vance also exhorted many audiences in North Carolina to hold fast in their support of the Southern cause. His ready wit, mastery of anecdote, solid reasoning, and compelling charm endeared him to his listeners and helped revive their drooping spirits. After Reconstruction Vance served again as governor and then was sent to the United States Senate, where he remained until his death in 1894.

In marked contrast to the particularism of Brown and Vance was the cooperativeness shown by Governors John Letcher of Virginia and John Milton of Florida in their relations with the Confederate administration. Letcher was lukewarm in his support of slavery and strongly opposed secession until Lincoln's call for troops on April 15, 1861. His tardiness in joining the secessionists, his deliberate manner and his complete lack of glamour, caused him to receive much criticism in the early period of the war. On November 23, 1861, John M. Daniel, the acerb editor of the Richmond *Examiner,* wrote in his paper: "There is nothing in the character, precepts or example of John Letcher to call upwards of sixty thousand volunteers to the tented field. . . . The only time our doughty Governor has been near to the field was when like a bird of evil omen he rode up in his carriage on the road to Rich Mountain, met the fugitives from a campaign he claimed to have planned and, in stern accents, with pocket-pistol in hand, bade them return to their duty and his driver to return to [the safety of] Staunton."

But "Honest John Letcher," as he was called when serving in Congress before the war, was much abler than his critics represented him to be. He was not always in agreement with Confederate leaders. He called Judah P. Benjamin sharply to task for intruding into army administration and provoking the resignation of Stonewall Jackson. He considered conscription unconstitutional, but he refused to oppose it. Shortly after the passage of the first draft law he declared that "harmony, unity and conciliation are indispensable now," and urged cheerful com-

Governor John Letcher of Virginia

pliance with its provisions. He realized the importance of teamwork and he gave the Confederate administration strong and loyal support until the end of his term on December 31, 1863.

John Milton was unlike Letcher in that he was an ardent secessionist and a firm believer in slavery. He was also more sensitive to state rights. But he was like Letcher in that he realized that harmony and amity were essential to Southern success. He doubted the constitutionality of conscription and had strong reservations concerning impressment. But he urged Floridians to acquiesce in these and other Confederate measures in the interest of the common good. He refused to grant wholesale exemptions to petty state officials, and he urged upon the Governor of Georgia the sensible course of postponing the agitation of state rights until the attainment of Southern independence. In the words of A. B. Moore, he "set a fine example" for all state executives. Early in the war he named one of his sons for Jefferson Davis, and his correspondence shows continuing cordiality toward the President throughout his administration. Hard work and chronic worry over the declining fortunes of the Confederacy so upset him that on April 1, 1865, he committed suicide.

In their relationships with the Confederate administration most of the governors fell between the extremes represented by Brown and Vance on the one hand and Letcher and Milton on the other, though as a group they stood closer to the former than the latter. Most of them maintained their own armies in the form of state militia or home guards, and by one device or another they were able to resist the repeated efforts of the Confederate Bureau of Conscription to take from state organizations men liable to Confederate service. Governor Rector of Arkansas in the fall of 1862 called into state service men whom agents of the central government were trying to draft into the Confederate army and then refused to turn them loose. In February, 1865, Governor Brown of Georgia furloughed "till the State is again threatened by the enemy" Georgia troops whom Beauregard had urgently requested for assistance in repelling Sherman.

One of the reasons for the unwillingness of the governors to render unto the central government that which both Confederate law and the common good required was exaggerated concern about the safety and welfare of their own people. Another reason was their lack of confidence in the Confederate government and its competency to make effective use of the country's resources. As the South's military fortunes declined, state governors and people in general came more and more to believe that Confederate affairs were being mismanaged and that the leaders in Richmond lacked the capacity to steer the South through to victory and independence. But the basic reason for each governor's trying to run his own show in his own way was the belief, sincerely held by most of them, that each state was an entity unto itself, sovereign, independent and self-sufficient, and hence not rightfully subject to the authority of

Jeff Davis and company. On February 10, 1865, Governor A. G. Magrath of South Carolina, who was by no means a self-seeking demagogue, but a leader of integrity and good intentions, wrote an acquaintance: "If in after times we shall analyse the causes which defeated the Revolution or multiplied the suffering & delayed the success of the cause, there will be but one opinion and that will be *our abandonment in its progress of the great truths which the Revolution was developed to establish* . . . [and] having permitted the sovereignty of the State to be degraded."

Working in close collaboration with the governors in resolving the problems incident to war were the state legislators. It is not surprising that the lawmakers found it necessary to meet more frequently during the conflict than before. Six Confederate states shifted from biennial to annual sessions during the war and the others resorted to the expedient of assembling occasionally in special session. North Carolina legislators supplemented their regular biennial meetings with seven extra sessions, while Texas and Mississippi held five called sessions and South Carolina held three. In several instances the conventions that enacted the secession ordinances and revised the state constitutions lingered on, or adjourned and reassembled, to exercise legislative functions. The North Carolina convention held four sessions, three of them during the period September, 1861, to November, 1862, when the legislature was in adjournment. The conventions generally reflected the viewpoint of the wealthy, conservative element and their assumption of the legislative function was in large measure a device of this element to increase its influence. In South Carolina and Florida the conventions established executive councils to advise the governor and help shape administrative policy.

Both the conventions and the councils were severely criticized for usurping legislative and executive authority, and they unquestionably caused confusion and conflict in the regulation of state affairs. The editor of the *Florida Sentinel* wrote on April 15, 1862: "Have we a constitutional government? Have we a Legislature? Have we a Judiciary? Or are all the powers of government . . . concentrated in and possessed by one set of men?" About the same time the editor of the Charleston *Courier* denounced South Carolina's Executive Council in these words: "It is a secret and irresponsible body, sitting with closed doors, without any check on its absolutism. We deny that the convention had any right to confer such powers on such a body." Some leaders defended conventions as more efficient and more representative of the popular will than the legislatures, but they were a minority. Opposition increased to such a point that both conventions and councils ceased to exist anywhere by the end of 1862.

The intrusion of conventions on their prerogative was only one of the many unusual difficulties confronted by the state legislatures, and it was of short duration. One of the first problems was the raising

The Governor's Mansion, Richmond, Virginia

of troops. As previously noted, the states took the initiative in mobilizing Southern manpower; the normal procedure was for regiments to be recruited and organized by state authorities and then turned over to the Confederacy. Frequently in the early period of the war units were delivered to Confederate officials fully uniformed and equipped. In addition to providing troops for Confederate service, the legislatures were responsible for raising and maintaining units for local defense.

The state legislatures cooperated with the governors to provide relief for soldier families, refugees and other indigent civilians. They instituted crop control to divert acreage from cotton and tobacco to corn, wheat and other food crops. They took emergency measures to procure and make available at reasonable prices scarce commodities such as salt, medicine, leather, textiles, farm implements and equipment for making homespun cloth. They gave bonuses to individuals to stimulate production, aided factories and subsidized railroads. In many instances they authorized the state to enter directly into production and distribution. To finance all these activities they provided for the floating of bonds and the issuance of state notes. They also increased taxes, though they showed considerably more timidity in taxing than in borrowing. Against

EMBATTLED
CONFEDERATES

tremendous opposition they passed stay laws for the relief of debtors. They devoted much attention to keeping courts in session and maintaining the normal processes of civil government. They showed less concern for maintaining schools, but this was due largely to the fact that at that time education was considered more of a private than a public responsibility. The lawmakers wrestled mightily with hoarding and speculation, but with only limited success.

The state legislatures worked under great handicaps and were subjected to frequent and scathing criticism. "I never saw such perfect, hopeless incapacity," remarked William H. Trescot after a visit to the South Carolina capital in December, 1861. A few weeks later Gideon Lincecum, an eccentric Texan, wrote a friend: "Don't you esteem our legislature . . . they passed a good many relief bills, protected the sabbath, enacted the damnable stay law and made a desperate effort to draw the last dollar from the treasury. . . . If ever one of them gets elected again . . . it won't be by my vote."

Much of the criticism directed at the general assemblies was unquestionably well-founded. The quality of most state legislatures left much to be desired in antebellum times and the war brought marked deterioration. Some of the most able assemblymen, actual or potential, preferred military service to lawmaking and others chose to stay at home to look after their families and businesses. Legislators often had to pay high prices for uncomfortable lodging and unpalatable food. They frequently had to listen to long-winded, pedestrian speeches. They were called on to deal with problems that defied solution. In their frustration and boredom some of them took to excessive drink; others imbibed freely from habit, or to forestall boredom. In liquor or sober, a few let their tempers get out of hand and made scenes in legislative halls or in places less respectable. Shortly after Alabama seceded, a legislator from Pickens County named Clitherall, during a discussion following passage of a stay law, said that had he known such a measure was forthcoming he would have preferred staying in the Union "even under Lincoln's administration." This provoked a hiss from a colleague. Clitherall then said if the gentleman—"no, the goose, as gentlemen did not hiss"—would reveal himself he would "put his mouth in such a condition as to make it impossible to engage in that pastime for a week." Immediately George C. Henry of Mobile announced himself as the hisser. Clitherall promptly hurled an inkstand at Henry and then leaped over his desk to push the attack with his fists. Friends broke up the melee but the newspapers reported the incident and the reputation of the body to which the participants belonged suffered in consequence.

Several legislatures had to shift their meeting place to elude the invaders. And some took to flight under circumstances which brought scorn from their constituents. A Nashville journalist who reported the departure of the Tennessee lawmakers after the fall of Fort Donelson, stated that the legislators evidenced "anxiety and fear" and "presented rather a ludicrous appearance as they trudged off towards the depot . . . each one with a trunk on his back or carpet sacks and bundle in hand." A Georgia girl who witnessed the demoralization of the legislators of that state when Sherman approached Milledgeville noted in her diary: "The scene at the State House was truly ridiculous; the members were badly scared; such a body of representatives make my cheeks glow with shame. What a time it was for the display of cool, wise legislation and undaunted courage and exalted patriotism; instead of that they passed a law levying troops *en masse*, excepting the legislators and judiciary. . . . [Two of them] paid three thousand dollars for the conveyance to move with speed from this place of danger."

Not all of the legislatures fled in panic in the hour of invasion. The Virginia assembly, for example, conducted itself with becoming calm and dignity when McClellan threatened Richmond in 1862. And the character and work of a number of legislatures was the subject of favorable comment in newspapers and correspondence of the times. The *Florida Sentinel* stated after the adjournment of a session in November, 1863: "We know of no better working body than the last general assembly for many years past." A veteran North Carolina solon wrote his wife on November 29, 1862: "The Legislature is giting along pretty well —we have perfected more legislation than at any previous session in the same time since I was a member of this body."

The performance of most wartime legislatures fell considerably below that suggested by these two comments. But when the circumstances under which they labored are taken into account, and full consideration given to the enormity and complexity of their problems, it must be acknowledged that they acquitted themselves reasonably well. In a comprehensive, unpublished study of Confederate state legislatures, Professor May S. Ringold of Clemson University summarizes their work as follows: "They devised paper schemes to support local and Confederate defense, to maintain business-as-usual economy and normalcy in the operation of social and political institutions. They abandoned traditions to set up relief programs. . . . But a pervading weakness sapped at the foundations of Southern society. Without money, credit and industrial productivity, Southern states could build only with straw. They could set the house in order but they could not prevent its collapse."

III. *The High Brass*

The Southern Confederacy was far more impressive in the realm of military activities than in politics and government. This was due in large measure to the high quality of its military leadership. The persistence of frontier conditions, the menace of hostile Indians, the threat of slave insurrection and attachment to the ideal of chivalry all tended to promote a martial spirit in the South and to lend prestige to the profession of arms. The military academy was a favored institution in antebellum times and many talented young Southerners obtained appointments to West Point. The highest-ranking officers in the Confederate army—the full generals and lieutenant generals—were all graduates of the United States Military Academy except Nathan Bedford Forrest, Wade Hampton and Richard Taylor. Of the 72 major generals and 328 brigadiers, 124 were West Point graduates and ten others had one or more years' schooling there.*

Southerners during, before and after the war attached great importance to military rank. The Confederacy had eight full generals and seventeen lieutenant generals, while the Union had no full generals and U. S. Grant was the only lieutenant general (Winfield Scott held the rank by brevet, which means that the title was honorary).

On the Federal side rank was designated as it is in the American army today, with one star denoting a brigadier, two stars a major general and three stars a lieutenant general. The stars were attached to shoulder straps. All Confederate generals wore the same insignia—three stars in a wreath, attached to the collar (three stars without a wreath indicated a colonel, two stars a lieutenant colonel and one star a major; captains wore three bars, first lieutenants two bars and second lieutenants one bar). In practice, high-ranking officers sometimes deviated from the rules specified in uniform regulations. General Lee, for example, appears in photographs wearing the unwreathed stars prescribed for colonels.

General Samuel Cooper

The eight full generals, in order of their seniority, were Samuel Cooper (the Adjutant General), Albert Sidney Johnston, Robert E. Lee, Joseph E. Johnston, P. G. T. Beauregard, Braxton Bragg, E. Kirby Smith and John B. Hood. The lieutenant generals, in order of seniority, were

* For a full list of Confederate generals, arranged alphabetically by rank, see pages 275–279.

James Longstreet, Leonidas Polk, William J. Hardee, Thomas J. Jackson, T. H. Holmes, John C. Pemberton, Richard S. Ewell, A. P. Hill, D. H. Hill, Richard Taylor, Jubal A. Early, R. H. Anderson, S. D. Lee, A. P. Stewart, Simon B. Buckner, Wade Hampton and Nathan B. Forrest. Joseph Wheeler and John B. Gordon were commonly listed as lieutenant generals, but Ezra J. Warner, author of *Generals in Gray* and best authority on the subject, concludes that they were never officially promoted to that rank.

Lieutenant General
Theophilus Hunter Holmes

As a group, Confederate generals represented tremendous variations. The eldest, David E. Twiggs, was seventy-one when the war began; William P. Roberts, the youngest, was only twenty at that time and only twenty-three when he got his wreathed stars on February 21, 1865. Septuagenarians were outnumbered by youngsters. Seventy Confederates who became brigadiers were still in their twenties when the war began and the average age of all the 425 men who were to wear the three wreathed stars was between thirty-five and forty. It is difficult to realize that most of the generals who peered out over a mass of whiskers in Confederate photographs were under forty.

The majority of the 425 generals had been lawyers, planters or businessmen in antebellum times. Twenty-four had been politicians and fifteen had been educators. Only 125 were career soldiers. Most of them could speak and write reasonably well. Extremes of cultural attainment were represented by Nathan Bedford Forrest, who had about six months' schooling; and James Johnston Pettigrew, who graduated from the University of North Carolina with an outstanding record at nineteen, taught two years at the naval observatory in Washington and then devoted two years to study and travel in Europe.

Lieutenant General
Richard Taylor

As representatives of a society steeped in chivalry, these military chieftains were inclined to venerate women, be fiercely loyal to their friends, resent quickly any personal affront, respect manly virtues and observe good manners in all their relationships. Sensitiveness to honor associated with chivalry, exaggerated individualism nurtured by the plantation system and the unusual tensions created by the war led to a shocking amount of strife among the generals. Robert Toombs challenged his superior, D. H. Hill, to a duel after Hill reproved him for the manner in which he handled his brigade at Malvern Hill. Nathan Bedford Forrest strode into Bragg's tent in October, 1863, after transfer of his troops to Joe Wheeler without notification or explanation and said: "You have played the part of a damned scoundrel, and are a coward, and if you were any part of a man I would slap your jaws and force you to resent it. You may as well not issue any more orders to me for I will not obey them. . . . If you ever again try to interfere with me or cross my path it will be at the peril of your life." Bitter controversy raged between Floyd and Wise, Longstreet and McLaws, Price and Holmes, Kirby Smith and Richard Taylor, and several others. In some instances differences were not confined to the exchange of angry words. In

EMBATTLED
CONFEDERATES

September, 1863, Brigadier General John S. Marmaduke killed Brigadier General Lucius M. Walker in a duel growing out of Marmaduke's alleged impugnment of Walker's courage in battle. Three days before Lee's surrender, Colonel George W. Baylor fatally shot Major General John A. Wharton during a heated argument in a Houston hotel. In June, 1863, Nathan Bedford Forrest, after receiving a bullet from an aggrieved subordinate, Lieutenant A. W. Gould, fatally stabbed his assailant with a knife.

Several distinct types were to be found among high-ranking military leaders. The romantic cavalier was represented by the dashing "Jeb" Stuart, who surrounded himself with gay companions, wore a feather in his hat and delighted in the smiles and plaudits of beautiful women,

ajor General George dward Pickett *Major General James Ewell Brown "Jeb" Stuart* *Major General Joseph Wheeler* *Brigadier General John Hunt Morgan*

but who was tremendously effective in reconnaissance and on the battle-field. The beau sabreur was typified by the handsome and able Earl Van Dorn, whose flirtations were the subject of much comment among both soldiers and civilians and who died of a bullet fired by a jealous husband at Spring Hill, Tennessee, in May, 1863. Hardly less glamorous than Stuart and Van Dorn were John Hunt Morgan, gallant and good-looking horseman from the Kentucky Bluegrass; "Fighting Joe" Wheeler, youthful, hard-hitting cavalryman of Georgia and Alabama; and George E. Pickett, the vain but valiant Virginian who led the desperate assault at Gettysburg on the third day. According to G. Moxley Sorrel, Longstreet's chief of staff, Pickett wore his hair in long ringlets, "trimmed and highly perfumed," and in the spring of 1863 slipped away from his command at night, sometimes without leave, to court the beautiful LaSalle Corbell whom he was to marry later that year.

Lieutenant General
Wade Hampton

Lieutenant General
Ambrose Powell Hill

Lieutenant General
Richard Stoddert Ewell

Brigadier General
Humphrey Marshall

The hail-fellow-well-met type was exemplified by Humphrey Marshall of Kentucky, who could hold his own with the best at the festive board or the hustings. Once, after a hearty drinking session, he urged his men to push the war through to a successful conclusion even if they had to wade waist deep in blood. One of the men who had not imbibed as freely as Marshall broke in at this point to remark: "General, that's too deep for me. I only contracted to go in knee deep."

The patrician warrior was exemplified by Wade Hampton, the giant South Carolinian who marshaled his neighbors, his sons and even his Negroes (as body servants) in Hampton's Legion and led them so effectively in the early battles that he rose steadily in rank and after Stuart's death was given command of the cavalry of Lee's army. He was thrice wounded, and in October, 1864, at Hatcher's Run, two of his sons, Preston and Wade, were wounded—the former mortally—in an action directed by their father. As the parent reached the scene of the tragedy, he leaped from his horse, took the dying Preston in his arms, poignantly muttered, "My son, my son," kissed him tenderly and then quickly remounted and rode forward to battle.

Scattered among the 425 generals were a considerable number of characters. One of these was Ambrose Powell Hill, who flaunted danger by wearing a red shirt on the battlefield, but whose prowess in combat was attested by the fact that both Jackson and Lee called for him in their dying deliriums. Despite the gaudy shirt and much reckless exposure he lived on until near the very end of hostilities when his life was snuffed out by a Federal bullet as he rode out to repel the Federal breakthrough near Petersburg on April 2, 1865. D. H. Hill was in many respects more unusual than A. P. Hill. Harvey, as he was called to distinguish him from the other Hill, was a caustic little man who ap-

EMBATTLED
CONFEDERATES

parently knew not the meaning of fear. In the thick of battle he would sit out in an open place on his horse, one foot thrown across the pommel of his saddle, the bullets whizzing about his head, surveying the scene as calmly as if he were back on the campus of Davidson College where he taught mathematics before the war. He was devoted to the men who carried the muskets but had little use for those in the supporting services. Once when a bugler applied for a furlough, Hill turned him down with the comment: "Disapproved—shooters before tooters." His frequent indulgence in sharp criticism, which may have been due in part to his ulcerous stomach, aroused much enmity among his associates and brought him into disfavor with President Davis. But he never lost the admiration and affection of his men.

*Lieutenant General
Daniel Harvey Hill*

Another odd character was R. S. Ewell, known as "Old Bald Head" by the soldiers. General John B. Gordon, who served under Ewell, described him as "a compound of anomalies, the oddest, most eccentric genius in the Confederate army." When Gordon first met him on the morning of First Manassas, Ewell shocked the young officer by saying: "Come and eat a cracker with me; we will breakfast together here and dine together in hell." Ewell had a high-pitched, squeaky voice and spoke with a lisp. His smooth dome, bulging eyes and tilted head gave him the appearance of a woodcock. He was an exceedingly modest man, and at a most serious moment was apt to pipe out the question, "Now why do you suppose President Davis made me a general anyway?" He was much given to profanity in the early part of the war but after his marriage to the widow Brown in 1863 he became more careful of both his language and his life. So absent-minded was he and so habituated to bachelorhood, that for some time after his marriage he would occasionally introduce his bride as "my wife, Mrs. Brown." Ewell was an aggressive and reliable division leader while operating under Jackson, but loss of a leg at Groveton impaired his mobility and possibly affected his mental outlook. He was considerably less impressive as a corps commander, entrusted with the discretionary authority habitually conferred by Lee on his principal subordinates. His failure to seize Cemetery Hill or Culp's Hill on July 1, 1863, is considered by many to have been the turning point at Gettysburg. True, in not pressing forward he was acting within the spirit of Lee's broad directive; but Major Sandie Pendleton, who served as adjutant to both Jackson and Ewell, expressed a widespread feeling when he quietly remarked late in the afternoon of July 1, 1863: "Oh for the presence and inspiration of Old Jack just for one hour."

No less of a character than Ewell was his friend and subordinate, Jubal A. Early. Both were profane, hard-fighting, rough-and-ready combat commanders. "Old Jubilee," when told at a critical point in a battle that the enemy could not be driven across a stream for lack of ammunition, replied: "Then, damn it, holler 'em across," and it was done. Another story about Early which was told about the campfires with much relish had to do with a chaplain. When "Old Jube" saw a uniformed

Lieutenant General Jubal Anderson Early

minister heading rapidly for the rear at Fredericksburg, he shouted: "Chaplain, where are you going?"

"General, I am going to a place of safety in the rear," replied the minister.

Early immediately retorted: "Chaplain, I have known you for the past thirty years, and all that time you have been trying to get to Heaven, and now that the opportunity is offered, you are fleeing from it, sir. I am surprised."

Still another Early anecdote relates to his conduct at a religious service near the end of the war. At the close of a sermon the minister stated with feeling: "Suppose, my Christian friends, that those who have laid for centuries in their graves should arise now and come forth from their quiet resting places, and, marching in their white shrouds, should pass before this congregation, by thousands and tens of thousands, what would be the result?" The hush that followed was broken by Early's loud whisper to his companion: "Ah, I'd conscript every damned one of them."

Early had a drive and a combativeness akin to that of Jackson, but he fell considerably short of Stonewall's resourcefulness and genius. He had his times of greatness, as at First and Second Manassas, but he seems to have become overconfident when sent to oppose Sheridan in the Shenandoah Valley and he never quite measured up as an independent commander. He lacked Ewell's modesty and warmth and he had more than his share of ambition. But there was never any question about his bravery and his total war record was one of which he could rightly be proud.

Except for Samuel Cooper, the Confederacy's full generals were army or department commanders. The most illustrious of these and the most revered of all the South's military leaders was Robert E. Lee. On March 1, 1862, William H. Trescot, distinguished South Carolina diplomat, wrote to a friend: "Lee is the only man in the revolution whom I have met that at all rises to historical size." This discerning estimate, made while Lee was relatively obscure, was to be abundantly confirmed by subsequent events.

Robert Edward Lee, fifth child of "Light-Horse Harry" and Ann Carter Lee, was born January 19, 1807. Following graduation as second in the class of 1829 at West Point, he was engaged in various engineer duties until 1846 when he joined the forces of General Winfield Scott in the campaign which led to the capture of Mexico City. His service in the Mexican War won him three brevets for gallantry and the high praise of his superiors. He was superintendent of West Point from 1852 to 1855 and was appointed lieutenant colonel of the Second Cavalry in 1855. He was promoted to colonel on March 16, 1861. His letters to his family during the secession crisis indicate deep devotion to the Union and great annoyance with extremists of both sections. Like many Southerners of the time, however, he felt a greater attachment to his state than

*General Robert
Edward Lee*

to the nation; when Virginia seceded, he turned down an offer to command the Federal forces and espoused the cause of the Old Dominion and the South. After a brief tour as commander of Virginia state forces he entered Confederate service on May 14, 1861. His initial assignment of repelling the Federal invasion of western Virginia was beset with many difficulties and was not successful. Jefferson Davis ignored the criticism unjustifiably directed at Lee and in March, 1862, made him military adviser to the President. After the serious wounding of Joseph E. Johnston at Seven Pines, Lee, on June 1, 1862, became commanding general of the Army of Northern Virginia. He held this position for the rest of the war. After February 6, 1865, he served also as general in chief of the Confederate armies.

In the Seven Days' Campaign, June 26 to July 1, 1862, Lee's command performance left much to be desired. His plan was overly elaborate, staff work was lamentably deficient and movements were poorly coordinated. But Richmond was saved and Lee learned valuable lessons from his first attempt to direct an army in battle. How well he learned was vividly demonstrated by his brilliant victory over Pope at Second Manassas, August 29–30, 1862. The Sharpsburg Campaign, coming immediately thereafter, might be called a draw, and Fredericksburg was such a great Federal blunder as to make relatively little demand on Lee's talents as a commander. At Chancellorsville, May 1–3, 1863, "Marse Robert," after being outmaneuvered in the initial stage, seized the initiative and won a smashing victory over "Fighting Joe" Hooker. Here in a most impressive manner Lee demonstrated the resourcefulness, boldness, character and genius of the truly great commander.

Never again did Lee shine with the brilliance manifested at Chancellorsville. At Gettysburg he revealed some of the weaknesses shown during the Seven Days. Staff work was poor, orders were imprecise (particularly those given to Stuart), and coordination was wanting. But Lee was operating at considerable disadvantage. His supply lines were overextended; he was unfamiliar with the country; two of his corps commanders were new; and Lee himself, according to Colonel W. W. Blackford, was sick with diarrhea. Moreover, the Union forces, in leadership, training and equipment, were greatly superior to those encountered in the early battles. After Gettysburg the increasing disparity between Lee's strength and that of his opponents forced him to assume a defensive role. In this capacity he proved a formidable antagonist. During the thirty days from the Wilderness to Second Cold Harbor he inflicted 55,000 casualties on Grant's forces and compelled the Union commander to shift to the slow but certain siege which, after nine months, brought about the surrender at Appomattox.

As great as Lee was as a field commander, he was even greater as a man. He was a considerate and affectionate father and husband. In January, 1864, he wrote his wife: "I would rather be in a hut with my own family than in a palace with others." But he scrupulously denied to

EMBATTLED
CONFEDERATES

himself and his family any comforts or favors not available to others. Early in 1864, Mary Lee wrote her husband asking him to appoint their son, Bob, to his staff. The General replied: "His company would be a great pleasure and a comfort to me and he would be extremely useful to me in various ways. . . . But I am opposed to officers surrounding themselves with their sons and relatives. It is wrong in principle and in that case the selection of officers would be made from private and social relations rather than the public good. . . . I should prefer Bob's being in the line, in an independent position, where he could rise by his own merit."

He was tolerant, tactful, modest and magnanimous. After Gettysburg, instead of criticizing the President for not sending reinforcements that he had requested or berating his subordinates for their shortcomings, he manfully assumed complete responsibility for the failure. One of the sublimest statements in the history of warfare is his remark to General Pickett after the climactic charge of July 3: "This has been my fight and upon my shoulders rests the blame. . . . Your men have done all that men could do. The fault is entirely my own." His one great weakness as a commander, according to Douglas Southall Freeman, was "excessive consideration for others."

He was a deeply religious man, and while he was not the teetotaler represented by his biographers (his war letters to his wife indicate that he occasionally drank brandy, and possibly whiskey, for medical purposes), he was remarkably chaste in habit and speech. Douglas Southall Freeman stated after completing many years of research for the four-volume biography that he had not been able to find any evidence of the use by Lee of a single profane or obscene word or phrase.

But Lee was no prig. He possessed a lively sense of humor. He liked to tease his daughters. He was keenly sensitive to feminine charm and from early manhood to old age he delighted in associating with beautiful women.

Duty was the guiding rule of his life. On one occasion he stated: "There is a true glory and a true honor, the glory of duty done, the honor of integrity of principle." To his son he wrote: "I know that wherever you may be placed, you will do your duty. That is all the pleasure, all the comfort, all the glory we can enjoy in this world."

In defeat he rose to supreme greatness. He accepted fully and finally the verdict of arms. He realized that Federal victory meant the triumph of national authority over local authority and that henceforth his first loyalty must be to the nation and not to Virginia. After laying aside his Confederate uniform and sword, he consistently and earnestly devoted himself to being a useful citizen, and he urged the same course on all his associates and former comrades. A part of being a good citizen, as he saw it, was to help restore the conquered and desolate South and to make it a healthy and prosperous region, fully attuned to the promise and progress of the great country of which it was a part. He spent his

General Braxton Bragg

General Pierre Gustave Toutant Beauregard

last years as president of Washington College, preparing young Southerners for lives of usefulness in a reunited country. The noblest Confederate thus became an exemplary American.

As certainly as Lee was the greatest of the South's army commanders, Beauregard was the most glamorous. Born on a plantation near New Orleans of an "ancient and honorable" French family, and reared in a household where only French was spoken, Pierre Gustave Toutant Beauregard was acutely conscious of his heritage. From his eleventh to fifteenth years he attended a New York school operated by two of Napoleon's officers. Here began an attachment to the dazzling Corsican that was to have an undying influence on Beauregard's life. As a Confederate leader he imagined himself a second Napoleon, and even in his photographs he assumed the pose of the hero of Ulm and Austerlitz. After graduating from West Point, second in a class of forty-five in 1838, he served with distinction in the Mexican War. Early in 1861 he resigned his captain's commission in the Federal army and was immediately commissioned a brigadier general in the Confederacy. His successful attack on Fort Sumter in April, 1861, rocketed him to fame.

A second spectacular victory at First Manassas made his name a byword in Confederate households. Babies, pet animals and marches were named for him, and his martial exploits were the subject of poems and songs. Numerous feminine admirers requested locks of his dark, curly hair. Few men ever enjoyed adulation more than he or responded to it more dramatically.

Beauregard's release of a report blaming Jefferson Davis with failure to follow up the victory at First Manassas brought him into the President's disfavor, and Davis was further annoyed by the General's order stopping the fight at Shiloh after Albert Sidney Johnston's death on April 6, 1862. When a few weeks later the "Grand Creole" went on sick leave without consulting authorities in Richmond, Davis summarily removed him from command of the Army of Tennessee. In August, 1862, Beauregard became commander of the Department of South Carolina, Georgia and Florida, and his successful defense of Charleston the following year was one of his most notable achievements. He was transferred to Virginia in the spring of 1864 and was credited with saving Petersburg and Richmond in June when Grant shifted his forces across the James River to launch an attack against Lee from the south. In October, 1864, he was given command of the Military Division of the West. He concluded his Confederate service as second in command of the forces opposing W. T. Sherman. After the war he managed the Louisiana Lottery and was Commissioner of Public Works in New Orleans. He died on February 20, 1893. Professor T. Harry Williams, author of the best and most recent biography of him, rates him as a good general, but not a great one. This seems to be a fair estimate.

The general who replaced Beauregard as commander of the Army of Tennessee in June, 1862, was Braxton Bragg, a native of North Carolina. Jefferson Davis had formed a favorable opinion of Bragg in the Mexican War and he expected great things of him. When Bragg failed to display a high order of generalship, and a chorus of complaint arose against him, Davis took the view that the criticism heaped upon the General was really directed at the President. He clung to Bragg through failure after failure with a persistence which caused many people to refer to the General as "Jeff Davis' Pet."

After graduating from West Point in 1837, Bragg served against the Seminoles and commanded a battery under General Zachary Taylor in Mexico. His superior leadership at Buena Vista was rewarded by a brevet lieutenant colonelcy. In 1856 he resigned from the army and devoted himself to planting and engineering in Louisiana. On February 23, 1861, he became a brigadier general in the Confederate army and took over the defense of the coastal area between Mobile and Pensacola. He was promoted to major general in March, 1862, and shortly afterward took command of a corps under Albert Sidney Johnston. He was in the thick of the fight at Shiloh and shortly afterward became a full general. A strict disciplinarian, with a special bent for administration, he was to aid the Southern cause substantially in noncombatant activities, but Shiloh marked his zenith as a battle leader. In the autumn of 1862 he led an expedition into Kentucky but, owing largely to his mismanagement, the results were meager. He failed to follow through after winning an initial advantage at Murfreesboro on December 31, 1862, and three days later yielded the field to the Federals. This failure was repeated after the victory at Chickamauga on September 20, 1863. As a result Bragg's corps commanders openly declared a lack of confidence in their superior. But the President refused to replace him until the overwhelming disaster at Missionary Ridge, November 25, 1863, led Bragg to ask for relief. Davis then assigned him to Richmond and made him responsible, under Presidential direction, for military operations of all the Confederate armies. Late in 1864 he was appointed commander of the Department of North Carolina, and on March 19, 1865, under Joseph E. Johnston, he led some of his old troops in the battle of Bentonville. After the war he was engaged in engineering activities in Alabama and Texas. He died in Galveston, September 27, 1876.

Bragg seems to have aroused more criticism than any other high-ranking Confederate general. On July 20, 1863, a Louisiana private wrote in his diary: "The most he is fit for is the command of a brigade and he would make a damned poor brigadier." Much of the adverse comment about Bragg was based on prejudice or hearsay. But William W. Mackall, who was Bragg's chief of staff and who credited him with industry, patriotism and integrity, considered him erratic and emotionally unstable. On September 29, 1863, Mackall wrote his family: "He is very earnest at his work, his whole soul is in it, but his manner is repulsive. . . . He is easily flattered and fond of seeing reverence for his high position. . . . If he don't want news to be true, he will listen to nothing . . . and if it proves true, he is not prepared to meet it. . . . I tell you frankly, I am afraid of his Generalship. . . . He has not genius. . . . His mind is not fertile, nor is his judgement good." In the light of history, this discerning commentary seems to hit very close to the truth.

One of the most controversial of the army commanders was Joseph Eggleston Johnston, who headed the Army of Northern Virginia (officially called the Army of the Potomac until March 14, 1862) from June 20, 1861, to May 31, 1862, and the Army of Tennessee from December 18, 1863, to July 17, 1864, and from February 23 to April 26, 1865. During the war some Confederate authorities, including Jefferson Davis, declared him overcautious, slow and uncooperative. Other contemporaries praised him for his tactical skill, his quiet dignity and the high esteem in which he was held by his officers and men. Present-day experts seem no nearer agreement concerning his personality and abilities than were his fellow Confederates. Gilbert E. Govan and James W. Livingood, in their biography, *A Different Valor*, give him a high rating; but Clifford Dowdey, a leading historian of the Confederacy, repeatedly refers to him as "Retreatin' Joe" in *The Land They Fought For*.

General Joseph Eggleston Johnston

Johnston was a native Virginian of distinguished parentage. He graduated from West Point in 1829 and in the years following held various artillery and engineer assignments. He made a splendid record in the Mexican War and came out of that conflict with five wounds and a brevet lieutenant colonelcy. In June, 1860, he became Quartermaster General of the United States Army with rank of brigadier general. When Virginia seceded, Johnston resigned from the Federal service and shortly afterward became a Confederate brigadier. He was the ranking general at First Manassas and shared with Beauregard the laurels won on that field. On August 31, 1861, President Davis, in nominating the five full generals authorized by Congress, specified the order of their rank thus: first, Samuel Cooper; second, Albert Sidney Johnston; third, R. E. Lee; fourth, Joseph E. Johnston; and fifth, P. G. T. Beauregard. A law of March 14, 1861, stated that Federal officers entering Confederate service should have the same relative rank that they had had in the old army. Since Johnston was the only Confederate who held a general's commission at the time of resignation from the Federal army, he expected to rank first among the Southern generals. When he learned that Davis had placed him below three others, he wrote the President protesting against "the wrong" which had been done him and asserting that "I still rightfully hold the rank of first general in the Armies of the Southern Confederacy." Davis, much offended by the letter, immediately wrote in reply: "Its language is, as you say, unusual; its arguments and statements utterly one sided, and its insinuations as unfounded as they are unbecoming." After the war Davis justified ranking Johnston fourth on the ground that he held his general's commission in the old army by virtue of a staff appointment; but the Confederate law made no distinction between the rank of line and staff officers and Davis was inconsistent in that he placed Samuel Cooper, whose highest line rank in the United States army was captain and who had never risen above colonel in a staff position, three notches above Johnston. Obviously the President did not want Johnston to outrank Cooper, Sidney Johnston and Lee, all of whom were Davis' good friends. It is possible, but not provable, that hostile feeling existed between Davis and Johnston because of an old quarrel, or because of friction between their wives. Be that as it may, the two were never on cordial terms after September, 1861. Johnston's subsequent actions were colored by a deep-seated suspicion that the President bore a grudge toward him and that Davis would not hesitate to use unfair means to undermine him. Relations were not helped by the fact that both men were proud, sensitive and hard-headed.

Johnston was greatly disappointed that Davis did not restore him to command of the Army of Northern Virginia when he recovered from the wound received at Seven Pines. He did not want the command of the Department of the West to which he was appointed in November 24, 1862. He took a more favorable view of the command of the Army of Tennessee when he received that assignment in December, 1863, for he liked an active field command and he was warmly received by both officers and men. But he knew that Davis had assigned him to the position reluctantly and with misgivings, and Senator Louis T. Wigfall and other prominent friends warned him to be on guard against the President's machinations.

With the odds heavily against him, Johnston put up a skillful and stubborn resistance to Sherman in the Georgia campaign of 1864. But he was forced to yield ground, and as he gradually fell back toward Atlanta he was subjected to increasing criticism, particularly by civilians. Natural reticence and distrust of Davis impelled him to keep his plans to himself. On July 17, 1864, he was relieved from command and ordered to turn the army over to General Hood. When news of his replacement reached the soldiers, many of them openly wept. An officer wrote on July 19: "With his troops nothing he did was wrong. He was

56   EMBATTLED
          CONFEDERATES

beloved far beyond any commander that ever controlled any portion of the army." The ragged remnant who survived Hood's disastrous Tennessee campaign the following winter gave Johnston a rousing welcome when Lee restored him to command in February, 1865, and in their last battle at Bentonville, on March 19, they showed their old commander that they would still fight gallantly under his lead. After the war he served a term in Congress and was commissioner of railroads. He died on March 21, 1891, from an illness precipitated by a cold contracted after standing bareheaded in the rain while acting as honorary pallbearer at the funeral of his friend and former antagonist, William T. Sherman.

The only army commander killed in battle on the Confederate side —and the only one to die during the war—was Albert Sidney Johnston. A thoroughly admirable man, he resembled Lee in character and personality.

General Albert Sidney Johnston

Johnston was born on February 2, 1803, at Washington, Kentucky, and attended Transylvania University before entering the United States Military Academy. Following his graduation from West Point in 1826, he performed routine tours at various army posts and took part in the Black Hawk War. He resigned his commission in 1834 and in July, 1836, moved to Texas where he served in the Texas army, first as a private, then as an adjutant general and finally as commanding general. During the war with Mexico he was colonel of the First Texas Rifles and inspector general under William O. Butler. In the 1850's he served successively as paymaster of the United States Army in Texas, colonel of the Second Cavalry and brevet brigadier in the Mormon war. In January, 1861, he took command of the Department of the Pacific, but when Texas seceded he resigned his commission and made his way overland to Richmond. President Davis appointed him general and put him in charge of the Western Department where he commanded the field forces that eventually became the Army of Tennessee. Appalling shortages of men and arms made it impossible for him to hold the long line for which he was responsible. He was severely criticized during the war and afterward for entrusting the defense of Fort Donelson to subordinates instead of taking on himself the protection of that vital point. But Professor Charles P. Roland, the best authority on Johnston, questions the validity of the censure, and Jefferson Davis' reply to those who urged Johnston's replacement after the fall of Fort Donelson was: "If Sidney Johnston is not a general, I have none." Following the loss of Donelson, Johnston evacuated Nashville, concentrated his forces at Corinth and set out on April 3, 1862, to defeat Grant before Buell could re-enforce him. Bad roads, inexperienced officers and poor discipline slowed the march and forced a day's postponement of the fight—a delay which very well may have spelled the difference between victory and defeat for the Southerners.

Johnston seemed confident as his troops began the attack early Sunday morning, April 6. "Tonight we will water our horses in the

Tennessee River," he said. At first the battle went well for the Confederates, but they soon ran into stubborn resistance. As General Johnston sat on his horse about 2:00 P.M., after leading a charge near the "Hornets' Nest," a Federal bullet severed an artery in his leg and he bled to death in a matter of minutes. A short time before, he had sent his personal surgeon, D. W. Yandell, to care for some captured Federals, so he died without medical attendance. Whether or not he would have won a victory if he had lived is a debatable question. So is his capacity for high command. He did not have ample opportunity to prove his abilities. Professor Roland makes the point that if Grant, Sherman, Lee and others who eventually achieved success had been killed as early in the conflict as was Johnston, their fame would be considerably less than it is. Certainly Johnston's death was regarded at the time as a crippling blow to the Confederacy. President Davis summed up prevailing sentiment when he said: "Our loss is irreparable. . . . There exists no purer spirit, no more heroic soul than that of the illustrious man whose death I join you in lamenting."

The youngest and one of the bravest of the army commanders was John Bell Hood. He is known in history as "the gallant Hood," and deservedly so. An equally appropriate designation would be "the tragic Hood." He affords a striking example of a person brilliantly successful in subordinate assignments, pushed by ambition and circumstances into a position beyond his capacities.

Born in Bath County, Kentucky, June 1, 1831, Hood entered West Point in 1849 and graduated in 1853, forty-fourth in a class of fifty-two. After service in the West, including a tour of duty in the Second Cavalry under Albert Sidney Johnston and Robert E. Lee, he resigned his commission in April, 1861, and became a Confederate lieutenant. His magnificent physique—he was six feet two inches tall, broad-shouldered and muscular—his kindly manner, his boundless energy and his determination to make his troops the best in the service soon attracted the favorable attention of his superiors and brought him rapid promotion. On March 2, 1862, he became a brigadier general, and shortly afterward he was given command of the Texas Brigade. Hood's brilliant leadership of this hard-fighting unit at Gaines' Mill, Second Manassas and Sharpsburg brought lasting fame to both the brigade and its commander. With the strong backing of both Jackson and Lee, Hood was promoted to major general on October 11, 1862. He was severely wounded in the left arm on the second day at Gettysburg and at Chickamauga he lost his right leg. During a long convalescence in Richmond he courted the lovely but unpredictable Sally Preston and ingratiated himself with President and Mrs. Davis. Sally Preston eventually tossed him aside but Davis evidently marked him for further observation and advancement. Hood was made a lieutenant general on February 1, 1864, and given a corps under Joseph E. Johnston. The defensive strategy of Johnston did not set well with Hood, and the latter's correspondence with Davis and Bragg

General John Bell Hood

EMBATTLED
CONFEDERATES

expressed sentiments bordering on disloyalty to his superior. On July 17, 1864, Hood superseded Johnston with the understanding that he was to fight for Atlanta. He fought on July 20 and 22 and lost. Then came the disastrous march to Tennessee culminating in the carnages at Franklin and Nashville, the near destruction of a splendid army and the ruin of the leader who had been one of the Confederacy's very best brigade and division commanders. He was unimpressive as commander of a corps, and an army was unquestionably beyond his ceiling.

Hood's misfortunes did not cease with the war. Business reverses in New Orleans reduced him to poverty. On August 24, 1879, his wife died of yellow fever. His eldest daughter passed away on August 30 and on the same day "the gallant Hood" breathed his last, leaving parentless ten young children.

The next to the youngest of the army commanders was E. Kirby Smith, who was born in St. Augustine, Florida, on May 16, 1824. Smith graduated from the United States Military Academy in 1845. In the Mexican War he served under both Taylor and Scott and was twice brevetted for gallantry. In April, 1861, he entered Confederate service as a lieutenant colonel. Two fortuitous changes in his orders sent him to Lynchburg, where creditable performance, good connections and favorable breaks combined to bring him quick promotion to brigadier general. Another fortunate series of events enabled him and his brigade to arrive at Manassas just in time to help deliver the Sunday punch that routed the Federals on July 21, 1861, and won for him the undying appreciation of Jefferson Davis. On October 11, 1861, Smith became a major general. In 1862 on the campaign into Kentucky with Bragg he demonstrated superior ability as a combat commander and as a result was promoted to lieutenant general. He was given command of the Southwestern Army in January 14, 1863, and the next month he succeeded T. H. Holmes as commanding general of the Trans-Mississippi Department. A year later he was elevated to the rank of full general. Smith made his reputation as a combat leader; as a departmental commander his duties were largely administrative. After the fall of Vicksburg the sprawling country west of the Mississippi was virtually a second Confederacy, and Smith's responsibilities and problems were enormous and onerous. He proved less successful as the administrator of a department than as a commander of troops in the field. But it is doubtful if any other high-ranking general, with the possible exception of Lee, could have done any better. After the war Smith became an educator. He concluded his academic career with eighteen years as professor of mathematics at the University of the South. The Confederacy's last surviving full general, he died March 28, 1893.

Nearly all of the lieutenant generals were corps commanders, and of these the most outstanding was Thomas Jonathan Jackson. Many regard him as the foremost combat commander of the Civil War and some rate him among the very best of all time. As is often the case with

General Edmund Kirby Smith

*Lieutenant General
Thomas Jonathan
"Stonewall" Jackson*

geniuses, he had some idiosyncrasies. He dressed shabbily and seemed to be utterly unconcerned about his appearance. He was a chronic lemon sucker. He liked to eat his meals standing up, to straighten out his intestinal tract and facilitate digestion. Imagining himself out of balance, he would walk around with one arm upraised to restore his equilibrium. He was deeply religious, but his piety was of the Old Testament sort that delighted in slaying the Yankee Philistines and giving God all the glory. He loved children, old women and preachers, but behind his soft eyes and his gentle expression smoldered an ambition and a sternness which caused him to drive his men relentlessly on a march and in battle flamed up to convert him into a ruthless killer. When he heard that General Ewell at Port Republic advised his men not to shoot a Federal officer who bravely exposed himself while exhorting his men, he rebuked his subordinate thus: "This is no ordinary war. The brave and gallant Federal officers are the very kind that must be killed. Shoot the brave officers and the cowards will run away and take the men with them." Because of his strange ways Jackson's men at first called him "Old Fool Tom Jackson," but after a while they gave him the nickname "Old Blue Light" and as long as they lived they took enormous pride in the fact that they were "Old Jack's boys."

Jackson was born on January 21, 1824, in Clarksburg, Virginia. His parents died in his early childhood and he was reared in humble circumstances by an uncle. At West Point, where he enrolled in 1842, he had great difficulty with his studies, but by diligent application he gradually overcame the handicap of poor preparation. When he graduated in 1846 he ranked seventeenth in a class of fifty-nine. After distinguished service in the Mexican War he was stationed at various army posts in the United States. In Florida in 1851 he and his superior became involved in a petty quarrel that reflected no credit on either of them. Before the controversy was settled Jackson accepted a professorship at Virginia Military Institute.

Jackson began his Civil War service as a colonel of Virginia militia in command of the state forces at Harpers Ferry. He became a Confederate brigadier on June 17, 1861. A month later, at First Manassas, he won the appellation "Stonewall"; henceforth it was his hallmark. He was promoted to major general on August 7, 1861, and after an unimpressive winter expedition against Romney he launched a campaign in the Shenandoah Valley which was so brilliantly executed as to assure him lasting fame as a military leader. This is not to say that his generalship was flawless, but measured in terms of what he accomplished against tremendous odds, the Valley campaign was a magnificent achievement.

In the Seven Days' battle against Richmond (June 26 to July 1, 1862), Jackson was slow and ineffectual. He was handicapped by ignorance of the terrain, but the most reasonable explanation of his substandard performance—and the one generally accepted by historians—is that he was benumbed by exhaustion. In the Second Manassas Campaign he was his old self again, and he won new glory at Harpers Ferry and Antietam. He became a lieutenant general on October 10, 1862, and was given command of the Second Corps. At Chancellorsville on May 2, 1863, he executed a flank march and a surprise attack which proved his remarkable genius and led to the most brilliant victory won by the Army of Northern Virginia. As he returned from a night reconnaissance on May 2, Jackson was mistaken for a foe and shot by his own troops. Following amputation of his left arm, complications set in and he died on May 10, after muttering the now famous words: "Let us cross over the river and rest under the shade of the trees." A Georgia lieutenant wrote his cousin a few days afterward: "There was very little rejoicing . . . over the late victory; the men would have much rather it had not been gained and Jackson still living, but we hope it is for the best." On May 11, General Lee wrote his wife: "We have to mourn the loss of the good and great Jackson. Any victory would be dear at such a price . . . I know not how to replace him. But God's will be done. I trust He will raise someone in his place." Lee's earnest hope failed to materialize for the simple reason that the Confederacy had no one who could match Jackson's greatness. James H. Hammond of South Carolina wrote a relative on August 22, 1863: "Stonewall is the only military development of the war on either side worth a sentence in history." This was an extreme statement but it conveyed the idea held by countless others then and since that Jackson deserves a unique place in the military hall of fame.

Lieutenant General James Longstreet

EMBATTLED
CONFEDERATES

Senior to Jackson as lieutenant general by one day and commander of Lee's First Corps from its inception was James Longstreet, familiarly known as "Old Pete" by his associates. The origin of the nickname is uncertain, but in 1890 Longstreet wrote a friend that it came "from adventures of old school boy days."

Longstreet was born in Edgefield, South Carolina, January 8, 1821, and spent his boyhood on a plantation near Gainesville, Georgia. He was a distant relative of Julia Dent, who married his good friend, schoolmate and Civil War adversary, U. S. Grant. After graduation from West Point in 1842 he served in the war with Mexico and was twice brevetted for gallantry. He resigned a major's commission on June 1, 1861, and was appointed Confederate brigadier on June 17; he became a major general on October 7. Confusion of orders and movements impaired Longstreet's effectiveness at Seven Pines on May 31, 1862, but he gave an admirable account of himself during the Seven Days' battles. His hard-hitting tactics at Second Manassas and Sharpsburg added further luster to his name. On the evening of September 17, 1862, as "Old Pete" stood with torn clothing and smudged face among the troops whom he had led so magnificently in that day's fighting, General Lee walked up to him, laid both hands on his shoulders and proudly exclaimed: "Here is my old war horse." When shortly afterward Lee divided his army into two corps he gave the first to Longstreet and the second to Jackson.

Longstreet's conduct at Gettysburg on the second and third days led to heated accusations after the war that his tardy and half-hearted execution of Lee's orders lost the battle for the South. Longstreet met these charges with vehement denials and thus was initiated a controversy that has raged ever since. "Old Pete's" reputation doubtless has suffered because of his affiliation with the Republican party in the postwar years and from the fact that the most gifted historians in writing about the Army of Northern Virginia have focused their attention on Robert E. Lee. In recent years, owing largely to Donald B. Sanger's detailed re-examination of what Longstreet did at Gettysburg, and Kenneth P. Williams' careful analysis of the situation on the Union side, the "Old War Horse's" star has regained some of its brilliance. One of the most convincing testimonials in his favor is the fact that Lee continued to seek his companionship and to manifest confidence in his generalship until the end of the war. Lee's relations with Pickett, after Lee learned the full story of Five Forks, indicated that he could be cold toward those whose conduct he considered reprehensible.

Longstreet distinguished himself at Chickamauga and in the Wilderness, but his record as an independent commander in east Tennessee in the winter of 1863–1864 left much to be desired. He died on January 2, 1904.

"Old Pete" was undoubtedly stubborn, argumentative and ambitious, and both during the war and after in his zeal to make a good case for himself he sometimes did less than justice to his fellow generals. He was less than brilliant and he was too often slow getting under way. But he was a brave and determined fighter and once he got up steam he was a formidable antagonist. All things considered, he appears to have justified the confidence and esteem which Lee reposed in him and to have rendered solid service to the Confederate cause.

Nathan Bedford Forrest was not a corps commander but the force which he led during the last months of the war was roughly equivalent to a corps. He was the most colorful of the Confederacy's lieutenant generals and one of the world's greatest commanders of mounted troops.

Born in middle Tennessee, July 13, 1821, the eldest son of William Forrest, a blacksmith, Nathan Forrest moved to Mississippi with his parents in 1834. When William Forrest died three years later, the fifteen-year-old Nathan took over the support of his widowed mother, five brothers and three sisters. By diligent application and good management as a laborer, livestock dealer, slave trader and planter, he rose from poverty to great wealth. In 1849 he moved to Memphis; nine years later he became an alderman there. When Tennessee seceded he was nearly forty years old, but he promptly enlisted as a private, along with his brother, Jeffrey, and Nathan's fifteen-year-old son, William. Within a month he was authorized to raise a battalion of cavalry; and in October, 1861, he became lieutenant colonel of this organization. After narrowly escaping capture at Fort Donelson and receiving a serious wound at Shiloh, he was promoted to brigadier in July, 1862. He then began to develop the type of operation that was to become his specialty—moving with lightning speed deep into enemy territory, surprising the foe, striking furiously, wreaking destruction and then moving on before the victims could recover their balance.

Following his profane denunciation of Bragg after Chickamauga, Forrest was transferred to Mississippi and made a major general. On June 10, 1864, at Brice's Cross Roads north of Tupelo, he won his greatest victory, routing with about 3,500 Confederates a Union force of approximately 8,100 commanded by General Samuel D. Sturgis. Near Okolona, on February 22, 1864, Forrest experienced a personal tragedy. As the Confederates launched a charge, Colonel Jeffrey Forrest, Nathan's youngest brother, whom he had reared as a son, received a bullet in the neck and fell from his horse. The General, who was nearby, rushed to his brother's aid, dismounted, gathered Jeffrey gently in his arms and called his name several times. When he realized that his brother was dead, he laid the body down, got back on his horse and led those about him in a fierce and successful attack on the Federals.

In February, 1865, Forrest was promoted to lieutenant general and given command of all the cavalry in Mississippi, east Louisiana and western Tennessee. He fought his last battle at Selma, Alabama, in April.

Forrest inspired his men to valor by personal example. During the course of the war he was wounded four times, had twenty-nine horses shot from under him and killed at least thirty Yankees in hand-to-

Lieutenant General
Nathan Bedford Forrest

EMBATTLED
CONFEDERATES

hand combat. His basic rule in fighting was, in his own words, to get there first with the most (he did not say "fustest with the mostest"). He had little use for leaders who rigidly fought by the book. "Whenever I ran into one of those fellers who fit by note," he is said to have remarked, "I generally whipped hell out of him before he could get his tune pitched." His spelling and grammar left much to be desired but he had no trouble making himself understood. When one of his officers asked for leave after twice being refused, Forrest wrote on the application: "I have tole you twict, goddamit no." In one of the few extant letters in his own hand, Forrest wrote his Memphis friend, D. C. Trader, on May 23, 1862: "I had a small brush with the Enamy on yesterday I Suceded in gaining thir rear . . . 8 miles from ham burg . . . they wair not looking for me I taken them by Suprise they run like Suns of Biches." He was frequently profane but never vulgar or obscene and he abstained totally from liquor and tobacco. In 1875 he quietly accepted the Christian faith and joined the Cumberland Presbyterian Church. He headed the Ku Klux Klan for a while after the war, but withdrew from the organization when it threatened to degenerate into an instrument of personal vengeance. He died in Memphis on October 29, 1877.

The overwhelming majority of the Confederacy's seventy-two major generals were commanders of divisions. One of the very best of the division commanders was Patrick R. Cleburne. Robert E. Lee referred to him as "a meteor shining from a clouded sky," and to many he was known as "the Stonewall Jackson of the West." On the basis of his brilliant record he should have been promoted to lieutenant general, and he might well have risen to that grade had he not incurred the disfavor of his superiors by prematurely advocating recruitment of slaves.

A native of Ireland, Cleburne attended Trinity College in Dublin for a while; then, in 1845, when he was seventeen, he enlisted in the British army. After three years' military service he migrated to the United States and settled in Helena, Arkansas, where he became a lawyer and an ardent Democrat. When Arkansas seceded he enlisted as a private and was soon commissioned captain in a local unit known as the Yell Rifles. In May, 1861, he was chosen colonel of the Fifteenth Arkansas Regiment. A few months later he and his unit were sent to Bowling Green, Kentucky, for service with Albert Sidney Johnston. Cleburne's military background and his exceptional qualities of leadership soon won the favorable attention of his superiors. He was promoted to brigadier on March 4, 1862; and at Shiloh, where his loss in killed and wounded exceeded that of any other Confederate brigade, he won praise for conspicuous gallantry. He commanded a division in the Kentucky campaign of 1862 and was wounded both at Richmond and Perryville. He became a major general on December 13, 1862. His division was in the thick of the bloody fighting at Murfreesboro and he was especially commended in Bragg's official report "for valor, skill and ability . . . throughout the engagement."

Major General Patrick Ronayne Cleburne

By repeatedly demonstrating gallantry in combat, consistently interesting himself in the welfare of his men and systematically attending to the details of administration, Cleburne won the respect and affection of his command and made his division one of the very best in Confederate service. Largely because of his superb leadership, Cleburne's division on the right stood firm against the powerful Federal attack at Missionary Ridge which penetrated the left center of the line and produced the first mass panic in any Confederate army. To Cleburne was assigned the difficult and dangerous task of covering the retreat. On November 27, at Ringold Gap, under instructions from Bragg "to hold his position at all hazards and keep back the enemy until the artillery and transportation of the army is secure, the salvation of which depends on him," Cleburne and his 4,000 men for six hours repelled a force several times their size and withdrew only after their mission had been accomplished. For this remarkable achievement Cleburne and his division received the thanks of the Confederate Congress.

Cleburne led his division with distinction during the Georgia campaign of May–September, 1864. After the fall of Atlanta he accompanied Hood to Tennessee, and there on the afternoon of November 30, 1864, at Franklin, he died at his accustomed place in battle, leading his troops where the fighting was hottest. Later one of his captains wrote: "[There] the gallant old soldier, General Pat Cleburne lay dead. He was the idol of his command, and a better soldier never died for any cause." In the *Rise and Fall of the Confederate Government,* Jefferson Davis paid the heroic Irishman this high tribute: "Around Cleburne thickly lay the gallant men, who in his desperate assault followed him with implicit confidence that in another army was given Stonewall Jackson and in the one case, as in the other, a vacancy was created which never could be filled."

The roll of brigadiers is too long to permit individual characterization of even the most distinguished. Among the very best were George Doles, who died in action near Bethesda Church, June 2, 1864; Samuel McGowan; John R. Cooke; W. H. Jackson; O. F. Strahl; Evander M. Law; Stephen Ramseur of North Carolina, who at twenty-seven became a major general, the youngest West Pointer to attain that grade, and who died at Cedar Creek not long after his promotion; M. P. Lowrey; G. B. Anderson; Junius Daniel; John Gregg; E. P. Alexander; Henry Lewis Benning, called "Old Rock" because of his sturdiness in combat, who at Gettysburg on the second day walked up and down in Devil's Den saying to his men, "Give them hell, boys, give them hell"; Dorsey Pender, who became a major general after Chancellorsville and who died of a wound received at Gettysburg; Lewis H. Little; A. R. Wright; John H. Kelly; Preston Smith; R. F. Hoke; Lewis Armistead and William Barksdale, both of whom died at Gettysburg; Joseph B. Kershaw, who like many other distinguished brigadiers eventually rose to division command; Paul J. Semmes, mortally wounded at Gettysburg; and three of the leaders

Brigadier General Junius Daniel

Major General Joseph Brevard Kershaw

Major General Cadmus Marcellus Wilcox

who followed Jackson as commanders of the famous Stonewall Brigade —Richard B. Garnett, Charles S. Winder and Elisha Franklin Paxton.

Other outstanding brigade commanders, to mention only a few, were Daniel C. Govan, Archibald Gracie, Cadmus Wilcox, Bryan Grimes, States Rights Gist, and John Pegram. The handsome and gallant Pegram was given command of a division after Rodes' death at Winchester, September 19, 1864, but did not live long enough to receive a major generalcy. At Hatcher's Run, February 6, 1865, three weeks after his thirty-third birthday and his marriage to the beautiful Hetty Cary, a Federal bullet pierced his breast and killed him. Four days before his death, bride and groom were riding at a review held in her honor when her horse brushed against a soldier. She reined up and started to apologize. But when the Reb looked up into her lovely face he broke in to say: "Never mind, Miss! You might have rid all over me, indeed you might."

In old-fashioned wars, of which the American Civil War was the last, generals were supposed to be brave, and it was not considered inappropriate for even the highest commanders to lead their men in

*Major General John
Brown Gordon*

combat. Confederate generals of all grades measured up especially well with respect to personal valor. Remarkably few showed the white feather in battle and many carried exhibition of bravery to the point of rashness by leading small units in front line assaults when they should have been in the rear directing the course of the battle. Striking evidence of their willingness to expose themselves is afforded by the fact that seventy-seven Confederate generals—more than one out of every six who wore the wreathed stars—died of hostile bullets. Among those who lost their lives in combat were a full general, Albert Sidney Johnston, and three lieutenant generals, Stonewall Jackson, Leonidas Polk and A. P. Hill. On one field alone, at Franklin, Tennessee, November 30, 1864, in a fight that lasted less than four hours, five Confederate generals were killed outright—Patrick Cleburne, John Adams, H. B. Granbury, O. F. Strahl and States Rights Gist—and a sixth, John C. Carter, was mortally wounded; one other, George W. Gordon, was captured; and five more— John C. Brown, A. M. Manigault, William A. Quarles, F. M. Cockrell and T. M. Scott—were wounded. The Wilderness-Spotsylvania Campaign of May 4 to June 3, 1864, took a toll of 37 percent of Lee's generals; of the twenty-two casualties, eight were killed, twelve wounded and two captured. The killed were Junius Daniel, George Doles, James B. Gordon, Micah Jenkins, John M. Jones, Abner Perrin, Leroy A. Stafford and "Jeb" Stuart. Truly, the life of a Confederate general was perilous and uncertain.

IV. *Officers and Enlisted Men*

Below the generals was a large corps of officers ranging in rank from colonel to third lieutenant. Most of the colonels were commanders of infantry regiments. Their principal assistants were lieutenant colonels and majors. Captains commanded the ten companies into which regiments were divided; each company was also authorized a first, second and third lieutenant, along with five sergeants and five corporals. Confederate regiments normally were not divided into battalions and platoons, though separate infantry battalions, commanded by lieutenant colonels, existed in considerable number, especially in the early part of the war. Artillery battalions, commanded by lieutenant colonels, consisted of four batteries, each commanded by a captain who was responsible for four or six guns. The authorized strength of infantry regiments in 1863 was 49 officers and 1,340 enlisted men, but few units ever attained full strength. In the latter part of the war many regiments dwindled to two hundred men or less, commanded sometimes by a captain or lieutenant.

In both Union and Confederate armies, as a general rule, regimental and company officers were elected. While this often led to unfortunate results, the system worked better in the South than in the North. Below the Mason and Dixon line, as above it, the persons generally elected as officers were those who took the initiative in raising units. In the North, where society was democratic, these frequently were men whose chief claim to office was their superior power of persuasion. They often made very poor unit commanders. In the South, on the other hand, regiments and companies normally were raised by planters or sons of planters and they became the colonels and captains.

Among the great majority of Confederate officers there was no question of their devotion to the Southern cause. The letters of David R. E. Winn of Georgia, who entered Confederate service as a lieutenant and rose to lieutenant colonel before his death at Gettysburg, repeatedly express his unwavering patriotism. "We came with the expectation and purpose of fighting," he wrote on May 19, 1861. "To God belongs the result, but we cannot fear it, fighting in a just cause." In two subsequent letters he stated: "No one can read . . . of the causes of the war and the manner in which it has been conducted by the enemy without having his blood to boil within him and being satisfied that our cause is dearer than life itself and deserves our whole devotion. . . . These may seem high-sounding expressions, but . . . I am certain that our cause is a righteous one, and consequently confident that it will succeed." Robert M. Gill of Okolona, Mississippi, who enlisted as a private and rose from the ranks to lieutenant before he was killed at Jonesboro, Georgia, in 1864, expressed it more simply in a letter to his wife after his first baptism of fire: "I [had] rather die and you be free than live and be slaves . . . I know that we will be victorious." Shortly before his death, when the prospects of victory looked bleak indeed, he wrote: "[I] think this cause a desperate one . . . there is no hope of defeating Lincoln . . . I wish I could be sanguine of success. I hope and pray for it." Gill, like so many of his countrymen, never gave up.

Recruiting for the Confederate army, Woodstock, Virginia

Louisiana Tigers

Regimental and company officers varied greatly in character, habits and ability, but the majority were steady, respectable men. Of course there were some gamblers, and there was the usual number who had loose morals, or were outright criminals, or problem drinkers. James C. Nisbet, who rose from captain to colonel before his capture at Atlanta and recorded his experiences in *Four Years on the Firing Line*, had to take over command of his Georgia regiment at Gaines' Mill when his colonel was incapacitated from "imbibing freely of the ardent." The colonel was arrested, released, but later asked to be relieved. Once Nisbet had to intervene on behalf of some of his soldiers who took whiskey from Richard Taylor's Louisiana Zouaves. After a rough and tumble fight Nisbet restored harmony by giving the bruised and beaten Zouaves a drink from his own bottle. Other officers drank infrequently or not at all. Lieutenant Gill of Mississippi reported in a letter home after participating in a charge near Marietta, Georgia, on June 22, 1864: "I saw a canteen on which a heavy run was made during and after the charge. I still like whiskey but do not want any when going into a charge for I am or at least was drunk enough yesterday without drinking a drop." Nevertheless, a stimulant of some sort was generally welcome. John Bratton of Winnsboro, South Carolina, who served as a captain and colonel before his eventual promotion to brigadier general, requested his wife to "always put liquor of some sort in every box, or coffee."

Some officers were deeply religious. Lieutenant Winn of Georgia could write his wife after the engagement at Malvern Hill: "It's astonishing that every man did not fall. . . . Grape shot swept the earth; shells burst over and among us, and yet I came from the bloody field, walking

Major John Pelham, commanding Stuart's Horse Artillery, mortally wounded in the battle of Kelly's Ford, Virginia, March 17, 1863

OFFICERS AND
ENLISTED MEN

71

Sergeant Stephen Clinton Adams and friend, Sixth Virginia Cavalry

Captain William Caleb Brown, Rough and Ready Guards, Fourteenth North Carolina Regiment

over the bodies of slain and wounded friends—without one scratch. Truly it was the hand of Providence that sheltered me." That religion could be carried too far—in the eyes of some—is evident in Winn's comments about General D. H. Hill: "He seems to be a morose, Puritanical, tyrannical Presbyterian, his whole soul centering in rigid discipline without regard to any possible circumstance of excuse . . . unless the delinquent happens to be a good Presbyterian." Captain Bratton of South Carolina did not consider himself an orthodox Christian, though he read the Bible frequently. Once when his wife expressed fear of a Yankee bullet cutting him off before he was prepared to die, he answered: "Sufficient unto the day is the evil thereof. . . . My ambition will be gratified if I can give satisfaction in life."

On the use of profanity there was also much variety, but the heat of battle could loosen the tongue of the most pious. Lieutenant Gill of Mississippi apologized to his wife for breaking a pledge to quit swearing during the fighting at Resaca, Georgia: "The men did not move out to suit me, and I forgot everything and began to curse a cowardly scamp who got behind." Six weeks later he confessed: "I am trying to do right but I find it very hard to control my worst passion, that of swearing. I do not intend it but as danger approaches I feel very wicked and I pray that the enemy may charge us as I know we will slay them by thousands.

. . . I have a man in my company who gets out his testament and begins to read whenever the pickets in front commence firing. His conduct disgusts me so I cannot read mine." And after the Battle of Atlanta, July 22, 1864, Gill closed a detailed description of the action with these words: "During the fight . . . I done some heavy swearing I am told. . . . I try to do right but it seems impossible for me to keep from cursing when I get under fire. I hope I will do better hereafter. I do not wish to die with an oath on my lips." Whether or not he achieved his wish was not recorded by the officers who wrote his widow of his death.

A great many officers had had some form of training, either in a militia unit or in one of the military academies that dotted the antebellum South, but many were pitifully ignorant of their duties when they first entered the service. When his company arrived in Richmond, Captain Nisbet of Georgia acquired a copy of *Hardee's Tactics*, the standard drill manual (it was also used by Union troops), and began to familiarize himself with the fundamentals of drill. To assist in his education and to expedite training, he engaged the services of an experienced sergeant from another regiment, who conducted daily drill for both officers and men of the company. "I went into the ranks with a musket," Nisbet wrote in his memoirs, "and was obedient under the drill-master's

Colonel Thomas P. Ochiltree of Texas, who served on the staffs of Lieutenant General Dick Taylor and Brigadier Generals Tom Green and Henry H. Sibley

Flag of the Dixie Rebels, First North Carolina Regiment

*Private Ivy W. Duncan,
Fifteenth Georgia Infantry*

orders." Nisbet himself paid the sergeant for this extra instruction. When John Bratton was elected colonel in 1862, he wrote his wife, "I am learning and doing at the same time. I shall have to work to make a colonel of myself."

Cowardice was frequently a subject for humor—especially if the coward was an enlisted man. Once when a Reb in front came dashing back on his supporting line, Nisbet called out: "Halt! What are you running for?" "Bekase I kant fly," the fleeing soldier replied. But, as in all armies, shirkers, self-seekers and cowards were a constant problem. Cowardice in a Southern officer was a particular disgrace. Describing the action at Malvern Hill, Captain Winn wrote his wife: "In our next charge we had the support of thousands of gallant troops from all parts of the Confederacy and thousands of dastardly cowards who did us more harm by running and shooting our own men [in greater number] than the Yankees did. I had only . . . [about 30] of the company in action. A majority of those not engaged were sick, but many were kept out by absolute cowardice. I am sorry to say . . . [Lieutenant] Sirene was in Richmond where he has been ever since we began to see dangerous times, walking around the streets complaining of being sick. . . . [Lieutenant] Hornaday between physical exhaustion and mental anxiety, barely managed to get through the day and has returned to the wagon camp. . . . This leaves me with pretty arduous duty, but my constitution thus far has nobly withstood the fatigue. . . . Without intending to boast, I was so perfectly cool and free from apprehension of personal danger as to be somewhat surprised at myself." Later Winn readily assented to the resignation of Sirene, and after the cowardly lieutenant had left for Georgia, Winn wrote: "He's gone and I'm glad of it. I cannot respect such men." In reporting a later instance of cowardice on the part of an officer in another regiment he stated: "I would rather be dead. . . . For generations to come it will reflect upon his children and children's children." Winn's reaction to an enlisted man who had tried to avoid exposure to fights like Malvern Hill by getting a substitute was less severe. "He is no account and I will be glad to get rid of him." Captain Bratton professed to have a higher regard for the enlisted men than for the officers, too many of whom, in his opinion, were "low, scheming, wire-pulling, self-servers"; while Robert Gill, when still a private, expressed his pleasure when Beauregard was replaced by Bragg because he had heard that Beauregard "has a train of concubines and wagon loads of champagne," and he approved of Bragg's stricter discipline. "Our soldiers act outrageously," he wrote shortly before Bragg took command, "They . . . have not left a fat hog, chicken, goose, duck, or egg, or onions behind."

It was perhaps in their devotion to duty, and particularly to the welfare of their men, that Confederate officers frequently showed their best qualities. They demonstrated this sense of responsibility in many ways. Colonel Nisbet several times directed and joined his men in snow-

EMBATTLED
CONFEDERATES

Confederates under Lieutenant General Early and Major General Gordon in York, Pennsylvania, June 28, 1863, just before the Battle of Gettysburg

ball fights, a winter diversion to keep up morale. In one of these melees Nisbet was dragged from his horse, captured and paroled. John Bratton, as a captain and later a colonel, frequently wrote home about the duties of keeping his outfit properly organized, supplied, and functioning. On January 9, 1864, Bratton wrote of his troubles: "It was my duty not only to make myself comfortable, but a whole Reg't of men . . . raking up old tents, building huts, trying to get shoes and blankets, keeping the camp in good order, and all the while drilling and inspecting and being reviewed and mustering. Muster and pay rolls, monthly and quarterly returns, returns of deceased soldiers and many other things too numerous to mention. All of which can be done very easily in a properly managed Reg't but I found mine [after an absence from illness] in a very deranged state. Reg't and Company papers have been lost or thrown away. My officers (a great many of whom . . . are new) seem to have forgotten that such things are required of us, and cannot do their part in making out the papers. It has been one protracted head-cracking job for me." His conscientiousness, while perhaps unusual, was undoubtedly a factor in his promotion to brigadier general.

In one of his earliest letters home, David Winn wrote, "I cannot leave my company. Many of our citizens placed their sons and brothers under my charge." His regiment, like many others, experienced heavy losses from illness during the first year of service. The surgeon and assistant surgeon were not able to care for all the patients and Winn was compelled during sieges of measles, malaria and typhoid to act as both

GENERAL ORDER.

General Order, No.

The Commanding General feels deeply sensible of his obligation to treat all persons in arms against the Confederacy, and who may fall into his hands, with the utmost humanity required by Christian charity and the usages of war. In like manner, all citizens who obey the laws, and repudiate their treason, will be treated with the clemency declared in the Commanding General's Proclamation. He has heard with deep mortification, that in a single instance, this rule has been departed from by the unauthorized order of one of his officers, but the wrong done will be promptly punished and redressed.

All persons who have received arms of the public enemy are invited to bring their arms into camp, and if they choose take service in the defence of the country. No punishment will be imposed on such persons.

By order of   MAJ. GEN. LORING.
                                              H. FITZHUGH,
                                              Chief of Staff.

physician and tactical officer. "I am physicking in spite of myself and am worn out at it," he wrote on October 29. "Poor John Foster will almost certainly die. I have been yielding my tent, cot and even bed clothing to the sick of our company." Being the good officer that he was, Winn did not hesitate to put the welfare of his men above his own comfort and convenience. In January he wrote that a sudden onslaught of snow and sleet had caught his company without shelter and that "we officers, desiring to have our men sheltered first, have yielded to them all the lumber, etc. furnished to us." When the huts were completed the officers moved in with the men until their own winter cabins were completed. Officers of the Sumter Light Guard also assisted their men in various other ways. On February 7, 1862, Winn informed his wife: "I regret very much that I have not sent some money home. . . . Every cent that Captain Johnson and myself have gotten has been spent for the company. In clothing, etc., for the men I have spent $200. I paid the whole expense of Ransom's funeral, coffin, etc., $60, and many other such constantly recurring expenses; $50 to get a rascally member of the company out of a stealing scrape, etc. These things have to be paid and I have tried to share some of these expenses with Capt. Johnson (for the other officers would not) and still have not been half as badly taxed."

The qualities that made these men outstanding company and regimental commanders were: diligent efforts to increase knowledge and efficiency; intelligence; integrity; a deep and abiding interest in the welfare of their men; resourcefulness; self-confidence; enormous pride in self and unit; bravery; and dedication.

THE RANK AND FILE

The common soldiers of the Confederacy, aggregating something less than a million, were a relatively homogeneous group. The majority of them were native Southerners, rural, Protestant and unmarried. Less than one-fourth of them possessed slaves or belonged to slave-owning families. In age they ranged from the early teens to the seventies, but four-fifths of them were between eighteen and thirty.*

Louisiana cartridge box plate with state coat-of-arms

Because of the vogue of wearing beards many Rebs looked much older than they were. Whiskers were worn partly for protection against the elements and partly because of the inconvenience of shaving. A pamphlet issued in 1862 to help Southern men adjust themselves to army life contained the advice: "Let your beard grow so as to protect your throat and lungs." Many soldiers followed the practice of wearing beards through the fall and winter and shedding them in the spring. A Mississippi private who rejoined his unit in November, 1861, after a sixty-day furlough wrote his home folks: "I did not recognize many of the boys on account of their hairy jaws." But some found their whiskers unendurable in any season. In the autumn of 1862 a Georgia private wrote his wife: "I shave off part of my beard the other day for the first time sense I left home. I don't want any beard dabling in my grub, let others do as they may."

About one out of every twenty or twenty-five Confederates was of foreign birth. The most numerous of the alien groups were the Irish and Germans, and they were excellent soldiers. Three brigades of Indians were organized for Confederate service in the Trans-Mississippi Department, and a few companies of red men were recruited in Tennessee and North Carolina. Most of the Confederate Indians were Cherokees, Chickasaws, Choctaws, Creeks and Seminoles. As the Southerners pitched into their foes at Wilson's Creek and Pea Ridge the savage whoop of the red men was blended with the high-pitched yell of the palefaces. The Indians were good fighters but they were hard to discipline between battles. In combat they sometimes insisted on scalping their foes and they appear to have been as proficient as their light-complexioned comrades

* For a detailed view of the composition of one infantry company see page 279.

Flag of the Van Dorn Guard of Texas

in appropriating the spoils of battle. After the fight at Pea Ridge, some of Stand Watie's Cherokees built a bonfire around a cannon that they had captured and started a war dance to celebrate their achievement. They did not know that the cannon contained an unexploded charge. When the barrel became hot the piece went off, inflicted some casualties on the dancers and brought the festivities to a sudden end.

Some of the rank and file were men of excellent education, refined in their tastes and well-versed in the classics. These were considerably

Flag of the Thirteenth Virginia Infantry

Flag of the Independent Blues, Company B, Third Florida Infantry

Flag of the Seventh Mississippi Infantry

Flag of a Kentucky Infantry Regiment

Flag of the Eighth Virginia Cavalry

outnumbered by Rebs at the opposite end of the scale who were completely illiterate. Original muster rolls in the National Archives show that in some companies more than half of the men could not sign their names. This was an uncommonly high percentage of illiteracy but almost every company had from one to a dozen men who had to call on comrades to read and write letters for them. An Alabama private wrote his home folks in January, 1862: "I do the love letter writing for about 20 men in our company. . . . I have engaged 3 young men of our Co. [to be married] in the last month. I get to read all the girls' letters of course."

Confederate authorities did not attempt to provide schooling for illiterate soldiers but a few Rebs learned to read and write on their own. On April 27, 1862, a Tarheel private wrote proudly to his mother: "Maw I have lurned to write in Camp well a nuf to write my leters my self." The recipient apparently had to rely on others to keep up her end of the correspondence, for the soldier wrote on June 4, 1862: "Mother when you wright to me get somebody to wright that can wright a Plain hand. . . . I cold not read your leter to make sence of it, it [was] wrote so bad. I have lurnd to do my one wrading and writing and it is a grate help to me."

The majority of Rebs had some education but the letters of most of them reveal serious deficiencies of spelling and grammar. Once frequently appeared as *wonst,* get as *git,* uneasy as *oneasy,* fit as *fiten,* any

EMBATTLED
CONFEDERATES

Sergeant Thomas Jefferson Rushin, Company K, Twelfth Georgia Infantry. Killed at Sharpsburg, September 17, 1862

as *airy*, ain't as *haint*, not any as *nairy*, it as *hit*, at all as *a tall*, until as *ontell*, and roasting ears (of green corn) as *roasting years*. Your was often written as *yore* or *yourn*, fought as *fit*, for as *fur*, peace as *peas*, drop as *drap*. Other common usages were *tuck* for took, *purty* for pretty, *laig* for leg, *afeard* for afraid, *ortent* for ought not to and *shore* for sure.

Long words were often divided, sometimes with strange results. One Reb complained about the "rashens" issued by the *comma sary;* another stated that he still hoped to get a *fur low* when some more *volen teares* joined the *ridge ment*. A third wrote that he was in very difficult *sur come stances*. Still another reported that he had seen the elephant and was *sad is fide*.

Some wrestled mightily and to little avail with the spelling of rivers and towns near which they encamped. Chattanooga was written *Chat a nooga*, Chickamauga as *Chick a mooga* and Mississippi as *Mascippia*. When Rebs became ill they wrote of going to the *horsepittle* and they spelled out their ailments in wondrous ways. Pneumonia was put down as *new mornion,* typhoid fever as *tifoid feaver,* erysipelas as *eri sipalous,* and yellow jaundice as *yaller ganders.*

Some semiliterate soldiers used colorful figures of speech. One Reb wrote: "The boys is all well sadisfide and in fine spirits pitching around like a blind dog in a meet hous." Another stated that "the dam Yankees . . . [are] thicker than lise on a hen and a dam site ornraier." A third reported that "it comentsed raining like poring peas on a rawhide." One Reb mutilated a trite simile thus: "Noose is as cerce as hen's teeth."

A basic concern of Johnny Rebs, and one about which they often commented in their letters, was food. The daily ration prescribed by Army Regulations in 1861 was "Three-Fourths of a pound of pork or bacon, or one and a fourth pounds of fresh or salt beef; eighteen ounces of bread or flour, or twelve ounces of hard bread, or one and a fourth pounds of cornmeal; and . . . [for every one hundred men] eight quarts of peas or beans, or, . . . ten pounds of rice; six pounds coffee; twelve pounds sugar; four quarts of vinegar . . . and two quarts of salt." The commissary department ordered a general reduction of this ration in April, 1862, and specific items were further curtailed by subsequent directives. In the autumn of 1863, Commissary General L. B. Northrop reduced the bacon issue to one-third of a pound, and the next year the flour or meal ration was cut to sixteen ounces. More often than not, soldiers in the field got considerably less than the allowances specified by the authorities in Richmond. The hunger experienced by Rebs was the more deplorable in view of the abundance produced on Southern plantations and farms. After 1861, much acreage normally devoted to cotton and tobacco was diverted to food crops, and throughout the war the yield of most items was more than ample to meet the needs of both soldiers and civilians. But speculation, hoarding, inadequacy of transportation, mismanagement on the part of commissary authorities and, in the instance of meat, scarcity of salt, prevented this abundance from reaching the people who needed it most. The near-starvation which bedeviled the common soldiers and many lowly civilians in the latter part of the war was due to failure of distribution rather than to inadequacy of production.

Hunger among soldiers was most common during periods of active campaigning and in times of siege. Soldiers penned up in Vicksburg and Port Hudson in the summer of 1863 came closest to starvation, but great suffering was experienced by Rebs who fought on the Virginia peninsula and at Sharpsburg in 1862, at Gettysburg in 1863, in Georgia and at Nashville in 1864 and in the final campaigns in Virginia in 1864 and 1865. In the withdrawal from Yorktown in 1862 some of D. H. Hill's men lived for several days on dry corn issued in the shuck and parched in the ashes of their campfires. The same was true of Rebs who accompanied Hood to Tennessee in 1864 and those who marched with Lee to Appomattox in 1865.

The mainstays of Johnny Reb's diet were cornbread and beef. These

Soldier's boot

Edmund Ruffin, honorary member of the Palmetto Guards of South Carolina, who fired one of the first shots at Fort Sumter and shot himself in 1865 because he was unwilling to live under the United States government

were supplemented as circumstances permitted with issues of pork, field peas, flour, soft bread, hardtack, potatoes, rice, molasses, coffee, sugar and fresh vegetables. As often as they could, the folks at home enriched camp fare with boxes of edibles, and soldiers roamed the countryside in search of milk, fruit, vegetables, fowls and home-cooked meals. Innumerable stray pigs were killed on the pretext of attacking unoffending Rebs or refusing to take an oath of loyalty to Jeff Davis. Few soldiers actually stole, but they learned to "forage" freely and without compunction. "Our troops rob friend or foe of everything edible when not well guarded," wrote a Confederate staff officer from near Atlanta on July 25, 1864. A chaplain of Lee's army, after deploring the wholesale plunder by Confederates of civilians near Fredericksburg in the winter of 1862–1863, stated: "Our country groans to be delivered of its friends."

The propensity of soldiers to pillage was due almost as much to the poor quality of rations as to scarcity. Bacon was often rancid, beef stringy and tough, and bread wormy and stale. One Reb claimed that the cows killed to feed his brigade were so feeble that "it takes two hands to hold up one beef to shoot it." A South Carolinian stationed near Petersburg wrote his wife in January, 1865: "We get corn bread now in place of wheat bread. . . . It looks like a pile of cow dung Baked in the sun. I could nock down a cow with a pone of it." Rebs became very tired of the monotonous offerings of beef and bread. One declared: "I have eat salt meat and bread so long that I hate for meal time to come."

While in camp soldiers frequently prepared and ate their food in small groups known as messes, with each taking his turn at the various

Capture of a part of the burning Union breastworks on the Brock Road on the afternoon of May 6, 1864

Corporal William H. Martin, Seventh Louisiana Volunteers, and his father Captain James Martin, Algiers Battalion, Louisiana Militia

chores. On the march every man was on his own, and the prevailing practice was to place the meat on the end of a stick and broil it over the campfire; flour bread was made by wrapping bits of dough about a pole or ramrod and baking it over the hot coals; meal was made edible by adding water to it and frying the mush in hot grease; if bits of meat were stirred in while the mush was cooking, the finished product was "cush" or "slosh." Some soldiers saved themselves the trouble of cooking by eating their meat raw and trading off their meal or flour for cornbread or hardtack. Cooking and eating practices of the rank and file may well be summed up by the comments of an Alabamian who wrote his wife: "Som times I git a nuff and Som times we dont have no Regeler way out here of Eatting we Eat Just when we git Hungery."

Clothing and shelter had an important bearing on the soldiers' comfort and morale. Regulations issued in 1861 prescribed the following uniform for enlisted men: long, double-breasted coat of "cadet gray," with two rows of buttons and stand-up collar, collar and cuffs to be trimmed with red for artillery, light blue for infantry and yellow for cavalry, and buttons of artillerymen to be stamped with the letter "A" while those of infantry and cavalry were to be marked with numerals designating the regiment; sky-blue trousers, cap modeled after the French kepi, with dark blue band and crown of red, light blue or yellow, depending on the wearer's branch of service; leather boots; and long, gray, double-breasted overcoat with cape. Fatigue garments (overalls) were authorized for engineer and ordnance soldiers but not for those of other branches. Shirts, drawers and socks were issued to all Rebs but regulations did not specify their color, pattern or material.

Sergeant John Eagen Howard Post, First Maryland Cavalry

These regulations were never fully observed and numerous modifications were made in the light of experience. Many units entering the service in the spring of 1861 wore their militia uniforms; these varied greatly in color and design, though most of them were of flashy hue and fancy cut. The long, double-breasted coats were replaced after a while by short, single-breasted jackets called "roundabouts." Sky-blue trousers were prescribed in each annual revision of the army regulations, but they were worn by only a few in 1861 and apparently by none after that time. Light gray was the prevailing color for both coats and pants until about 1863, when the blockade reduced the stock of imported dye to such an extent that Confederates had to rely mainly on a homemade product made of walnut hulls which gave to uniforms a yellowish-brown tint called butternut. Wide use of this color was responsible for Johnny Reb receiving the popular nickname of "butternut."

Robert B. Hurt, Jr., Adjutant, Fifty-fifth Tennessee Infantry Regiment. Killed at the Battle of Franklin

Heavy brogans, cut so straight that they could be worn on either foot, were the prevailing type of shoes throughout the war. Soft felt hats were much preferred over caps, and the caps that were worn usually had crowns of gray rather than the colors denoting branch as prescribed in regulations. Shirts varied greatly in color and pattern. Drawers were usually ankle-length, cotton garments, and flannel was a popular material. Many Rebs considered underclothing an unnecessary bother but some who had not worn drawers at home came to appreciate the protection which they afforded against the harsh winters of Virginia and Tennessee and others began to wear them to guard against the chafing of legs on a hard march.

Until late 1862 the government permitted Rebs to draw money in lieu of part or all of their clothing according to a prescribed scale of prices (in May, 1861, the annual cash clothing allowance was fixed at $42). Many soldiers took advantage of this arrangement to obtain clothing from private sources. Even after cash commutation was discontinued, Rebs continued to rely on the home folks for much of their apparel. In 1864 the wife of one of Lee's soldiers took to her husband in camp a

*Night amusements in a
Confederate camp*

complete outfit of clothing, spun, woven, dyed and fabricated by her own hands. Home letters of most Rebs contained requests for clothing, especially for shoes, shirts, socks and drawers.

Despite the best efforts of individuals, societies, state authorities and the Confederate government, many Rebs suffered for lack of clothing. Overcoats were in short supply after the first year of the war, but greater discomfort resulted from a chronic deficiency of shoes. Thousands of Rebs were unable to accompany Lee to Sharpsburg in September, 1862, owing to lack of shoes, and many who went with Longstreet to Knoxville in 1863 and with Hood to Nashville the next year wore out their shoes on the march and walked for miles over rocky, ice-coated roads in their bare feet, leaving traces of blood along the way. In both the eastern and western armies men resorted to the expedient of making crude moccasins from untanned hides furnished by commissaries, but this footwear gave little satisfaction. One Reb stated that his rawhide contrivances "stretch out at the heel . . . whip me nearly to death . . . flop up and down . . . stink very bad and i have to keep a bush in my hand to keep the flies off of them." This soldier made a joke of his discomfort, and so did many others who were reduced to rags and tatters in the latter part of the war. A Texan entrenched near Atlanta wrote to his wife in June, 1864: "In this army one hole in the seat of the breeches indicates a captain, two holes a lieutenant, and the seat of the pants all out indicates that the individual is a private."

Shortage of clothing would have produced less suffering had the soldiers been adequately provided with blankets and tents. Blankets became increasingly difficult to obtain after 1862 and "the tented field" was practically unknown to men who wore the gray. Some Rebs obtained pieces of Yankee-made canvas or oilcloth on the battlefield and fashioned pup tents or shelters after the mode of the Federals, but most of them lived in the open during the greater part of the year. When cold weather came and the army settled into winter quarters, Rebs erected huts of logs, usually over an excavation two or three feet deep, built fireplaces, furnished their dwellings with crude bunks, stools, tables and shelves, placed pegs about the walls on which to hang weapons, clothing and cooking utensils and improvised candleholders from bayonets or tin cans. Many contrived various additional touches to increase the attractiveness and comfort of their huts; in the relative calm, leisure and security of their winter homes some achieved the greatest contentment of their army service.

Johnny Rebs of all branches learned to "travel light" as the war progressed. Early in the conflict infantrymen wore heavy belts adorned with brass buckles, carried their food in haversacks, packed wearing

Confederate picket post near Charleston, South Carolina

apparel, books, stationery and razors in knapsacks and loaded themselves down with an assortment of cooking utensils. But most of them eventually shed all but the bare essentials. The seasoned veteran was sparsely dressed and carried only a gun; a leather cartridge box holding forty rounds of ammunition; a small leather box full of percussion caps; a knapsack containing rations, toilet articles, writing materials, an extra garment or two, and sundry miscellaneous items; a tin plate; a tin cup; a canteen, sometimes a Confederate article made of wood but more often a metal container captured from the Yankees; and a blanket wrapped into a tight roll, tied together at the ends and draped from left shoulder to right hip. Many Rebs would have considered this an excessive load.

Powder horn of soldier in the Fifteenth Arkansas Infantry

The monthly pay of Confederate enlisted men during the first three years of the war was as follows:

Infantry and artillery privates	$11.00
Cavalry privates	12.00
Sergeant majors, infantry, artillery, cavalry	21.00
First sergeants, infantry, artillery, cavalry	20.00
Corporals, infantry, artillery, cavalry	13.00
Engineer privates, 1st class	17.00
Engineer privates, 2nd class	13.00
Engineer corporals	20.00
Engineer sergeants	34.00

On June 9, 1864, President Davis signed a bill giving all enlisted men a raise of seven dollars a month but by that time inflation had reached such a point that the increase had little meaning. The eighteen dollars drawn by infantry privates in the summer of 1864 woud hardly buy a peck of meal or two pounds of bacon, and almost six months' pay was required for the purchase of a pair of shoes or trousers. To make matters worse, pay was rarely received when it was due. Soldiers' letters revealed many cases of men getting no pay for six months and some Rebs went for more than a year without a peep at the paymaster.

Skimpy rations, shoddy clothing and poor pay were only a part of Johnny Reb's misery. Health was precarious and medical service was impaired by the ignorance of doctors and a woeful inadequacy of facilities. Measles, malaria, typhoid, smallpox, pneumonia and other maladies took a far heavier toll of life than did Yankee bullets, and inadequate care of the wounded made hostile missiles far more deadly than they should have been. Of the 258,000 estimated deaths on the Confederate side, 164,000 were said to have resulted from disease and other causes not associated with combat as against 94,000 from enemy fire.

Harsh and capricious discipline was another deterrent to the soldiers' welfare and happiness. This does not mean that the Confederacy was heartless and reckless in shooting and hanging deserters, cowards and criminals, for relatively few Rebs were executed for any cause, and many serious offenders were given surprisingly light sentences. But punishments short of death were often cruel in the extreme and many of them were meted out for relatively minor breaches of discipline. Soldiers were tied up and severely flogged for absence without leave, backtalk to their officers and overindulgence in intoxicating drink. The Confederate Congress early in 1863 passed a law prohibiting the whipping of soldiers, but this act was sometimes ignored. In some instances cowards had the letter *C* burned on their faces or hips with a hot iron, and deserters were branded with the letter *D*. Rebs guilty of insubordination, brawling, malingering and various other misdeeds were "bucked and gagged"—that is, placed in a sitting position, hands bound together and slipped over the knees, a pole run beneath the knees and over the arms and a stick or bayonet tied in the mouth. One of the most brutal punishments was the suspending of offenders by their thumbs, with toes barely touching the ground, and leaving them hanging thus for long periods of time. Another inhuman penalty was to strap a soldier to the extra wheel attached to the back of a caisson; the torture was sometimes increased by giving the wheel a half turn so as to shift the body from a vertical to a horizontal position.

The most common punishments for lesser offenses were: reprimand by the commanding officer; confinement under guard, sometimes on bread-and-water rations; carrying a rail, log, or bag of sand; wearing a ball and chain, attached to the ankle; walking around camp inside a barrel "shirt"; wearing a placard indicating the offense, such as "thief," "coward," or "drunk"; performing extra duties; marking time on a box; or forfeiture of pay.

Confederate wooden water cask

Virginia belt buckle with state coat-of-arms

Virginia belt plate with state coat-of-arms

Deserters and other serious offenders, far more often than being shot or hung, were sentenced to long imprisonment at hard labor or dishonorably discharged and drummed out of camp. Sometimes the culprits were further disgraced by having their heads shaved.

When the death sentence was imposed, it was carried out under circumstances calculated to make the most profound impression. The culprit was usually hauled to the place of execution sitting on his coffin and shot in the presence of a brigade of his comrades formed in a hollow square about the open grave.

Another unattractive feature of army life was the monotony and drabness of camp routine. In September, 1861, a Louisiana Reb, stationed

EMBATTLED
CONFEDERATES

Florida belt buckle

Texas belt plate

in Virginia, outlined in a letter the regimen observed in his brigade and indicated his disgust with it: "To give you a slight idea of our duties, I will give you them as they come in military order—No. 1 Reveille at 5 oclk am—Roll call—Then we cook our breakfast which of course we are supposed to eat—Half past eight company drill until 10 oclk, after which we are free until 12 oclk when we have the dinner call, after which comes what is called fatigue duty which means Spades are trumps—and when there is no digging to be done, we have to clean up Quarters, after which we are again free until ½ past four when we have regimental drill until 6 oclk then dress parade & dismiss cook our supper eat loaf and spin yarns until 9 oclk when tattoo beats & we are all sent to bed like a parcel of school boys—fifteen minutes after which 3 taps are sounded & all lights put out & the tired soldier is soon asleep, now this occurring every day makes it very tiresome."

Privates John T. McKee and James S. Mackey, Liberty Hall Volunteers, Company I, Fourth Virginia Infantry, Stonewall Brigade

Johnny Rebs were hard put to escape the monotonous grind of military life. Furloughs were rarely to be had and neither the government nor the army attempted to provide recreational facilities. Post exchanges, libraries and reading rooms were unheard of and sutlers were hardly ever seen in Confederate camps. As a general rule, soldiers had to provide their own entertainment. Singing was the most popular diversion. The songs most frequently heard about Confederate campfires were "Home Sweet Home," "Annie Laurie," "Lorena," "Dixie," "Bonnie Blue Flag," "Juanita," "The Girl I Left Behind Me," "Annie of the Vale," "Her Bright Eyes Haunt Me Still," "Listen to the Mocking Bird," "Sweet Evalina," "Just Before the Battle, Mother," "Belle Brandon," and familiar hymns such as "Amazing Grace," "On Jordan's Stormy Banks," "There Is a Fountain Filled with Blood," "Rock of Ages," and "All Hail the Power of Jesus' Name." Almost every company had a violinist or two who entertained his associates with repertoires which included "Arkansas Traveler," "The Goose Hangs High," "My Old Kentucky Home," "Billy in the Low

Louisiana Zouave

Private Thomas Kitchen,
Eighth Georgia Infantry

EMBATTLED
CONFEDERATES

Grounds," "Oh Lord, Gals, One Friday," and "Hell Broke Loose in Georgia." Sometimes Rebs would pair off and dance to these lively tunes. Regimental bands occasionally gave serenades in the evening. When opposing armies were camped near each other as at Fredericksburg, Petersburg, Murfreesboro and Vicksburg, Yankee and Rebel musicians sometimes took turns playing their own patriotic songs and then joined together to render some piece well-known to both sides.

Interesting books were hard to obtain. Newspapers were in great demand but their circulation was limited by lack of distribution facilities and the poverty of the soldiers. Any newspaper or periodical that reached camp was passed from comrade to comrade until it was literally worn out in the reading.

Baseball, football, wrestling, boxing, quoits, marbles, chess and checkers—all had their devotees among the men who wore the gray. Cavalrymen raced their horses and occasionally rode in ring tournaments. Swimming, fishing and hunting were all pursued as season and circumstance permitted. Sham trials afforded merriment to many Rebs, and some delighted in staging amateur theatricals. Religiously inclined soldiers derived much pleasure and comfort from sermons, prayer sessions and "class meetings" featured by scripture reading, hymn singing and testimonials. Occasionally, and especially in the last two years of the war, great revivals swept through Confederate camps, bringing scores of wicked to repentance and causing the faithful to sing and shout with joy. But these outbursts were usually short-lived, both in duration and in their reforming influences.

Evil—or what people of the time regarded as evil—flourished to a greater extent in Confederate camps than did righteousness, and far more Rebs found diversion in drinking and gambling than in hymn singing and praying. J. W. Jones, a chaplain in Lee's army, stated that in the months following First Manassas "the vices common to most armies ran riot through our camps. Drunkenness became so common as to scarcely excite remark, and many who were temperate, and some who were even total abstinence leaders at home, fell into the delusion that drinking was excusable, if not necessary, in the army. The drunken brawls of even high officers were the common talk around the campfires, and the men of the rank and file claimed the privilege of imitating their leaders. . . . Gambling became so common, so open and so unrebuked, that men wearing 'the bars,' and even 'the stars' of rank would win from the soldier his scant pay."

Drinking was more common early in the war than later, owing to the fact that soldiers had more money in 1861 than 1865, and whiskey was more abundant. At any period in the war, except possibly during the peak of revivals or when battle was imminent, most Rebs would drink when they had an opportunity. Many of them would continue to swig the "Oh Be Joyful" until they were uproariously drunk. Intoxication was especially common at Christmas and New Year.

Background of Forest

Texans of Longstreet's
Corps retaking the outer
entrenchments on the
south side of the James
River, June 15, 1864

Gambling was even more pervasive than drinking. The most common games of chance were poker, euchre, twenty-one, keno, faro, craps, and chuck-a-luck, the last played by rolling three dice from a cup, with the contestants betting on number combinations indicated by figures in squares on a board or cloth.

The prevalency of drinking and gambling was due largely to boredom and loneliness. And many soldiers who indulged in these activities desisted from them when they returned to their homes. Admittedly, the Southern army had its quota of weaklings, shirkers, cowards and knaves. But the majority were solid, trustworthy, admirable characters deeply attached to their families, loyal to their comrades, faithful in the discharge of their duties, sound in their reactions, and abundantly endowed with the simple virtues. Letters of fathers to their children reveal high idealism, deep affection, and a concern for education. Typical of many was the following note of a Virginia soldier to his son: "I hope you have been a good little boy since I have been from home and when I get back I hope I may find you still a good boy. I hope my son you are trying to learn your books. Tell your Sis Susa I say she must heare your lessons for you. I want you to try and be a good and smart boy. I hope my son you

Winter quarters,
Confederate army,
Manassas, Virginia

are good to your ma and little sister. I hope my child it will not be very long before I can come home and stay with you. May the Lord bless you my son."

Another trait often demonstrated by the common soldiers was pride. The greatest fear of most Johnny Rebs as they faced the ordeal of battle was not that they would be killed—though concern for physical safety was deep and real—but rather that they would show the white feather, disgrace themselves before their comrades and bring shame on themselves and their families. Sometimes the subject of humorous stories, cowardice was a genuine concern on the part of many soldiers. A Georgian wrote home with pride after the battle of Franklin in 1864: "One of Old Abe's boys pluged me in the right foot making a severe wound [but] I am proud to say that there was no one between me and the Yankees when I was wounded."

EMBATTLED
CONFEDERATES

Another quality conspicuously demonstrated by the Rebel rank and file was an acute sense of duty. Shortly after the battle of Chancellorsville, one soldier wrote his wife: "I was very near not going into the fight; I had been sick so long; but when I got to thinking about it, I could not stay behind if it had killed me. I do not think I could have kept out of the fight."

When put to the test on the field of battle, most Rebs measured up well with respect to courage, and many displayed heroism of the highest order. Colonel Roger Q. Mills of the Tenth Texas Regiment paid high

Private William Harrison Rockwell, Company H, Eighteenth North Carolina Regiment

Drummer Boy William Shores, City Guards, Company C, First Arkansas Infantry. Killed at Shiloh, April 7, 1862

tribute to a Rebel hero of Chickamauga. "Private McCann was under my own eye. He stood upright, cheerful, and self-possessed, and after he had expended all his ammunition, gathered up the cartridge boxes of the dead and wounded and distributed them to his comrades. He bore himself like a hero through the entire contest, and fell mortally wounded by the last volleys of the enemy. I promised him during the engagement that I would mention his good conduct, and as he was borne dying from the field he turned his boyish face upon me and, with a light and pleasant smile, reminded me of my promise."

Still another trait abundantly demonstrated by those who wore the gray was staunchness in adversity. Confederates had an enormous capacity for hardship and suffering. Hunger was habitual, raggedness was normal, and lousiness was well-nigh universal. Disease and enemy bullets made life perilous and uncertain. Literally thousands of wounded Rebs were subjected to the ordeal of having bullets extracted or limbs sawed

Homemade playing cards made by John Hill Hewitt of Augusta, Georgia

off without benefit of anesthesia. But deprivation, discomfort and suffering were all borne with remarkable patience and cheerfulness. An Alabama nurse assigned to a Virginia hospital wrote in 1861 to her superior: "While I grow sick at the sight of the amputated limbs and ghastly wounds, I must testify that a groan has rarely reached my ears and the heroism of our men has developed itself more thoroughly and beautifully in enduring bodily suffering." Phoebe Yates Pember, matron of Chimborazo Hospital, told a story illustrating the calm with which dying Rebs met their fate. Fisher, one of her patients, was a young soldier whose optimism and fortitude during ten months' convalescence from a hip wound had won the admiration and affection of all his associates. On the night following his first success in walking the length of the ward, Fisher cried out in pain as he turned in his bed. A quick examination indicated that a splintered bone had pierced an artery.

Mrs. Pember pressed her finger against the wound to curb the hemorrhage and sent for the surgeon. The doctor found that the severed artery was too deeply imbedded in the thigh to permit repair. When Fisher was told of the hopelessness of his plight he gave the matron his mother's address and asked: "How long can I live?"

"Only as long as I keep my finger on this artery," the matron replied. Then followed a period of silence broken by the simple remark, "You can let go."

"But I could not," wrote the matron in her memoirs. "Not if my own life had trembled in the balance. Hot tears rushed to my eyes, a surging sound to my ears and a deathly coldness to my lips."

"The pang of obeying him was spared me," Mrs. Pember added, "and for the first and last time during the trials that surrounded me for four years, I fainted away."

Thus a brave boy died, and the strength and character that he reveals from the time of his wounding until the tragic moment of his passing reflected great credit on him and the thousands like him who marched among the Rebel rank and file. The manner in which the common soldiers of the Confederacy acquitted themselves is a heritage of which all Americans may be justly proud. These men endured, and the record of their endurance stands as an imperishable monument to their greatness.

v. *Armament* *and Industry*

When Johnny Rebs first entered the army in 1861 they frequently loaded themselves down with extra weapons such as bowie knives, daggers and pistols. Many photographs of the period show the recruit holding a musket by his side and carrying knives and pistols in his belt. After a little while the soldier shed his surplus weapons and carried only the one authorized in army regulations. In the case of the infantry private this was normally a rifle musket, though in the first year of the war, owing to the scarcity of arms, many Rebs carried smoothbore muskets loaded with "buck and ball" (one large and three small pellets) and some were equipped with shotguns. Many types and varieties of shoulder arms were in use throughout the war but the mainstays were Enfield rifle muskets, caliber .577, imported in large quantities from England, and Springfield rifle muskets, caliber .58, most of which were captured from the Federals. Other shoulder arms issued in considerable numbers were the Mississippi rifle, caliber .54, and the Harpers Ferry rifle (model 1855), caliber .58, many of which were manufactured in the Confederacy with equipment captured at Harpers Ferry in May, 1861. All of these guns were muzzle-loaders. The Confederacy had few breech-loading or repeating rifles, and most of these were taken from the Yankees.

Rifle muskets got their name from the fact that they were shaped like the old smoothbore muskets that they superseded, but had spiral grooving or rifling in the barrels which gave a spin to the bullets. The Enfields were 73 inches long with bayonet attached and weighed 9.19 pounds; the length and weight of the Springfields were 74 inches and 9.75 pounds. The bullet for both was a Minié ball, which was conical, with the base hollowed out so that it would expand on firing to engage the rifling and utilize fully the energy released by the explosion of the powder. Bullet and powder were packed in a paper cartridge which the soldier had to bite open with his teeth. He then poured the powder into the rifle barrel, set the bullet in the muzzle, pushed it home with a ramrod, placed a percussion cap on the tube leading into the base of

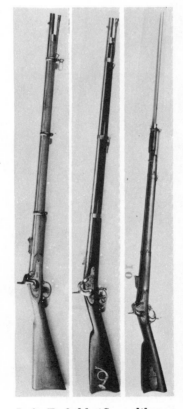

Left, Enfield rifle, caliber .577; center, Springfield musket, caliber .58; right, Harpers Ferry rifle, Model 1855, caliber .58

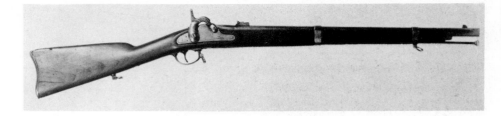

Richmond musketoon

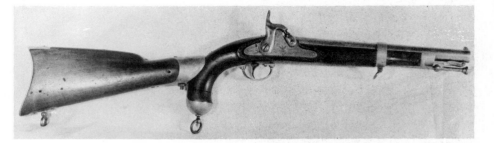

Pistol-carbine, used by Confederate cavalry, caliber .58, made by Fayetteville Arsenal, North Carolina. Copy of U.S. Model 1855 pistol-carbine

Morse Confederate breech-loading carbine

First Sergeant Charles Stevens Powell, Company E, Fourteenth Regiment, North Carolina Volunteers (redesignated in November, 1861, as Twenty-fourth Regiment, North Carolina Volunteers), holding a short-model Colt revolving rifle

the barrel, pulled back the hammer, took aim and fired. All this required nine separate motions (outlined in the manual) and under favorable conditions consumed fifteen or twenty seconds; and the sustained rate of fire averaged less than three shots a minute. But the effective range against troops was about four hundred yards, and with good luck a soldier might kill a foe one-half mile away.

Cavalry were usually armed with carbines, which were shorter, lighter weapons than rifle muskets. Most carbines were muzzle-loaders, though some were breechloaders fabricated in the Confederacy or obtained from outside sources.

Pistols were carried by some enlisted cavalrymen and by officers of all branches. Most of these weapons were revolvers, principally of Northern or foreign manufacture. Colt's six-shooters were the most popular. Confederates preferred the .36 caliber navy Colt over the heavier .44 caliber army version. Other brands of revolvers used by Confederates included the Remington, Whitney, Joslyn, Starr, Savage, Beal, and Smith and Wesson, made in the North; the Kerr, Deane and Tranter manufactured in England; and the LeMat, invented by Dr. Jean LeMat of New Orleans but produced in France. The LeMat, carried by "Jeb" Stuart, Beauregard and other Confederate generals, was a ten-shot revolver with two barrels, one above the other.

Sabers were issued to the rank and file of both cavalry and artillery, but these had far greater use as accessories than as death-dealing weap-

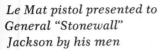

Le Mat pistol presented to General "Stonewall" Jackson by his men

John Hunt Morgan's pistol, a Colt Navy model 1851

Leech and Rigdon Confederate Colt percussion revolver, .36 caliber. One of the best six-shooters made by the Confederacy

Confederate water battery at Warrington, entrance to Pensacola Bay, Florida, February, 1861, showing old Columbiad guns of about 1812, mounted on Gribeauval carriages, and sandbag parapets, the gun crew in the act of loading and the drummer about to roll the drum

ons. The same was true of bayonets. An analysis by Federal medical authorities of 246,712 Civil War wounds revealed that only 922, less than four-tenths of 1 percent (.0037) were inflicted by sabers or bayonets.

Confederate artillerymen stationed in forts along coasts and rivers manned the "big guns"—huge, fat-bellied Columbiads, Dahlgrens and other siege pieces, some of which were so heavy that giant sling carts had to be built to move them; and short, dumpy mortars that lobbed tremendous balls into enemy works or vessels. But the great majority of Rebs who wore the red trimmings of the artillery serviced the lighter

A Dahlgren 11-inch smoothbore naval gun in the Confederate fortifications opposite Yorktown, Virginia, June, 1862

A Columbiad gun with reinforced breech by Brooke, at Howlett House, Trent's Reach, James River, Virginia, April, 1865

A giant sling cart to transport siege guns

EMBATTLED CONFEDERATES

Confederate water battery at Warrington entrance to Pensacola Bay, Florida, February, 1861. The mortar gun here shown was an old-style piece dating from before the Mexican War

Confederate water battery, with Rodman smoothbore siege guns, Yorktown, Virginia, June, 1862

Confederate 12-pounder howitzers captured at Missionary Ridge, November, 1863. The guns were made in Macon, Georgia, arsenal earlier that year

Far left, Confederate 12-pounder brass mountain howitzers; left, French 12-pounder bronze field guns made by Le Place Frères in Paris, and run through the blockade

and smaller fieldpieces which backed up the men who wielded the muskets and carbines. Fieldpieces were of many varieties and calibers. All fell within the general designation of cannon; but cannon were classified as guns if their projectiles followed a fairly level course, as mortars if their shots were arched high into the air, and as howitzers if the trajectories were between those of guns and mortars. Some cannon were smoothbores and others were rifled; most of them were loaded from the muzzle but a few were breechloaders; some were made of iron, some of brass and others of steel. Cannon were also classified by the weight of their projectiles and the diameter of their barrels, as is indicated by the designations "12-pounder howitzers" and "3-inch rifles."

The most widely used fieldpiece on the Confederate side was the 12-pounder Napoleon, a smoothbore gun-howitzer, caliber 4.62 inches, operated by a crew of five or six men. Most Napoleons were of bronze but in the latter part of the war shortage of brass caused Confederates to cast some from iron. Napoleons could fire a 12-pound cannon ball about 1,600 yards, but they were most effective when loaded with canister and used against troops no farther removed than 400 yards.

Ranking next to Napoleons in extensiveness of use were the 3-inch rifles, also worked by a crew of five or six men. These guns fired 10-pound conical shells and their effective range was about 2,400 yards. Many of the 10-pounders were cast-iron Parrotts captured from the Fed-

Lieutenant Andrew Blakely, Second Company, Washington Artillery

ARMAMENT
AND INDUSTRY 101

Right, Federal soldiers by Parrott gun in Fort McAllister, near Savannah, Georgia; far right, Armstrong gun, Fort Fisher, North Carolina

Right, a light 3-inch Brooke rifle, invented by John M. Brooke, C.S.N.; far right, a modified 12-pounder breech-loading Whitworth gun that ran the blockade

EMBATTLED CONFEDERATES

Confederate shells and torpedoes, Charleston Arsenal, Charleston, North Carolina, 1865

Sergeant Edward S. Duffey and his
associates firing what they claim was
the last Confederate shot at Gettysburg,
after Pickett's repulse.

*Brigadier General Edward
Porter Alexander, Chief of
Artillery of Longstreet's
Corps*

erals. (They were named for the inventor, Robert P. Parrott.) Others
were Confederate-made Brooke guns, also of cast iron, named for
John M. Brooke, designer of the battleship *Virginia*. The distinctive feature
of both Parrott and Brooke rifles was a breech banded with an extra
sheet of iron to give additional strength at the point of greatest strain.
These guns also were made in larger sizes; but the bigger guns, especially
those firing projectiles heavier than 20 pounds, had only limited use on
the battlefield.

Confederates imported some breech-loading rifled cannon from
England. Among these were 3-inch Armstrongs, 12-pounder Blakelys,
and 6- and 12-pounder Whitworths. The Whitworths were highly praised
for their range and accuracy.

Many types of ammunition were used in Confederate fieldpieces.
Solid shot, round or conical, was normally used for long ranges and
when the purpose was the battering of hostile works or the harassing of
enemy formations. For intermediate distances, when the prime consideration was the silencing of opposing artillery, or the breaking up of an
incipient assault, explosive spheres filled with small balls were fired
from smoothbores, and conical shells, similarly filled, were hurled from

Private John O'Farrell,
Crenshaw's Battery

Private Adolphus P. Williamson,
Company B, Fifth Battalion,
Virginia Artillery

Private James M. Kasey, Company A,
Lee Battery, Braxton's Battalion,
Virginia Artillery

Brigadier General Walter H.
Stevens, chief engineer of the
Army of Northern Virginia

rifled pieces. At close ranges, when the objective was to kill masses of charging foes, crews of all pieces generally shifted to canister and in desperate circumstances two and even three loads were fired at one shot. Canister was a can full of lead or iron balls varying in diameter from ⅝ to 1½ inches and in number from 25 to 76. The can contained no powder but was fragmented by the blast which drove it from the muzzle.

To produce the arms, powder, and all the appurtenances of war needed by the army and navy, and the rolling stock to move it, was a tremendous undertaking for the agrarian South. In his address to the Alabama Legislature in October, 1861, Governor A. B. Moore declared: "Mechanical arts and industrial pursuits hitherto practically unknown to our people are already in operation. The clink of the hammer and the busy hum of the workshop are beginning to be heard through our land. Our manufacturers are rapidly increasing. . . . The return of peace would find us a self-reliant and truly independent people."

Southerners in 1861 showed almost as much zeal for achieving economic self-sufficiency as for winning political independence. The efforts of towns and cities to mobilize troops for the fighting fronts were accompanied by ambitious attempts to manufacture products formerly obtained from the North and from Europe. In terms of the number and diversity of new factories brought into being as well as in the expansion of those already in existence, the bid for economic self-sufficiency was impressive. In 1861 *DeBow's Review* published an industrial survey which listed scores of plants that had recently been established in Norfolk, Charlottesville, Wilmington, Macon and other Southern towns to produce textiles, rope, leather, candles, cots, saddles, plows, stoves, stationery, steam engines, guns, uniforms, swords, spurs, canteens, gun carriages, tent cloth, and numerous other articles needed by soldiers and civilians.

Cadet Marcellus N. Moorman, V.M.I., Class of 1856, and Captain of Moorman's Battery of Virginia Artillery

Tredegar Iron Works, Richmond, Virginia

Brigadier General Joseph Reid Anderson, "The Krupp of the Confederacy," superintendent of Tredegar Iron Works, Richmond, Virginia

DeBow's survey did not include larger towns and cities, but if it had, the emerging industrialism would have appeared even more impressive. Richmond was as much the center of the Confederacy's industrial activity as it was the focal point of political life. At the outbreak of the war the Virginia capital was the South's first city in iron manufacture with four rolling mills, fourteen foundries and machine shops, fifty iron and metal works, two circular saw factories, a nail factory, and other industries representing a total investment of nearly four million dollars and employing more than sixteen hundred mechanics. It was the home of the famous Tredegar Iron Works, the South's foremost industrial plant and one of the very few establishments in the Confederacy capable of manufacturing locomotives. Owned and directed by Joseph Reid Anderson—a remarkably able executive trained at the United States Military Academy—Tredegar began early in 1861 to shift to war production. On January 17, Anderson, in response to an inquiry from the state of South Carolina, sent the following telegram: "Will make anything you want—work night and day if necessary, and ship by rail." Shortly

Ruins of State Arsenal, Richmond, Virginia

afterward he received orders from several Southern states and as the war progressed Tredegar became the Confederacy's mainstay for munitions and, until completion of the government arsenal at Selma, Alabama, its sole reliance for heavy ordnance. During the conflict it produced more than one thousand cannon including many large siege guns, numerous gun carriages and enormous quantities of artillery projectiles. It

EMBATTLED
CONFEDERATES

provided armor plating and machinery for battleships, built submarines and torpedoes and manufactured essential equipment for other arsenals scattered throughout the South. It was also an important center for research and development. Tredegar expanded its facilities enormously to serve its war mission and acquired various subsidiaries, including pig iron furnaces, coal mines, a tannery, a sawmill, a brick factory, a blockade runner and nine canal boats. At the peak of its war activity in 1863 it employed no less than 2,500 men.

Working in close cooperation with the Tredegar Works was the Richmond Armory and Arsenal, a government concern. This establishment provided, either through its own facilities or by contract with other firms (including the Tredegar Iron Works), about one-half of the ordnance material distributed to the Southern armies. Between July 1, 1861, and January 1, 1865, it issued 1,647 cannon, 921,441 rounds of artillery ammunition, 357,928 muskets and carbines, 6,074 pistols, about 72,500,000 rounds of small arms ammunition and large quantities of other ordnance material.

In Richmond were concentrated the principal directors, designers and inventors on whom the Confederacy depended for devising and producing the tools of war. Among these were Josiah Gorgas, the brilliant and resourceful head of the War Department's Ordnance Bureau; John M. Brooke, inventor of the Brooke gun and designer of the ironclad *Virginia;* George Minor, the navy's Chief of Ordnance and Hydrography; and, until his assignment to duties in England in the fall of 1862, the great oceanographer and naval inventor, Matthew Fontaine Maury.

Richmond was also the Confederacy's principal center for the making of flour and tobacco, and both of these industries were stepped up to meet the increased demands incident to war.

Nashville, before its fall in February, 1862, was another important center for the manufacture of war materials, and it experienced an industrial expansion similar to that of Richmond. Selma, Alabama, after 1862, became a key site for the manufacture of Confederate ordnance. Here was located both a state and Confederate arsenal, a navy yard and a naval foundry equipped with machinery made in England and run through the blockade. The government works at Selma, using coal and iron mined in Alabama, cast many cannon, large and small, manufactured armor plate for Confederate battleships and made large quantities of shot, shell, swords, rifles, pistols and caps. The Selma navy yard built the Confederate armored ram *Tennessee* and the gunboats *Selma, Morgan* and *Gaines.* The Confederate factories and foundries in this Alabama town consisted of more than a hundred buildings and employed about six thousand men.

Selma was also an important powder-making center. The principal ingredient of powder was saltpeter or niter (by weight, the content of powder was fifteen parts of niter, three of charcoal and two of sulphur), and procurement of niter was one of the Confederacy's major concerns.

McLeish Vulcan Iron Works, Charleston, South Carolina

Brigadier General Josiah Gorgas (in uniform of colonel), chief of the Confederate Ordnance Department

*James Gabriel Rains,
superintendent of the
Confederate Torpedo
Bureau*

In 1862 a Niter and Mining Bureau, headed by Isaac M. St. John of Augusta, Georgia, was organized in the War Department and charged with developing the South's niter resources. Limestone caves in Tennessee, Georgia and Alabama yielded some niter but the government found it necessary to resort to niter beds or nitriaries for the production of this important commodity. Government nitriaries were established in Selma, Mobile, Montgomery and other Southern cities and many individuals and private concerns throughout the Confederacy produced niter on a contract basis. Niter-making was a slow and unpleasant business. Dead animals, manure and rotting vegetable matter were dumped into shallow pits or beds and doused from time to time with urine and other liquids. After eighteen months of soaking and mixing, the putrid soil was dug up from the beds, placed in hoppers and drained of niter by the application of water. Captain Jonathan Haralson, Selma agent of the Niter and Mining Bureau, is said to have run an advertisement in the Selma newspaper requesting ladies of the town to save all the "chamber-lye" collected around their premises for use in making niter. Haralson's request inspired Thomas B. Wetmore, a local citizen possessed of a lively sense of humor and a bent for poetry, to write some doggerel chiding the captain for his unusual appeal. The risqué verses, printed in broadside form in both North and South, were circulated in Union and Confederate camps, much to the amusement of the soldiers. Most of the niter obtained in Tennessee and Alabama was taken to the Confederate works at Selma to be made up into powder.

The Confederacy's largest powder plant was located at Augusta, Georgia. Augusta, also the site of a Confederate arsenal, a clothing bureau and other government establishments, as well as a number of privately owned factories, enjoyed a war boom comparable to that of Selma. The Confederate States Powder Works at Augusta was planned and built by one of the Confederacy's scientific geniuses, George Washington Rains, whose elder brother, Gabriel James Rains, was superintendent of the Confederate Torpedo Bureau and a pioneer in the use of land mines. George Washington Rains was a native of North Carolina and a graduate of the United States Military Academy. After a varied career in the United States Army, including a tour as assistant professor of chemistry, geology and mineralogy at West Point, he resigned his commission in 1856 and became president of two iron works in New York. He entered the Confederate army as a major in July, 1861, and eventually rose to the rank of colonel. He served in the ordnance department throughout the war.

Rains had hardly donned the Confederate uniform when Gorgas put him in charge of expediting powder production and told him to do whatever was necessary to accomplish his mission. The appointment proved to be one of Gorgas' wisest moves. After exploratory trips to Nashville and New Orleans, Rains visited Augusta, where he found an admirable site for a new plant, on the Augusta Canal near the city's

*Confederate powder
works, Augusta, Georgia*

western limits. Here he decided to erect a large powder works. From rough sketches prepared by Rains, architect C. Shaler Smith drew up plans for the buildings. Construction began in September, 1861, and the plant opened for operations on April 10, 1862. The works when completed consisted of twenty-six substantial buildings stretching for two miles along both sides of the canal. Equipping of the works was an "all Southern" project. Tredegar contributed twelve large iron beds and twenty-four five-ton rollers; an Atlanta flour mill provided a large steam engine; an Augusta factory made pipes, coolers and retorts; some machinery was obtained from the Nashville armory; and other equipment was gathered from various private and government establishments.

The Powder Works at Augusta proved to be the Confederacy's most spectacular success. Its daily output averaged more than 7,000 pounds of superior powder. Total production during the three years of operation was 2,750,000 pounds and the cost per pound was one-third of the price paid for powder run through the blockade. At the end of the war Rains had a surplus of 70,000 pounds in storage at Augusta; to him, to Gorgas, and to their corps of able assistants is to be credited the remarkable fact that Confederates never lost a battle for lack of powder.

Another Georgia town which experienced a manufacturing boom was Macon. A key figure in this town's industrialization was John W. Mallet, a Dublin-born chemist who migrated to the United States in 1853 and later settled in Alabama. Mallet enlisted as a private in the Confederate army in the spring of 1861 but the next year Gorgas obtained his transfer and placed him in charge of the Confederacy's ordnance laboratories. His duties included supervision and standardization of the production and packaging of Minié balls, percussion caps, artillery projectiles, fuses and rockets.

In the interest of promoting uniformity and efficiency in the production of ammunition, Mallet established at Macon a central ordnance laboratory. He worked in close collaboration with James H. Burton, the Ordnance Bureau's Superintendent of Armories, who was completing a Confederate armory at Macon. A large Confederate arsenal was also located at Macon, and in the various government establishments small arms, heavy cannon and fieldpieces were produced. The output of Macon's Confederate plants was supplemented by that of numerous private firms engaged in the production of pistols, swords and other army equipment as well as a large assortment of civilian materials.

Atlanta experienced an even greater war boom than Macon. The Atlanta Arsenal, established by the Confederate government early in the conflict, made and repaired arms of various types, and manufactured ammunition, haversacks, knapsacks, saddles and other army equipment. The Confederate Quartermaster Department, utilizing cloth and other materials obtained under contract, produced large quantities of uniforms, blankets, drawers, wool hats and shoes. The Commissary Department maintained a large depot for the collection, storage and distribution of meat, flour, lard and other provisions. State commissary and quartermaster departments had headquarters and supply depots in Atlanta. Four railroads, all operating at peak capacity during the war, greatly stimulated trade, kept hotels and boardinghouses overflowing with customers and caused an expansion of maintenance, drayage and storage facilities. The Southern Express Company did a thriving business in the handling of mail, money and packages. In 1862 E. N. Spiller, a German gunsmith, formed a partnership with J. H. Burr to manufacture pistols for the Confederate government, and the weapons which began to come from the shop near the end of the year were pronounced by the Atlanta *Southern Confederacy* to be "as serviceable pistols as Colt of Hartford ever turned out." A woodwork shop on Decatur Street, owned by Peck and Day, turned to the assembling of muskets and the manufacture of long handles for the famous "Georgia Pikes" with which Governor Joe Brown proposed to arm Southern troops. Four machine shops and a large rolling mill were expanded to meet the increasing requirements of the army and navy. Among other Atlanta firms established or enlarged to supply government and civilian needs were a leather tannery, printing house and book bindery, flour mill, several whiskey distilleries, and factories for the manufacture of shoes, shoe polish, friction matches, stationery, soap, candles, trunks and dental and surgical supplies.

VI. *Life in Town and Country*

The experiences of Mobile, Montgomery, New Orleans, Memphis, Raleigh, Charleston and other Confederate cities were very similar to those of Atlanta, Macon, Augusta, Selma and Richmond. All felt the stimulating influence of the new demands created by mobilization and war. The large towns and cities and especially those which became centers of government activity continued to grow and thrive—though in varying degree—throughout most of the war, or until Federal invasion brought demoralization and destruction. But in the smaller towns and in cities less favored by government business, the boom at the beginning of the war proved to be short-lived. Most of the new industries were small, their financial resources were limited and in the ever increasing competition for raw materials they could not maintain sufficient stocks to fill orders and continue profitable operation. After a few months most of them withered away or sold out to larger firms. The government absorbed more and more of the output of the establishments which continued in existence; and scarcity and high prices drove many consumers to improvisation and home manufacture.

Before the war was a year old, residents of most Southern towns were crying hard times, and the cry increased as the blockade tightened, transportation facilities deteriorated, prices soared and the twin evils of speculation and hoarding grew to monstrous proportions.

A considerable number of Southerners, some by legitimate methods and others by practices which would not have borne close scrutiny, prospered greatly and lived well even in the last years of the war. But they were a small minority. Most town and city dwellers were middle- and lower-class people, and as a general rule their plight worsened with the passing of time. Even in the war industries, where the pay scale was relatively high, the purchasing power of wages and salaries steadily decreased as scarcity and inflation boosted the prices of consumer goods. In February, 1863, master machinists in government armories received $5.00 a day; and carpenters, $2.00 a day. At that time beef was selling

EMBATTLED CONFEDERATES

in Richmond at $1.00 a pound; bacon, $1.25; butter, $3.00; meal, $6.00 a bushel; flour, $30.00 a barrel; and shoes, $25.00 a pair. By January, 1865, wages at the Tredegar Iron Works had increased to about $10.00 a day for machinists, blacksmiths and carpenters, but a day's pay bought far less than in 1863. Flour sold at $1,000.00 a barrel in Richmond early in 1865; meal, $100.00 a bushel; field peas, $80.00 a bushel; white beans, $5.00 a quart; beef, $8.00 a pound; butter, $15.00 a pound; wood, $100.00 a load; and plain cotton cloth, $15.00 a yard. To hold the laboring force and assure a livelihood for them, the War Department in 1863 began to provide food and other essentials at cost prices. Other government agencies and private concerns engaged in war production took similar steps. Even so, the plight of the laborers continued to deteriorate. In October, 1863, a Columbus, Georgia, mechanic wrote: "I once got 25 pounds of bacon for a day's work. What do I get now? Only two. I once got fifty pounds of beef for a day's work. What do I get now? Only six. I could once get 8 bushels of sweet potatoes for a day's work. What can I get now? Not one."

Confederate laborers were not organized, but some of them resorted to strikes in an effort to improve their lot. These were only moderately successful. Many skilled workers were exempted from conscription on the basis of their occupations and they were reluctant to strike for fear of being drafted. Some who did dare to quit their jobs in protest against low wages were enrolled in the army and their pay reduced to that of infantry privates.

Managers, foremen, clerks and other salaried workers in government and private employ were little better off than the day laborers. The compensation of most was meager at the beginning of the war and the increases which they received during the conflict fell far short of advances in the cost of living.

Street in Fredericksburg, Virginia

The difficulties and anxieties of white-collar workers are well illustrated by the experience of the family of John Beauchamp Jones, a clerk in the Confederate War Department, as set forth in *A Rebel War Clerk's Diary*. In the spring of 1861 Jones obtained employment in the Confederate War Department at a salary of $1,200 a year, and in August his son, Custis, joined him in the war office at a salary equal to his own. Two years later, when they were beginning to feel the pressure of inflation, Jones had the good fortune to find a large furnished house for $80 a month, with fruit trees and garden plot that provided vegetables for the table. About the same time his salary was increased to $3,000 a year, and his son's likewise, raising the family's annual income to $6,000. But the raise was more than offset by mounting inflation. On July 17, 1863, Jones wrote: "We are in a half-starving condition. I have lost twenty pounds and my wife and children are emaciated to some extent."

In January, 1864, Custis started a night school which added $100 a month to the family income. Still, the Jones family was ragged and undernourished. On January 17, 1864, Jones wrote: "With flour at $200 a barrel, meal $20 per bushel and meat from $2 to $5 a pound what

*Merchants cotton mill,
Petersburg, Virginia*

Ruins of Gallego Flour Mill, Richmond, Virginia

Baptist church, Yorktown, Virginia

income would suffice?" The plight of the Joneses steadily deteriorated, despite a salary increase that brought the family income to $10,200 by the end of the year. On April 8, 1864, the diarist wrote: "I cannot afford to have more than an ounce of meat daily for each member of my family. . . . This is famine." On January 24, 1865, Jones confided to his diary: "What I fear is starvation." Six weeks later he reported that bacon was selling at $13 a pound and meal at $100 a bushel. He did not starve but he grew thinner and weaker and there can be little doubt that his death on February 4, 1866, at age fifty-five, was due in part to malnutrition experienced during the war years.

Country folk as a general rule lived better than city dwellers. In most cases rural families were able to produce their own food and, as indicated elsewhere, the women became expert at spinning, weaving, tailoring, improvisation and home manufacture.

The war required many adjustments on farms and plantations. Absence of adult males in the army threw increased burdens of supervision and labor on women, children and old men. The army's enormous demand for horses greatly reduced the supply of work animals and led to an increasing reliance on mules and oxen. When vehicles and tools were broken or worn out it was often difficult, if not impossible, to repair or replace them. Neighbors frequently pooled their labor, their work

Stacking wheat near Culpeper, Virginia, 1863

animals and their implements to get the greatest return from what they had. Even so, resort to primitive practices and devices was not uncommon in the last two years of the war. Sleds and two-wheel carts often replaced wagons for hauling. Hand-swung cradles were substituted for reapers in the harvesting of wheat and oats. Wheat was threshed by flailing the stalks against barrels or laying them in troughs and beating the heads with wooden mauls; the winnowing was done by pouring the grains on sheets from containers held high in the air, so the breeze would sweep away the chaff. Rice was threshed in a similar manner and the husks removed by dumping the grains in a partially hollowed stump and beating them with a wooden pestle. Juice was extracted from sorghum cane by crushing the stalks between wooden rollers; the liquid was then boiled in pans or kettles to produce molasses.

Rural folk often were unable to get their wheat ground into flour owing to lack of milling facilities. But almost every community had a corn mill of some sort which would convert the kernels into meal on a share basis. As a result cornbread almost completely replaced biscuits on country tables after the first year of conflict and bolted meal was used as a substitute for flour in making cakes and pastries. Shortage of salt for preserving meat deprived many families of their highly cherished pork save for brief periods after hog killing. Some households resorted to the practice of taking turns killing hogs and beeves and distributing the meat among their neighbors for quick consumption. Standard winter fare for many was cornbread, molasses, dried field peas and sweet potatoes, supplemented occasionally by turnips, dried fruit (stewed or converted into fried pies) and pork. Coffee, as noted elsewhere, virtually disappeared from Southern tables early in the war, though some families resorted to substitutes made from roasted cereals, peanuts or sweet-potato particles and others drank tea brewed from sassafras roots or blackberry leaves. The more fortunate had a cow or two to supply their tables with milk, but many families went for long periods with no other beverage than water, laboriously drawn from wells or carried from springs.

Summer fare of country folk was enriched by fresh vegetables from fields and gardens. Shortage of sugar curtailed desserts in both winter and summer. But molasses, which provided "long sweetening" for beverages, was widely used in the making of cakes, pies and candy.

Slave-owning families felt the pinch of war far less than did those of the yeoman class. Planters usually had more of a reserve in the way of clothing, equipment and means to cushion themselves against adversity, and their Negroes relieved them from the labor and drudgery of cultivating their fields and running their households. In the interior

Brigadier General William R. Peck, Louisiana plantation owner

View of Culpeper, Virginia

South many planter families lived comfortably throughout the war. But in invaded areas slaveowners were hardest hit of all. Their Negroes frequently ran away or refused to work; their fields were often devastated by the invaders, their homes pillaged or burned, their horses and mules confiscated and their poultry, hogs and cows slaughtered. It is not surprising that many planter families elected to flee on approach of the Federals, taking along as much of their property as possible. But what they left behind was usually seriously damaged, if not destroyed; and when the refugees returned their lot was much harder than in former times.

In both country and towns the war led to many changes in day-to-day living. Cutting off of the Northern supply of oil caused a widespread shift from lamps to homemade candles. Many families had no other light except that afforded by open fireplaces. Women learned to knit, crochet and perform other manual tasks in the dark. Letters

Quarles mill on the North Anna River, Virginia

were written with homemade ink on coarse brown paper; and for economy of space, correspondents gave the sheets a half-turn after filling them in the usual manner and scribbled across the lines previously written. Envelopes, sometimes made of wallpaper and old business forms, were reversed and used a second time. For computing and making temporary notations, slates and boards often were substituted for paper. Needles and pins became so scarce that the loss of either might be the occasion for a search involving the whole family. Thorns and splinters sometimes sufficed for pins. Blacksmiths attempted to make substitutes for needles, but their products were not satisfactory. Nails and screws were in great demand and much care was taken to conserve the limited supply. The increasing shortage of these and other metal items such as hinges, locks and wire severely restricted construction of buildings and furnishings and prevented proper maintenance of homes and premises.

Plates, cups and saucers were fashioned of clay to replace glass- and chinaware; gourds were converted into ladles and dippers; and home-woven baskets supplanted boxes and kettles. An Alabama mother wove willow switches into "a beautiful and ornate baby carriage."

Women made fans of palmetto, rushes, paper and goose feathers. They obtained starch by soaking wheat bran, grated corn or sweet potatoes in water until fermentation, skimming off the surface and then running the solution through sieves and cloths. They produced soap by mixing lye, drained from ashes, with refuse grease.

Confederate families blacked their shoes with polish made at home by mixing soot with lard or with oil pressed from cottonseed or peanuts. They cleaned their teeth with twigs chewed at the end to separate the fibers or with crude brushes made of hog bristles; pulverized charcoal was the most widely used tooth powder. Lard, scented with rose petals, was substituted for hair oil. Women arranged their coiffures with combs carved from wood or cow horns, and hairpins improvised from thorns. They adorned themselves with rings and bracelets whittled by their menfolk from bone or wood and with necklaces made by stringing together dried and varnished melon seeds.

Shortage of doctors and drugs compelled many Southerners to treat themselves with medicines made at home or by local apothecaries. Both professional and amateur practitioners and druggists received valuable

LIFE IN TOWN
AND COUNTRY

*Street in Warrenton,
Virginia, August, 1862*

assistance from *Resources of Southern Fields and Forests*, a book prepared during the war by a distinguished Charleston surgeon, Francis P. Porcher, and first published in 1863. In this thick volume were listed the medical properties of plants obtainable in the South: dogwood berries, the roots and bark of chestnut and chinquapin trees, willow bark, poplar bark, sweet gum, tea made from cottonseed, boneset, pleurisy root, mandrake, roots of white or prickly ash and Sampson's snakeroot, mustard seed, hickory leaves, and pepper. Opium was extracted from poppies. Hops were used for laudanum; corncob ashes for soda; pleurisy root, dandelion and butterfly root for calomel. Brandy for medicinal and other uses was made from apples, peaches and watermelons. So many dentists entered the army that their services rarely were obtainable in rural sections. The same was true in many towns. The Shreveport, Louisiana, *News* of June 21, 1864, carried this notice: "There are many ladies and gentlemen in this city who are greatly in need of dental operations. Cannot General [E. Kirby] Smith detail some competent dentist for the benefit of the sufferers?"

Money played an important role in the life of all classes in both town and country. In the first months of the war currency was scarce. Federal specie in circulation when the war broke out quickly disappeared; some of it was hoarded, some acquired by the Confederate government through the sale of bonds, and some sent to the North or abroad in exchange for goods. The Confederate Congress on March 9, 1861, authorized the issue of one million dollars in Treasury notes but the lowest denomination was fifty dollars. On May 16, 1861, Congress provided for the issuance of five-dollar notes, but these did not get into circulation until summer.

In the meantime, to provide a circulating medium in denominations small enough for routine business, states, cities and banks issued large quantities of notes and business houses flooded the country with shinplasters. The latter were small bills ranging in denomination from five cents to a half-dollar. They had no legal status, but were issued for convenience. At first they served a useful purpose, but irresponsibility, excess and fraud on the part of firms and individuals who put them in circulation eventually made them a worthless nuisance.

By the end of 1861 the currency situation had changed from crippling sparseness to damaging abundance. A Staunton, Virginia, lawyer wrote in his diary on December 26, 1861: "Money was never so plentiful —Confederate States Treasury Notes, Bank Notes of all sorts and sizes, and 'shinplasters' issued by towns, corporations and Tom, Dick and Harry. Gold and silver are never seen."

By the end of 1863 more than $730,000,000 in Confederate notes, in denominations extending from $0.50 to $1,000.00, were in circulation. In 1864 and 1865 presses ground out even greater quantities of Confederate paper, bringing the total issue of Treasury notes during the war to the enormous figure of $1,554,087,354.00. The Confederacy issued

Chattanooga, Tennessee

no coins of its own though a die was made for a fifty-cent piece from which four "proofs" were struck.

The currency became so cheap that people contemptuously referred to it as fodder, rags, shrunken cabbage and oak leaves. A common saying late in the war was that "you take your money to market in a basket and bring home what you buy in your pocketbook."

Inflation caused debtors to seek out their creditors in an effort to redeem old obligations with depreciated paper, and creditors ran from debtors to keep from being paid. As a Confederate diarist put it in May, 1864: "Never were debtors more eager to pay or creditors so loth to receive."

Depreciation of currency caused an increasing resort to barter and exchange of services for goods. Farmers who refused to sell their produce for money willingly traded for salt, sugar, tools, clothing and other essentials. Factories had no difficulty in obtaining meat in exchange for textiles. On July 9, 1864, the Savannah, Georgia, *Republican* carried the following notice: "I will barter salt from my salt factory on the following terms. . . . 4 bushels of salt for 5 bushels of corn and peas; 1 bushel of salt for 5 pounds of lard or bacon; 2 bushels of salt for 7 pounds of sugar; 10 pounds of salt for a barrel of 'super' flour; 2 bushels of salt for 1 pr. of shoes." A New Orleans woman traded a bonnet which she valued at $600 in Confederate money for five turkeys. Doctors preferred provisions to money in payment of their services and schools encouraged pupils to pay their tuition and board in bacon, potatoes and other produce.

Street in Atlanta, Georgia, 1864

The disruption, deprivation and tragedy of war bore heavily on the spirit of the Southern people, but many were able to rise above their woes and to achieve a fair degree of happiness. Newspapers, correspondence and diaries of the time reveal a varied program of diversions. In the towns and cities theatrical groups, amateur and professional, played to large and appreciative audiences. Their offerings consisted largely of comedies and musicals, though most companies occasionally presented tragedies of Shakespeare. Leading performers included Charles Morton, Harry Macarthy, E. R. Dalton, Walter Keeble, D'Orsay Ogden, Jennie Powell, Ella Wren, Ida Vernon and Mary Parrington. Shortage of men led in some instances to the use of women disguised as males in secondary roles.

In the fall and winter of 1864 the Montgomery Theater, run by W. H. Crisp—whose family comprised a considerable portion of the cast—presented the following:

November   1, *The Lady of Lyons*
November   4, *London Assurance*
November   8, *Leap Year* and *Black-Eyed Susan*
November 11, *Richard III*
November 13, *Lucille: The Story of a Heart*
November 16, *Lady of the Lake*
November 17, *Tobin's Honey Moon* and *Beauty and the Beast*
November 18, *Don Caesar de Bazan* and *Pleasant Neighbor*
December 18, *The Death of Rolla*
December 19, *Our Wife*
December 20, *Serious Penalty*
December 22, *Ellen Wareham, The Wife of Two Husbands*
December 24, *Richelieu*

The Montgomery *Daily Mail* ran an editorial on November 1 praising the local theater as "the neatest in the South and among the most tastefully arranged on this side of the Atlantic." It also complimented the cast but added this note reflecting the impingements of war: "One thing is greatly needed . . . a good orchestra. The present one is simply a first-rate musician without support—a leader without a band."

Home of Robert Barnwell Rhett, Sr., Beaufort, South Carolina

View of Fredericksburg,
Virginia

View of Meeting Street, Charleston, South Carolina,
St. Michael's church (center), Circular church (distance)
and the South Carolina Club House (right)

EMBATTLED
CONFEDERATES

Mule team crossing a brook in Virginia

Colored minstrels performed occasionally in Confederate towns, as did a famous Negro pianist named "Blind Tom." Jugglers, organ-grinders, tumblers, jig-dancers, sleight-of-hand artists and other enter-tainers made their rounds during the war as before. Almost every community had occasional benefit programs consisting of tableaux, charades, songs, and readings, presented by local talent. Typical of many such performances was the "Tableaux and Charades" presented by the women of Uniontown, Alabama, for the benefit of the "brave Missouri soldiers cut off from friends and home." Admission for the show was "$2 or a pair of socks."

Dinner parties, dances, picnics, "singing sprees," candy pullings (with molasses providing the sweetening), fishing and hunting were also popular. So were chess, checkers, dice games and cards. Shortage of ammunition curtailed the use of guns, but a good dog sufficed to bag opossums, and rabbits could be stalked or clubbed after a heavy snow. Blockade runners occasionally brought in shipments of playing cards. On June 9, 1864, the triweekly *South Carolinian* reported importation by way of Nassau of several sets of Yankee-made cards bearing the likenesses of Confederate generals and statesmen, with the hearts, diamonds, spades and clubs located in the corner. "Our leaders are thus ingeniously made to turn up as trumps," the editor humorously observed.

Some communities continued to observe the Fourth of July, but many Southerners ignored this anniversary on the ground that it had been taken over by the Yankees. On July 4, 1861, Kate Stone of Louisiana wrote in her journal: "This is the first Fourth in our memory to pass without a public merry making of some kind, but we do not hear of the day's being celebrated in town or country. There are sterner duties

before us. It would ill become us as a Nation to be celebrating a day of independence when we are fighting for our very existence."

Christmas was celebrated with all the merriment that circumstances would permit. On December 25, 1862, S. P. Richards, an Atlanta businessman, wrote in his diary: "We had a fine rooster for Christmas dinner which tasted quite as well as turkey. Santa Claus, as usual, brought the children some presents and they had a fine time." On December 26, 1862, a North Carolina woman wrote her soldier husband: "Our children had no Christmas tree as there was a scarcity of fruit, but they hung up their stockings and were much pleased with their contents—cake, sugar, candy (home-made), an apple apiece, nuts, etc. The fire crackers from dear papa pleased them better than anything else."

After 1862 the content of Christmas stockings dwindled and took on more of a homemade quality, and many parents improvised toy horses out of cornstalks and dolls out of rags. For adults, the greatest problem was a dearth of alcohol. When liquor was obtainable, it was sometimes of an exceedingly poor quality. On January 6, 1862, Kate

EMBATTLED
CONFEDERATES

Stone wrote in her journal: "Christmas passed very quietly with us. . . . Had the customary eggnog before breakfast, but not a prize nog. It was made of borrowed whiskey with a strong flavor of turpentine." With or without the aid of alcholic stimulants, people of staunch character, optimistic disposition and the will to be gay were able to find enjoyment during the darkest periods of the war. This was especially true of the young people, for they had a vitality and exuberance which made them impervious to the troubles which surrounded them.

GENERAL ORDER.

**HEAD QUARTERS,
DEPARTMENT OF WESTERN VIRGINIA,**
Charleston, Va., Sept. 24, 1862.

General Order, No.

The money issued by the Confederate Government is secure, and is receivable in payment of public dues, and convertible into 8 per cent. bonds. Citizens owe it to the country to receive it in trade; and it will therefore be regarded as good in payment for supplies purchased for the army.

Persons engaged in trade are invited to resume their business and open their stores.

By order of   **MAJ. GEN. LORING.**
H. FITZHUGH.
Chief of Staff.

VII. *Transportation and Communication*

For transportation beyond their home communities the people of the Confederacy relied mainly on railroads. At the beginning of the war the eleven states comprising the Confederacy had 9,000 miles of railroad. Virginia had 1,800 miles; Georgia, 1,400; and Tennessee, 1,284. Louisiana had only 328 miles of railroad; Florida, 327; and Arkansas had even less. The rail system of Texas consisted of some short lines radiating from Houston and a few miles of track running out of Marshall and Sabine Pass.

Southern rail lines rarely exceeded two hundred miles in length, but in some instances a number of short lines connected (or almost connected) to comprise something approaching trunk systems. The longest of these major routes was the series of lines running southwestward from Richmond through Lynchburg, Bristol, Chattanooga, Corinth, Grand Junction, and Jackson, Mississippi, to New Orleans. Another principal route extended from Richmond through Weldon, Wilmington, Charleston, Savannah and Atlanta to Montgomery and beyond. These east-west arteries were tied in to some extent with three major routes running north and south. The Georgia-owned Western and Atlantic connecting Atlanta and Chattanooga was the central link of a system extending northward to Nashville and southward to Macon and points beyond. Farther west the Mobile and Ohio pushed northward from the Gulf through Meridian, Corinth and Jackson, Tennessee, to Columbus, Kentucky. This route was paralleled by still another series of roads running from New Orleans through central Mississippi to Grand Junction and Jackson, Tennessee.

Confederate railroads were ill-prepared to meet the enormous demands created by war. Some of the main routes had huge gaps which necessitated long and costly detours. An incompleted stretch between Meridian and Selma deprived Louisianians and Mississippians of direct service to Montgomery and lengthened the route to Richmond. To get to the Confederate capital for his first inauguration Jefferson Davis had to

EMBATTLED
CONFEDERATES

make a roundabout trip of 750 miles from Jackson, Mississippi, through Grand Junction, Chattanooga, Atlanta and West Point. If the road through Selma had been complete, the distance would have been only 250 miles. With pressure and financial help from the Confederate government the gap between Meridian and Selma was completed in December, 1862, with the exception of the Tombigbee River, which remained unbridged for the duration of the war. No rail service was available between Selma and Montgomery, since these towns were connected by the Alabama River; passengers and freight made this part of the journey by boat. Another gap of about fifty miles between Tensas Station and Pollard, Alabama, denied Mobile a direct rail connection with Montgomery and a short route to Virginia until November, 1861.

One of the most serious flaws in the Southern network was the lack of a rail line covering the forty-eight miles between Danville and Greensboro. Connection of these towns would provide a third and relatively secure rail route from Richmond to the deep South. The Confederate Congress in February, 1862, on President Davis' strong recommendation, appropriated one million dollars to subsidize the building of this important link. But various impediments, including the opposition of state rights leaders who questioned the constitutionality of government aid, and of stockholders in the Weldon railroad who objected to additional competition, delayed completion of the new route until May, 1864.

Another deterrent to efficient rail service was a diversity of gauges. Some companies followed the practice, standardized after the war, of laying the rails four feet, eight and one half inches apart; others used a five-foot gauge; and still others spaced the rails at five and one-half feet. This lack of uniformity prevented through service and interchange of equipment. The only major route which had the same gauge (five feet) throughout was that running from Petersburg to New Orleans by way of Knoxville, Chattanooga and Grand Junction. The confusion of gauges is well exemplified by the lines running between the capitals of Virginia and South Carolina. From Richmond to Petersburg the gauge was four feet, eight and one-half inches; Petersburg to Danville, five feet; Danville to Charlotte, four feet, eight and one-half inches; Charlotte to Columbia, five feet.

Even if gauges of all lines had been the same, long hauls would still have been an impossibility, for many towns, owing to opposition of draymen, would not permit the junction of lines coming to their borders. The five railroads serving Richmond in 1861 were unconnected. Here, as at Petersburg, Augusta, Savannah and other cities, passengers and freight had to be unloaded and hauled through the streets before continuing on the way. Often these transfers resulted in long layovers and additional expense for lodging or storage.

From the beginning, Confederate railroads were handicapped by weak rails, poorly constructed roadbeds, flimsy trestles and deficient maintenance. Rails were made of wrought iron instead of steel. The

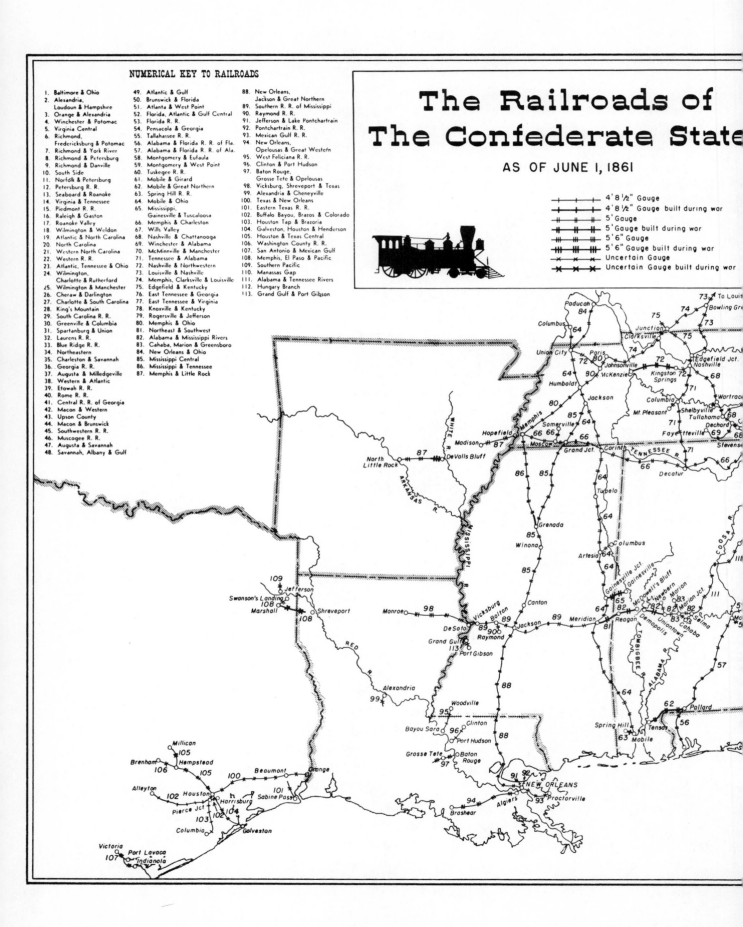

The Railroads of The Confederate State[s]

AS OF JUNE 1, 1861

NUMERICAL KEY TO RAILROADS

1. Baltimore & Ohio
2. Alexandria, Loudoun & Hampshire
3. Orange & Alexandria
4. Winchester & Potomac
5. Virginia Central
6. Richmond, Fredericksburg & Potomac
7. Richmond & York River
8. Richmond & Petersburg
9. Richmond & Danville
10. South Side
11. Norfolk & Petersburg
12. Petersburg R. R.
13. Seaboard & Roanoke
14. Virginia & Tennessee
15. Piedmont R. R.
16. Raleigh & Gaston
17. Roanoke Valley
18. Wilmington & Weldon
19. Atlantic & North Carolina
20. North Carolina
21. Western North Carolina
22. Western R. R.
23. Atlantic, Tennessee & Ohio
24. Wilmington, Charlotte & Rutherford
25. Wilmington & Manchester
26. Cheraw & Darlington
27. Charlotte & South Carolina
28. King's Mountain
29. South Carolina R. R.
30. Greenville & Columbia
31. Spartanburg & Union
32. Laurens R. R.
33. Blue Ridge R. R.
34. Northeastern
35. Charleston & Savannah
36. Georgia R. R.
37. Augusta & Milledgeville
38. Western & Atlantic
39. Etowah R. R.
40. Rome R. R.
41. Central R. R. of Georgia
42. Macon & Western
43. Upson County
44. Macon & Brunswick
45. Southwestern R. R.
46. Muscogee R. R.
47. Augusta & Savannah
48. Savannah, Albany & Gulf

49. Atlantic & Gulf
50. Brunswick & Florida
51. Atlanta & West Point
52. Florida, Atlantic & Gulf Central
53. Florida R. R.
54. Pensacola & Georgia
55. Tallahassee R. R.
56. Alabama & Florida R. R. of Fla.
57. Alabama & Florida R. R. of Ala.
58. Montgomery & Eufaula
59. Montgomery & West Point
60. Tuskegee R. R.
61. Mobile & Girard
62. Mobile & Great Northern
63. Spring Hill R. R.
64. Mobile & Ohio
65. Mississippi, Gainesville & Tuscaloosa
66. Memphis & Charleston
67. Wills Valley
68. Nashville & Chattanooga
69. Winchester & Alabama
70. McMinnville & Manchester
71. Tennessee & Alabama
72. Nashville & Northwestern
73. Louisville & Nashville
74. Memphis, Clarksville & Louisville
75. Edgefield & Kentucky
76. East Tennessee & Georgia
77. East Tennessee & Virginia
78. Knoxville & Kentucky
79. Rogersville & Jefferson
80. Memphis & Ohio
81. Northeast & Southwest
82. Alabama & Mississippi Rivers
83. Cahaba, Marion & Greensboro
84. New Orleans & Ohio
85. Mississippi Central
86. Mississippi & Tennessee
87. Memphis & Little Rock

88. New Orleans, Jackson & Great Northern
89. Southern R. R. of Mississippi
90. Raymond R. R.
91. Jefferson & Lake Pontchartrain
92. Pontchartrain R. R.
93. Mexican Gulf R. R.
94. New Orleans, Opelousas & Great Western
95. West Feliciana R. R.
96. Clinton & Port Hudson
97. Baton Rouge, Grosse Tete & Opelousas
98. Vicksburg, Shreveport & Texas
99. Alexandria & Cheneyville
100. Texas & New Orleans
101. Eastern Texas R. R.
102. Buffalo Bayou, Brazos & Colorado
103. Houston Tap & Brazoria
104. Galveston, Houston & Henderson
105. Houston & Texas Central
106. Washington County R. R.
107. San Antonio & Mexican Gulf
108. Memphis, El Paso & Pacific
109. Southern Pacific
110. Manassas Gap
111. Alabama & Tennessee Rivers
112. Hungary Branch
113. Grand Gulf & Port Gibson

Legend:

+-+-+	4' 8½" Gauge	
+-++-+	4' 8½" Gauge built during war	
-+++-	5' Gauge	
-++++-	5' Gauge built during war	
-##-	5' 6" Gauge	
-####-	5' 6" Gauge built during war	
-x-x-	Uncertain Gauge	
-xx-xx-	Uncertain Gauge built during war	

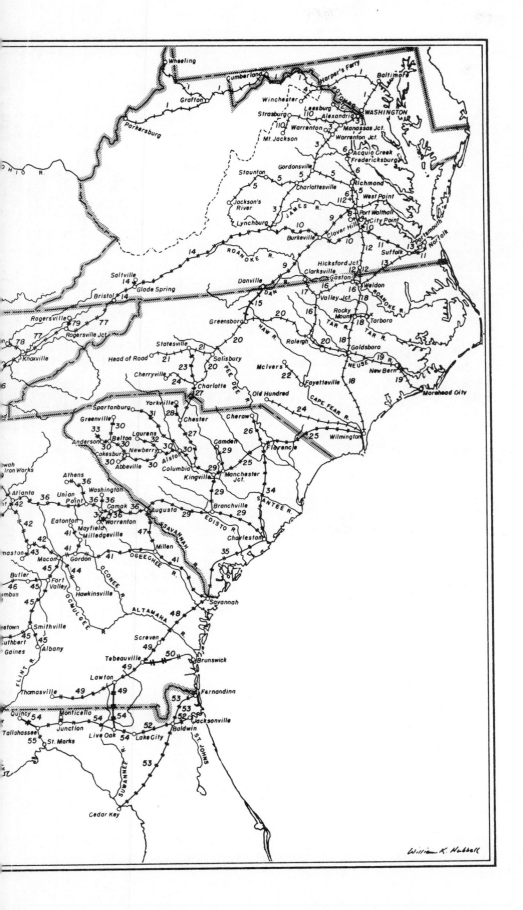

The railroads of the Confederate States

Ruins of railroad roundhouse, Atlanta, Georgia

prevailing type was the "T" rail, but some of the major routes contained sections laid with antiquated "U" and "strap" rails which were nothing more than thin strips of iron affixed to the surface of wooden stringers. Locomotives and cars were generally less substantially built than those used in the North, and the supply of both was exceedingly limited.

The typical freight train seen on Southern railroads early in 1861 consisted of an eight-wheel (4–4–0), wood-burning engine weighing about twenty tons and about fifteen wooden cars of various design including boxcars, gondolas, and flatcars, and with no caboose. Passenger trains usually had smaller locomotives and fewer cars; the cars, made of wood, were heated by stoves and, like their freight counterparts, were individually braked by hand. Sleeping cars were a rarity. Stops were made along the way to enable passengers to obtain meals and refreshments. The normal speed was about twenty miles an hour, but Louisville and Nashville trains sometimes attained a rate of forty miles. Passenger fares in antebellum times averaged four and one-half cents a mile.

EMBATTLED CONFEDERATES

The stress and strain of conflict caused a great deterioration of both equipment and service. The tremendous increase of traffic wore out rolling stock and rails. Soldiers en route to war or to new assignments thought nothing of knocking holes in the walls of boxcars to improve ventilation or wave at pretty girls. Diversion of shops, factories and labor to the manufacture of war materials greatly impeded repair and replacement of equipment. Not one rail was rolled in the Confederacy after 1861; occasionally rails in areas of lesser need were used to repair or extend track in sections where traffic was heavy. Many Yankee engineers and mechanics inevitably returned home, and a considerable number of experienced crewmen and laborers entered Confederate military service. Losses and damage inflicted by the Federals were heavy, beginning in Virginia in 1861, and extending into Tennessee, Mississippi and Alabama in 1862 as the invaders cut some of the South's most important routes and captured and destroyed valuable shops and equipment. The tragedy was repeated and compounded in 1863 and 1864 as the Union forces pushed deeper into Dixie.

Rufus B. Bullock of Georgia, Southern Express Company official who established railroad and telegraph lines on interior routes during the war

On the invitation of Postmaster General John H. Reagan, railroad owners met in Montgomery in April, 1861, and promptly indicated their desire to cooperate with the government by voting to transport soldiers and military freight at half the regular rates. But after a while their patriotism and enthusiasm cooled, rates went up, and competition, jealousy and shortsightedness prevented the various lines from working together effectively for the public good. Military commanders and their supply officers did not help, sometimes making high-handed and unreasonable demands upon the rail lines. One of their most serious abuses was long retention of loaded cars on sidings for storage purposes. The government should have assumed control of the railroads early in the war. In July, 1861, President Davis made a move in this direction by making William S. Ashe coordinator of rail transportation to Confederate forces in Virginia. Ashe, a native of North Carolina and former president of the Wilmington and Weldon Railroad, was an experienced, farsighted and able administrator. But he had to depend largely on persuasion, and his accomplishments fell far short of his hopes and the needs of the country. Frustration and disappointment led to his resignation in April, 1862.

Late in 1862 the President appointed William L. Wadley of Georgia, recognized as the ablest railroad administrator in the South, to the position vacated by Ashe, gave him a colonel's commission and extended his supervision to all the Confederacy's railroads. Wadley called a convention of railroad executives and outlined to them a plan calling for through train schedules and interchange of freight cars, but the principal accomplishment of the meeting was to vote an increase in passenger and freight rates. Wadley organized in the War Department what amounted to a railroad bureau, but his efforts to promote better utilization of rail facilities and closer cooperation between the companies and the government were caught between lack of understanding and power on the part of the government and exaggerated concern for prerogative and profit on the part of the companies, and he was relieved of his duties in May, 1863. Wadley's successor, Captain Frederick W. Sims, a co-owner of the Savannah *Republican*, worked well with his friend, Confederate Quartermaster General A. R. Lawton, and he was somewhat more successful than Wadley in dealing with the railroad presidents. But he was never able to achieve more than a token response to his pleas for a pooling of the South's rapidly deteriorating transportation facilities.

After much hesitation and debate, in May, 1863, Congress passed a law making the railroads subject to government control under the supervision of the Quartermaster General. This law empowered the President to compel any carrier to devote its facilities to army needs, except for one train a day, and to adhere to schedules prescribed by the government. It also provided for the transfer of rolling stock, rails, shops and equipment from one road to another and authorized the impressment of those roads refusing to comply with the law. Yet in one of the major ironies of Confederate history, the government failed to exercise its sorely needed authority. President Davis, Southern nationalist though he was in a relative sense, was so enthralled by the doctrine of state rights that he was unwilling to exercise the authority placed in his hands.

Cedar Creek Bridge, near Franklinton, North Carolina, Raleigh and Gaston Railroad

So, localism continued to hold sway in transportation, as in other realms, while conditions steadily deteriorated and the South moved inexorably toward defeat. In March, 1865, Congress passed another and more drastic act placing all railroads, steamboats and telegraph lines under War Department control and empowering the government to order officers and employees into military service. Davis withheld his approval for ten days and when he finally signed the measure into law on March 15, the time for remedying the Confederacy's ills had passed.

During the war, railroad and military authorities did manage some remarkable feats of transportation. After the fall of Fort Donelson more than 40,000 troops, from Kentucky, Louisiana, Alabama and Florida, were rapidly concentrated at Corinth to oppose Grant and Buell. In July-August, 1862, 25,000 soldiers of the Army of Mississippi, along with field equipment and ammunition, were moved 776 miles over six separate rail lines from Tupelo to Chattanooga. Owing to Federal seizure of portions of the Memphis and Charleston line through North Mississippi and Alabama, the route ran southward through Meridian to Mobile and thence northeastward by way of Montgomery and Atlanta to Chattanooga. Soldiers received several days' cooked rations before they boarded and changed lines and trains several times, but the elapsed time from the first departure to the last arrival was less than

Schedule B.
LABOR AND TRANSPORTATION.

LABOR AND TRANSPORTATION.	Average rate of pay for the five y'rs next preceding the war.		Quantity.	Distance.	Time.	Price proposed to be fixed by the Secretary of War.	
	Dlls.	Cts.				Dlls.	Cts.
Baling long forage,	—	—	Pr 100 lbs.	—	—	—	30
Shelling and bagging corn, sacks furnished by the government,	—	—	" 56 "	—	—	—	05
Hauling,	—	—	" cwt.	per mile,	—	—	04
Hauling grain,	—	—	" bush.	"	—	—	02
Hire of two horse team, wagon and driver, rations furnished by owner,	—	—	—	—	per day,	5	00
Hire of same, rations furnished by the government,	—	—	—	—	" "	3	00
Hire of four horse team, wagon and driver, rations furnished by owner,	4	00	—	—	" "	8	00
Hire of same, rations furnished by the government,	—	—	—	—	" "	4	00
Hire of six horse team, wagon and driver, rations furnished by owner,	5	00	—	—	" "	10	00
Hire of same, rations furnished by the government,	—	—	—	—	" "	4	25
Hire of laborer, rations furnished by owner,	—	75	—	—	" "	1	50
Hire of same, rations furnished by the government,	—	50	—	—	" "	1	00
Hire of same, rations furnished by the owner,	—	—	—	—	per month,	30	00
Hire of same, rations furnished by the government,	—	—	—	—	" "	20	00
River transportation by batteaux,	—	—	pr. cwt.	for 20 miles, and under,	—	—	25
" "	—	—	"	over 20 and under 30 miles,	—	—	35
" "	—	—	"	30 miles and under 50 miles,	—	—	45
" "	—	—	"	50 miles, and over,	—	—	50
" " grain,	—	—	pr. bush.	for 20 miles, and under,	—	—	11
" " "	—	—	"	over 20 and under 30 miles,	—	—	16
" " "	—	—	"	30 and under 50 miles,	—	—	20
" " "	—	—	"	50 miles, and over,	—	—	23
Canal transportation between Lynchburg and Richmond, and intermediate points,	—	—	pr. cwt.	—	—	—	25
Same between above points, for grain,	—	—	" bush.	—	—	—	10
Same from Buchanan and Lexington and other points above Lynchburg to Richmond,	—	—	" cwt.	—	—	—	35
Same between above points, for grain,	—	—	" bush.	—	—	—	16
Same between Buchanan and Lexington, and Lynchburg and intermediate points,	—	—	" cwt.	—	—	—	10
Same between above points, for grain,	—	—	" bush.	—	—	—	06
Transportation by batteaux on tributaries of James river, from highest point of navigation on same, and all intermediate points to James river and K'wha canal,	—	—	" cwt.	—	—	—	25
Transportation by same, between same points, for grain,	—	—	" bush.	—	—	—	08
Transportation by batteaux on James river and Kanawha canal from Lynchburg and intermediate points to Richmond,	—	—	" cwt.	—	—	—	25
Transportation by same, of grain,	—	—	" bush.	—	—	—	10

NOTE.—Where farmers cannot procure the necessary nails for baling forage, government to furnish the same at cost: which will be deducted from the established price for baling.

NOTE.—In addition to the established price of transportation, the government to pay all legal tolls.

The above are approved as maximum rates, not to be exceeded in contract, and on which, when necessary, impressment is authorized, as more fully stated in written power given the Q. M. General.

(Signed)   J. A. SEDDON,
                                                                          Sec'y of War.

Dec. 26, 1862.

three weeks. In September, 1863, 12,000 troops of Longstreet's First Corps were transported from Virginia to northern Georgia to assist Bragg in his campaigns about Chattanooga, traveling as far as Atlanta by alternate routes, one of which ran through Charlotte and Augusta and the other through Wilmington, Charleston and Savannah. From Atlanta all proceeded the rest of the way over the Western and Atlantic. The first contingent left Richmond on September 9. More than half of those making the trip reached the destination in North Georgia in time to take part in the second day's fighting at Chickamauga on September 20.

As the war progressed, travel by train became increasingly unpleasant, expensive and hazardous. Civilian fares on some routes rose as high as forty cents a mile near the end of the war, and deterioration of equipment necessitated reduction of speed to less than ten miles an hour and led to numerous delays. Even so, long trips were a perilous venture. In 1863 collision of two trains on the Mississippi Central Railroad killed thirty-five passengers and injured about fifty more, and eighty persons were drowned when a train ran into a river near Meridian. A Jackson, Mississippi, editor complained that "there is less risk in fighting a battle than in traveling a short distance on that road [running from Vicksburg to Meridian]." In May, 1863, an English officer, Arthur Fremantle, noted after traveling from Jackson to Meridian in sixteen hours: "After we had proceeded five miles our engine ran off the track which caused a stoppage of three hours. All passengers had to get out to push along the cars. We reached Meridian . . . only five hours late." In the spring of 1863 the Jackson, Mississippi, *Daily Southern Crisis* published the following dialogue:

First person: Have you heard of the railroad accident?
Second person: No, where was it?
First person: The Western train left Meridian and arrived at Jackson on schedule time.

Passenger trains, crowded to overflowing, ran with diminishing frequency, and schedules virtually ceased to have any meaning. "Ladies' cars" were usually cleaner and more comfortable than the other coaches, but even there the traveler's rest was often disturbed by whimpering children and screaming infants. "I never saw such crowds of people . . . such a cram and mess, as is daily witnessed on the Mobile and Ohio Railroad . . . between Meridian and Jackson," wrote a Confederate major in 1862. "It reminds me of what you see when you throw a stick into a beehive," he added, "and the children and babies how they do cry and fret."

A considerable portion of the Confederacy's scant rolling stock was absorbed by the Southern Express Company, a firm established in 1861 to take over the Southern business of the Northern-owned Adams Express Company. The Southern Express Company by military permission rented cars from the railroads and provided the swiftest and safest shipment obtainable in the Confederacy without any government regulation of rates and cargoes. The only real competitor was the Pioneer Express Company, which did considerable business in the Southwest at rates said to be much lower than those of the Southern. As a patriotic gesture the Southern transported free of charge soldiers' packages weighing no more than a hundred pounds, but citizens claimed that it was a Yankee concern interested only in making huge profits, and Confederate Senator W. S. Oldham in his memoir denounced the Southern Express Company as a monopoly.

The expense and uncertainty of rail transportation caused Southerners to rely increasingly on inland waterways, stagecoaches, wagons, private carriages, horses, and walking. Travelers had great difficulty finding comfortable lodgings. Hotels and inns frequently were crowded, dirty and costly. Meals were unsavory and expensive. Hungry, ragged soldiers traveling through the country were often turned away when they sought food or shelter at the more pretentious homes, but they were usually accorded a hospitable reception by the humbler folk.

The swiftest means of communication available to people of the 1860's was the telegraph; and both Northerners and Southerners made such extensive use of Morse's remarkable invention as to cause their conflict to be called "the first telegraph war." Because of its more abundant resources in money, metal and mechanical skills the Union had many more miles of telegraphic lines and far better service than did the Confederacy. But the secession of the Southern states was flashed through the country by telegraph, as was the election of Jefferson Davis to the Presidency and the report of the firing on Fort Sumter. The Confederate government communicated with military commanders by telegraph, newspapers devoted much of their space to telegraphic messages, and soldiers often relieved the anxiety of their home folks after battles by telegraphing that all was well.

A number of small telegraphic companies operated in the Confederacy, but the lion's share of the business was done by the Southern Telegraph Company (an offshoot of the American Telegraph Company) headed by William S. Morris. The South-Western Telegraph Company, presided over during most of the war by John Van Horne, had lines running from Louisville to New Orleans. West of the Mississippi the principal firms were the Arkansas State Telegraph Company and the Texas Telegraph Company, but service in this area was limited and Texas had no telegraphic connection with other portions of the Confederacy.

In May, 1861, the Confederate Congress subjected all telegraphic lines to the control of the President. Davis made Postmaster General Reagan superintendent of telegraphs, but as with the railroads, the Chief Executive showed little disposition to exercise his supreme authority. Reagan delegated immediate supervision of telegraphic service

Railroad yards, Atlanta, Georgia

to William S. Morris, president of the Southern Telegraph Company. Morris acquitted himself in a manner which won Reagan's warm praise, but he used his position to further the interests of his firm and he made an unsuccessful effort to have its chief competitor, the South-Western Telegraph Company, taken over by the government. He and other telegraph executives used the threat of conscription to thwart efforts of operators to obtain an increase in wages and reduction of their long working hours.

Destruction wrought by the invaders and increasing scarcity of wire, chemicals, glass and other materials needed to replace and maintain equipment, caused a deterioration of the South's telegraphic service. For two weeks at the end of 1864 there was no telegraphic service at all between Mobile and Richmond. In the latter part of the conflict wires were taken down in areas of lesser need and used to patch lines deemed of greater importance in maintaining the flow of communications.

Railroad depot, Nashville,
Tennessee

Confederate military authorities made far less use of the telegraph as an instrument of war than did their foes, such as Sherman at Kennesaw Mountain and Grant and Meade in the Spotsylvania–Cold Harbor Campaign. This was due in part to the South's relative lack of facilities, but Southern leaders, with the possible exception of Beauregard, seem to have been less alert than their adversaries to the military potential of this improved means of communication. Forrest, Morgan and other cavalry leaders took telegraph operators along on their raids; and these men, especially Morgan's George Ellsworth, performed valuable service by tapping Federal lines to obtain information about Yankee movements and sending spurious messages to create confusion in enemy camps. In 1864 General Lee's confidential operator, C. A. Gaston, tapped a Federal line and for about six weeks listened to messages passing to and from Grant's headquarters; one bit of information that he obtained enabled the Confederates to capture 2,586 beeves intended for Union consumption.

In directing field operations Confederate generals relied mainly on flag-waving signalmen (the "wigwag" system) and mounted messengers, who usually were staff officers, to transmit orders, collect information and keep in touch with subordinates. The Southerners had at least one observation balloon, made early in 1862 of silk dresses

EMBATTLED
CONFEDERATES

contributed by Confederate women, but it was captured after only token use, in the Seven Days' Campaign.

The principal medium of communication in the Confederacy among both soldiers and civilians was the handwritten letter. Transmission of mail was the responsibility of Postmaster General Reagan and, as previously noted, this able official was beset with the problems of the inadequacy of the railroads on which he had to depend, and shortage of personnel. The Confederate Constitution required the Post Office Department to be self-supporting and Reagan was never able to maintain anything like an adequate corps of helpers. As a result, delays in the delivery of letters increased and soldiers sometimes were out of communication with their families for many months. "I haint got nary letter from you for somtime," wrote an Alabama private to his wife in June, 1863. "When you fail to Rite it ceeps mee uneasy all the time." Mail service between the Trans-Mississippi Department and the eastern Confederacy was especially poor. In April, 1863, a Texas officer stationed in Mississippi noted in his diary the receipt of a letter written by his wife in July, 1862.

Soldiers and civilians turned increasingly to transmitting letters and packages via furloughed soldiers, or traveling ministers, friends and relatives who gathered up mail at each end of their journey for delivery at the other. Intent of making such a journey was passed about by word of mouth and in some instances published in newspapers, so that correspondents might have an opportunity to place letters in the hands of the transient for delivery at his destination.

In the latter years of the war, military authorities established a courier service to maintain official communications in some of the more remote sections of the Confederacy. The Shreveport *News* of March 31, 1863, ran a notice stating that a line of couriers had recently been set up between that city and General John B. Magruder's headquarters in Houston. Relays of cavalrymen, stationed at ten-mile intervals, carried dispatches from Shreveport to Navasota where other

Confederate signal station near Beverly Ford, Virginia, September 20, 1863

messengers picked up the communications and carried them by rail to Houston. The horsemen made the two-hundred-mile trip from Shreveport to Navasota in about thirty hours. Other official courier lines were established between Shreveport, Mobile and Richmond. Apparently some of the couriers carried both government and private communications, the latter on a fee basis. Soldier correspondence leaves the impression that some of the mail passing to and from camp was carried by persons not having any official connection, for fees ranging from fifty cents to a dollar per item.

Files of the Shreveport *News* afford some information on the activities of couriers operating between western and eastern sections of the Confederacy during the last year of the war, though their status rarely is specified. A notice of March 15, 1864, stated: "A courier will

EMBATTLED
CONFEDERATES

leave Shreveport for Mobile and Richmond about the first of April. He will take all letters that may be forwarded to Shreveport care of Dr. Gilbert. Put a dime stamp on single letters and inclose $1 for the courier." Several of the announcements pertain to the comings and goings of Major A. S. Rose, who was described as the "pioneer courier," the "champion courier" and the "government courier." Rose operated between various Trans-Mississippi towns—including Shreveport and Houston—and Richmond, stopping along the way as business required. His fee for correspondence taken across the Mississippi, regardless of the distance, seems to have been ten dollars a letter for civilians and five dollars for soldiers. Recipients were permitted to send back a reply free of charge. Rose worked on a regular schedule with an estimated time of five or six weeks for the round trip between Shreveport and Richmond. The journey announced for April 29, 1864, was said to be Rose's twenty-seventh, and he was still in business seven months later.

The passage of couriers across the Mississippi River must have been difficult and perilous. The Federals kept a close watch on the stream and the country lying along it. Congressman A. M. Branch of Texas, in making the trip from his home to Richmond in December, 1863, crossed the Mississippi in a boat that had been hauled seven miles through flooded lowlands, and after he got to the eastern bank he had to hide two nights in a swamp before continuing his journey. About the same time an Arkansas congressman, G. D. Royston, made two efforts to get across the river, but Yankee patrols proved so threatening that he turned back both times. He finally returned home and in consequence missed the final session of the First Congress.

Faulty communication did serious injury to the Southern people and their cause, especially to soldier and civilian morale. Isolation of detached military units from high commanders weakened discipline and reduced efficiency. Lack of reliable information gave rise to floods of rumor; and the frequent circulation of false reports, particularly those representing military disasters as great victories, tended to impair the confidence of the masses in their leaders.

A people nurtured in the doctrine of state rights would have found it difficult under propitious circumstances to develop a strong attachment to the Confederate government. Richmond and the central authority which it represented seemed far away. The breakdown of communication enhanced this sense of remoteness and made it more of a reality. This was especially true of the Trans-Mississippi region, which in many respects ceased to be a part of the Confederacy after the fall of Vicksburg. But it was also true to some extent of other parts of the South. Factors other than communication contributed to this centrifugal drift but there can be no doubt that diminishing contact with Richmond caused a people already provincially disposed to look more and more to local authorities and less and less to Jefferson Davis and the government that he represented.

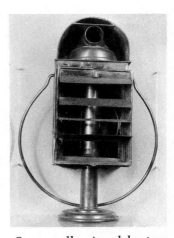

One-candle signal lantern, E. P. Alexander's equipment at Bull Run, Virginia, 1861

VIII. *A Navy from Nothing*

The South's conduct of the war on the water was marked by pettiness and magnanimity, bungling and brilliance, shameful failure and shining achievement. Shortcomings were due, in large measure, to lack of resources, men, matériel and technical skill; but they resulted in part from errors of judgment, loose management, divided command and poor cooperation. Before the loss of Roanoke Island in February, 1862, uncertainty existed as to whether an important floating battery was under naval or military command. After the fall of New Orleans, Major General Mansfield Lovell testified that military and naval authorities charged with that city's defense were "entirely independent of each other." Failure to complete the ironclad rams *Arkansas* and *Tennessee* in time to assist in the defense of Memphis was due in part to refusal of General Leonidas Polk to detail carpenters to assist in their construction. Too little, too late, was the story not only at New Orleans and Memphis, but also at many other vital points where harmonious and efficient collaboration was imperative.

Even so, the Confederacy succeeded in developing a navy that won renown not only for superb performances in combat but also for important innovations in naval warfare. Although Napoleon III had successfully used iron-plated floating batteries in the Crimean War, and both France and England before 1861 had begun the construction of ironclad war fleets, the Confederacy had the distinction of sending the first ironclad warship into naval combat on March 8, 1862, at Hampton Roads. This vessel, the *Virginia*, also initiated the famous "first fight between ironclads" when the next day, March 9, it attacked the Federal *Monitor*. The Confederacy achieved another outstanding "first" in naval warfare when, as previously noted, the submarine *H. L. Hunley*, on the night of February 17, 1864, sank the U.S.S. *Housatonic* near Charleston, South Carolina. Confederates were pioneers in the use of various types of stationary, floating and spar-borne torpedoes; these deadly in-

Submarine torpedo boat H. L. Hunley at Charleston, South Carolina, December 6, 1863

struments sank more than fifty Union vessels and proved to be the South's most effective defense against naval attack.

The basic requirement of the Confederate navy was men, and procurement of personnel was one of the first problems to which Stephen R. Mallory devoted his attention. The law of February 21, 1861, by which the Navy Department was established provided only a skeleton organization; but a more comprehensive law, approved on March 16, 1861, authorized creation within the department of four bureaus and the recruitment of a corps of officers and enlisted men not to exceed three thousand. The bureaus and their first heads were: Orders and Detail, Captain Franklin Buchanan; Ordnance and Hydrography, Commander George Minor; Provisions and Clothing, Paymaster James A. Semple; and Medicine and Surgery, Surgeon W. A. Spotswood. The Lighthouse Board—a bureau of the Treasury Department—was headed by Captain Raphael Semmes. Two key officers not included among bureau heads were Engineer-in-Chief William P. Williamson, and John L. Porter, director of construction. Outside the capital the principal officers initially were Captain Victor Randolph, who commanded the naval forces at Mobile; Commodore Josiah Tattnall, at Savannah; Commodore French Forrest, at Norfolk; and Commodore Duncan N. Ingraham, at Charleston. To Commander James D. Bulloch was given the important assignment of procuring ships and equipment in England.

Captain French Forrest, Chief of Bureau, Navy Department

Most of these men had long and distinguished records in Federal service. Buchanan, who was to reach the pinnacle of fame as commander of the ironclad *Virginia* in its spectacular baptism of fire on March 8, 1862, and to become the Confederacy's only full admiral, had spent forty-six of his sixty-one years in the United States Navy and had won the commendation of Secretary of the Navy, George Bancroft, for successfully launching the Naval Academy at Annapolis.

Semmes, destined to win renown as captain of the *Alabama,* was a veteran of thirty-four years' service and had been cited for gallantry in the Mexican War. Forrest, who was sixty-four when he donned the Confederate uniform, had entered the United States Navy in 1811, participated in the Battle of Lake Erie in 1813 and directed the landing of Scott's forces at Vera Cruz in 1847. Tattnall, also a veteran of two wars, and a year older than Forrest, had completed eleven years as captain when he resigned his Federal commission in February, 1861. Ingraham's forty-eight years in the United States Navy included service against England in 1812–1814 and against Mexico in 1846–1847. Bulloch, a Georgian whose half-sister married Theodore Roosevelt, Sr., in 1853, was only thirty-eight in 1861, and his record included no combat service.

The Confederacy's principal source of officers for both staff and command was the large group of Southerners who left the United States Navy after the secession of their respective states. By June, 1861, 320 of the 671 Southerners who held commissions in the Federal Navy had resigned or had been dismissed, and some of the remaining 351 subsequently left the Union service. Because of the lack of ships, this mass exodus was to create a surplus of naval officers in the Confederacy during the initial period of the conflict, compelling many to spend months at routine desk chores, or as makeshift artillery officers, supervising the erection of batteries and drilling recruits in the rudiments of gunnery. Eventually the Confederacy acquired enough vessels and stations to provide naval assignments for most of them, but the heavy loss of ships later in the war created another surplus of commissioned personnel.

Meanwhile Secretary Mallory began to make plans for the establishment of a school for the training of naval officers, and in the autumn of 1863 the Confederate States Naval Academy opened with some fifty midshipmen and about thirteen instructors, headed by Captain William H. Parker. The Academy was located on board the steamer *Patrick Henry* which was anchored at Drewry's Bluff in the James River near Richmond. Captain Parker was a distinguished alumnus of the United States Naval Academy, and he modeled the curriculum on the one used at Annapolis. Confederate midshipmen were frequently called from the classroom to help work shore batteries and man ships of the James River squadron. During the campaigns about Richmond in the spring and summer of 1864, the students were more often on battle vessels or in the fighting lines than in class.

The Confederate Navy was never burdened by a surplus of enlisted men. The prewar South had relatively few seafaring men serving in the United States Navy, or among its civilians, for the ocean-going vessels which entered its ports and even the steamers that plied its rivers were in most instances owned and manned by outsiders. Most of the few experienced Southern sailors rushed into army service after

Fort Sumter, believing that independence would be won in one short campaign and wanting to get in a lick at the Yankees before peace was declared. When it became apparent that the war would not be short, some of the "water men" who had enlisted in the army tried to transfer to the navy, but laws authorizing the shift were of little avail. On October 31, 1864, Secretary Mallory reported that "recruiting for the navy has been barely sufficient to supply the deficiencies occasioned by death, discharges and desertions."

But the Confederacy was fortunate in having other sources. The *Alabama* and other ships built abroad were manned largely by foreigners, and the same was true of many smaller vessels operating on rivers and along the coast. Captain William H. Parker, who commanded the steamer *Beaufort* before taking over the direction of the Naval Academy, wrote after the war: "I made up a crew principally of men who had been in the prizes captured by the *Winslow*. I had but one American in the crew—a green hand who shipped as a coal heaver. . . . The crew was composed of Englishmen, Danes and Swedes." Parker's foreign seamen gave a good account of themselves. "I never knew them to fail in their duty," he wrote; "indeed I used to wonder at their eagerness to go into battle, considering the fact that they knew nothing at all about the cause of the war; but a sailor is a sailor all the world over."

Figures on the aggregate strength of the navy in officers and men are not available for all periods of the war. But Secretary Mallory's report of November 30, 1863, showed a total of 693 officers and 2,700 enlisted men in service at home and abroad. By April 30, 1864, the numbers had increased to 753 and 4,460, respectively, or a total of 5,213, and this was probably the navy's peak strength.

In 1863 Congress made two organizational changes affecting naval personnel. The first of these was a law of April 16 authorizing the President to organize privateers and their officers and crews into a volunteer navy. Vessels had to have a capacity of one hundred tons to be accepted into this service and the highest rank permitted was that of commander. The Confederate government was to receive 10 percent of the value of prizes taken by vessels of the volunteer navy and 90 percent was to be divided among owners, officers and crews. It was hoped that the new organization would lead to a substantial increase in the Confederacy's sea power; but these expectations apparently were never realized.

On May 1, 1863, President Davis signed a law creating a "Provisional Navy of the Confederate States." One of the purposes of the act was to facilitate the rapid advancement of younger officers of exceptional ability by transferring them to the new organization, as the rule of seniority was too strongly entrenched to permit "graybeards" of long service in the old navy to react kindly when younger men were jumped to high rank. After establishment of the provisional navy most of the

Deck of the steamer Hudson, *blockade runner captured by the Federal navy*

officers on ship duty were transferred to the new organization, and the regular navy, according to Raphael Semmes, became "a kind of retired list."

Another important part of the organization headed by Mallory was the Confederate States marine corps, established on March 16, 1861, with only six companies, but shortly enlarged to a regiment similar in organization and size to the infantry unit. However, as most prospective recruits were in the army and it was almost impossible to pry

Robert E. Lee, *Confederate blockade runner that was captured by the Union Navy and renamed U.S.S. Fort Donelson* them loose, the marine corps at its peak strength in 1864 had only 539 officers and men. The marines were commanded by Colonel Lloyd J. Beall, but they never functioned as a unit. They operated in detachments of company size or smaller and were used chiefly as guards on ships and shore. Some, however, experienced the thrill of combat, fighting gallantly in the Battle of Mobile Bay and the defense of Fort Fisher. Posted as sharpshooters on the bank of the James River, they helped repel the attack of the Union gunboats at Drewry's Bluff, May 15, 1862. One of the last actions in which they participated was the Battle of Saylor's Creek, April 6, 1865, for which they won a commendation for bravery. The *esprit* of the marines must have been high. John R. F. Tattnall, who gave up the colonelcy of an infantry regiment in December, 1862, to become a captain of marines, stated that he "would rather command a company of marines than a brigade of volunteers."

Of equal importance to manpower was the procurement of boats and ships, and it proved considerably more difficult to accomplish. The first vessels acquired by the South were obtained by the states, most of which established navies of their own soon after leaving the Union. These consisted largely of revenue cutters, lighthouse tenders and other small vessels formerly in Federal service and seized by secessionists. But some states purchased steamboats and schooners from private owners and converted them into war vessels. Governor Francis Wilkinson Pickens of South Carolina bought the steam tug *James Gray* from a Richmond firm, had her adapted for war service and renamed her the *Lady Davis* in honor of the Confederacy's First Lady. Lieutenant W. B. Hall purchased in New York for the Georgia navy an old mail

Lieutenant Francis Hawks Cameron, Confederate States Marine Corps

Gun of the gunboat Teaser, one of the first Confederate gunboats

C.S.S. Stonewall, at Washington, D.C., April, 1865

Paymaster Douglas F. Forrest, C.S.S. Rappahannock

Blockade runner Old Dominion *at Bristol, England*

steamer, *The Huntress*, obtained a crew and brought her to Savannah. After entering the Confederacy the states turned over their war fleets to the central government, though some of them later purchased or constructed war vessels for Confederate service. In 1862 Alabama bought and placed at Secretary Mallory's disposal the steamer *Baltic*, and South Carolina authorities the same year financed and built for Confederate use the ironclad steamer *Chicora*.

The floating battery *Georgia* was built with funds contributed by "patriotic citizens of Georgia," and ladies of Charleston raised a considerable portion of the money required for construction of the C.S.S. *Charleston*. Unfortunately the *Georgia* was so poorly constructed as to be virtually useless and both the *Georgia* and the *Charleston* had to be destroyed by the Confederates to prevent their capture by Sherman's forces during the invasion of 1864–1865.

The Confederacy obtained a substantial number of war vessels by capture. The *Star of the West*, which had provoked the first hostile shot of the war near Charleston, was seized at Indianola, Texas, by soldiers of General Earl Van Dorn's command on April 17, 1861. Taken to New Orleans, she was converted into the Confederate receiving ship *St. Philip*. When the Federals approached New Orleans the next year, the *St. Philip* was loaded with money from the mint and banks of the city and run up to Vicksburg. Early in 1863 she was sunk in the Talla-

EMBATTLED
CONFEDERATES

hatchee River to protect Fort Pemberton and thwart the Federals in their attempt to attack Vicksburg from the north. In October, 1861, near Roanoke Island, North Carolina, a joint army-navy expedition commanded by Colonel A. R. Wright of the Third Georgia Regiment captured the steamer *Fanny* and $100,000 worth of supplies intended for Federal troops on Hatteras Island. The *Fanny* was added to Lynch's "mosquito fleet," but she flew the Confederate flag less than five months. On February 10, 1862, during the battle of Elizabeth City she was run aground and destroyed to prevent her recapture by the Federals. Other important captures by the Confederates included the steamer *Harriet Lane,* taken by General John B. Magruder's forces when they drove the Federals out of Galveston on January 1, 1863; the iron-protected steam ram, *Queen of the West,* seized on the Red River by soldiers of General Richard Taylor's command on February 14, 1863; and the steamer *Diana,* captured by Trans-Mississippi troops on the Atchafalaya River on March 23, 1863.

The champion captor of Union war vessels was apparently Commander John Taylor Wood. On February 15, 1864, the Confederate Congress voted a resolution of thanks to this officer and his command "for the daring and brilliantly executed plans which resulted in the capture of the U. S. transport schooner *Elmore* on the Potomac River; of the ship *Alleghany* and the U. S. gunboats *Satellite* and *Reliance* and the U. S. transport schooners *Golden Rod, Coquette* and *Two Brothers* on the Chesapeake; and more recently in the capture from under the guns of the enemy's works of the U. S. gunboat *Underwriter* on the Neuse River."

Officers of C.S.S. Sumter, *photographed at Gibraltar, February, 1862. Standing, left to right: Fourth Lieutenant W. E. Evans, First Lieutenant (Marine) B. Howell, Third Lieutenant V. M. Stribbing, First Lieutenant J. M. Kell, Second Lieutenant R. T. Chapman, Engineer M. J. Freeman, W. B. Smith, Clerk. Seated: Captain Raphael Semmes*

The Federal evacuation of the Norfolk navy yard on April 20, 1861, placed in possession of the South several partially destroyed war vessels valued at more than $300,000. One of these, the steam frigate *Merrimack,* was raised and converted into the ironclad *Virginia.* Two splendid sloops, the *Plymouth* and the *Germantown,* were found to be in reasonably good condition and were well along toward restoration to service when the order to abandon the city in May, 1862, necessitated their destruction.

The Confederacy's English-built cruisers captured, equipped and put into service at sea several commerce destroyers, including the *Lapwing* (renamed the *Oreto*), the *Clarence* and the *Tuscaloosa.* These vessels all had brief but successful careers as raiders. The *Clarence,* captured by the *Florida,* seized and commissioned the bark *Tacony,* which in turn captured and converted into a commerce destroyer the fishing schooner *Archer.*

The Navy Department, of course, arranged for the purchase or construction of a substantial portion of the Confederacy's war vessels.

EMBATTLED
CONFEDERATES

Mallory was able to purchase in Southern ports a few vessels adaptable to war service. One of the most important was the *Habana*, a propeller-driven commercial steamer bought in New Orleans in April, 1861. She was small and slow, but under the expert supervision of Semmes, who obtained permission to convert and command her, she was transformed into the C.S.S. *Sumter*. The five guns of the *Sumter*—one 68-pounder and four 32-pounders—were obtained from the recently acquired Norfolk navy yard and the ammunition from the Baton Rouge arsenal. With a crew "nearly all green" and a corps of promising young officers, Semmes slipped his vessel out of the Mississippi and into the Gulf on June 30, 1861. She headed for Cuban waters and began her career as the

C.S.S. Atlanta *after its capture at Trent's Reach, James River, Virginia*

first of the Confederate raiders. During her six months of active service before being sealed up at Gibraltar, she took seventeen prizes and did considerable injury to the North's carrying trade.

Of much greater significance than ships bought at home were those purchased abroad. The principal agent for procurement of foreign vessels was James D. Bulloch. His first purchase was the *Fingal*, an iron-hull merchant steamer obtained in October of 1861. After loading a large cargo of arms and ammunition on the vessel and disguising her ownership and destination, Bulloch ran her through the blockade to Savannah. He returned to England on another ship and the *Fingal* was converted into the Confederate armored ram *Atlanta*. On June 17, 1863, shortly after the conversion was finished, the *Atlanta* was captured in Wassaw Sound by two Federal ironclads, the *Weehawken* and *Nahant*.

In September, 1864, Bulloch purchased the cruiser *Shenandoah*. Under the command of Captain James I. Waddell, the *Shenandoah* took thirty-six prizes before her belated cessation of hostilities on August 2, 1865; not until then did Waddell learn that the war was over.

Captain James Iredell Waddell, commander of C.S.S. Shenandoah

G. Perk

U.S.S. Brilliant *with cargo of grain, captured and burned by C.S.S.* Alabama, *October 3, 1862*

Flag of the Shenandoah

Bulloch also contracted for the construction in Great Britain and France of about a dozen other vessels (including two powerful ironclad rams, the "294" and "295," built by the Laird Brothers of Birkenhead), but of these only three, the *Alabama, Florida* and *Georgiana*, actually entered Confederate service. The *Alabama*, known also as the *Enrica* and the "290," was built in Liverpool by the Lairds. When construc-

Midshipman William H. Sinclair, C.S.S. Alabama

Midshipman James H. Dyke, C.S.S. Florida

Chief Engineer Charles W. Quinn, C.S.S. Florida

EMBATTLED
CONFEDERATES

tion was completed in August, 1862, the ship proceeded unarmed and with British papers—to avoid seizure for breach of English neutrality—to the Azores. There she received her guns and stores, and on August 24, 1862, while a band played "Dixie," she was commissioned as a Confederate ship of war under the command of the bold and resourceful Semmes. The *Alabama* was a fast ship, capable of making fifteen knots when utilizing sails and propeller. She mounted ten guns, including a Blakely 110-pounder rifle pivoted forward and six 32-pounders in broadside. Before her destruction in the English Channel on June 19, 1864, by the U.S.S. *Kearsarge,* she cruised the Atlantic, Pacific and Indian Oceans and took more than sixty prizes. As commander of the *Sumter* and *Alabama,* Semmes captured eighty-two merchant vessels worth more than six million dollars, and sank a man-of-war. In recognition of this unparalleled achievement, he was promoted to rear admiral.

The *Florida,* originally christened the *Oreto,* built by William C. Miller and Sons at Liverpool, was not quite as fast or as heavily armed as the *Alabama,* but she had an outstanding career as a Confederate raider. Between the time of her delivery to her captain, John N. Maffitt, at Nassau on April 28, 1862, and her sinking, in flagrant violation of the recognized usages of war in the neutral harbor of Bahia, Brazil, by the U.S.S. *Wachusset,* October 7, 1864, she made a total of thirty-seven

Admiral Raphael Semmes

A NAVY
FROM NOTHING   155

captures. The *Georgiana*, commanded by George T. Sinclair, had only a brief service. She departed from Liverpool on January 21, 1863, and was wrecked two months later trying to enter Charleston.

Captures and seizures were only a part of the success achieved by Confederate raiders. Their very presence on the seas compelled many American merchantmen to lie idle in ports for long periods and caused scores of them to be transferred to foreign ownership. In one year, 1863–1864, American shipping employed in the trade with England decreased nearly 50 percent. Most of the shipping lost by Americans was taken over by the British.

Mallory worked diligently to promote construction at home, but shortages of essential material and skilled laborers were tremendous obstacles. Difficulties were enhanced by Mallory's decision to concentrate on ironclads. As he stated in a letter to Congressman C. M. Conrad, the only way to offset the North's naval superiority was by "fighting with iron against wood." Mallory's strategic judgment was sound. To establish her independence the South had to defend her inland waterways, break the blockade and keep open the avenues of foreign trade. Ironclad ships offered the best hope of attaining these goals. Unfortunately, two basic requirements—metal plate and motive power—were almost completely lacking, for in 1861 the South had "not a rolling-mill capable of turning out a 2½-inch iron plate nor a workshop able to complete a marine engine." Southerners demonstrated much ingenuity and resourcefulness in improvisation and adaptation, but the results fell far short of the needs.

The first and most famous of the ironclads was the *Virginia*, built by the government at the Norfolk navy yard, May, 1861–March, 1862, from the sunken remains of the *Merrimack*. John M. Brooke, E. C. Murray and John L. Porter all claimed credit for her design, attributed by Mallory to Brooke, which set the pattern for other Confederate ironclads. Raised and pulled into Norfolk dry dock on May 30, 1861, the *Merrimack* was cut down almost to the water line, and a flat-top house, or shield, 170 feet long, with sloping sides and ends, built over the central portion of the 275-foot hull. The underside of the shield was of wood two feet thick, and the surface consisted of two layers of iron plating, each two inches thick, rolled at the Tredegar Iron Works; the flat roof, or upper deck, some twenty feet wide, was overlaid with iron grating. The *Virginia* was armed with ten guns: six 9-inch Dahlgren smoothbores and two 6-inch Brooke rifles in broadside; and a 7-inch Brooke rifle at both stern and prow. The *Virginia* kept the same engines, and though they were overhauled and modified slightly by Chief Engineer William P. Williamson their performance left much to be desired.

Building the *Virginia* required close cooperation between naval officers, the Tredegar Iron Works, shipping firms and construction crews. According to the naval historian J. Thomas Scharf, "in many instances

Captain Franklin Buchanan

EMBATTLED CONFEDERATES

the very tools required by the workmen had to be improvised and made." In the latter stages of construction some 1,500 workmen were employed on the project at Norfolk, many of whom volunteered to labor extra hours without pay in order to hasten the ironclad's completion.

The ship was finished in late February and turned over to Captain Buchanan and a crew of 320 officers and men. Among the latter were eighty volunteers from a Louisiana infantry regiment who were quickly converted into sailors so that the navy might have the benefit of their prior service on merchant vessels operating out of New Orleans.

In addition to her undependable engines, the Virginia's propeller and rudder were not sufficiently protected; her speed was only five or six knots; she was so sluggish and unwieldy that it took thirty minutes to turn her around; her draft of twenty-two feet greatly limited her usefulness for coastal operations and she was too unseaworthy to venture far from shore. Even so, she was a formidable floating arsenal, capable of wreaking destruction on any wooden vessels that came within range of her powerful guns. The introduction into naval warfare of this novel

THE NAVAL ENGAGEMENT BETWEEN THE MERRIMAC AND THE MONITOR AT HAMPTON ROADS
ON THE 9TH OF MARCH 1862.

battleship reflected great credit on the young and struggling Confederacy.

While the *Virginia* was under construction at Norfolk, two other large ironclads, the *Louisiana* and the *Mississippi,* were in preparation near New Orleans, under contracts made by Secretary Mallory in September, 1861. The *Mississippi* was designed and built by the Tift brothers, Asa and Nelson, natives of Connecticut, who migrated to the South in boyhood. Nelson Tift resided in Albany, Georgia; and Asa, in Key West, Florida. Both were prosperous businessmen and patriotic Confederates, but neither was experienced in the construction of ships. Their plans for the *Mississippi* had the original feature of utilizing straight timber in the construction of the hull and avoiding the curved frames, crooks and knees that were a part of traditional designs. This innovation meant that ordinary house carpenters were able to do most of the basic construction.

The contractor for the *Louisiana* was E. C. Murray, a "practical shipbuilder" who had constructed 120 sailing vessels and steamboats in antebellum times. Murray and the Tifts began their ironclads in adjoining shipyards on the Mississippi in October, 1861. Murray had the good fortune to obtain engines and other machinery from the steamer *Ingomar.* The *Louisiana*'s protective shield was made of railroad iron —some five hundred tons—purchased from the president of the Vicksburg and Shreveport Railroad. Guns for both vessels were provided by the Confederate government from the supply captured at Norfolk.

Machinery for the *Mississippi,* with the exception of the massive center shaft—which the Tredegar Works recast from a huge salvaged bolt—was manufactured in New Orleans. The iron plating was rolled by Schofield and Markham of Atlanta.

Builders of both vessels were hindered by carpenters' strikes, inability of iron manufacturers to fill orders on schedule, transportation bottlenecks on materials ordered from afar, and a shortage of metalworkers and mechanics. The few artisans that were available were repeatedly interrupted to parade with local militia units, despite orders from Governor Thomas O. Moore that they were not to be disturbed. It is not surprising that neither ship was completed when the Federal fleet attacked the forts below New Orleans on April 24. The *Louisiana* was towed down-river, moored to the bank and used as a floating battery until her destruction on April 29. But the *Mississippi,* only partly armored and equipped, had to be burned without firing a shot. Arthur Sinclair, her commander, later told an investigating committee: "If the *Mississippi* had been completed, and with her armament and men on board, she alone would have held the river against the entire Federal fleet coming up from below; and she would have been the most formidable ship that I ever knew or heard of—very creditable to her projectors, builders and country."

At the time of the fall of New Orleans two other ironclads, the rams *Arkansas* and *Tennessee,* were being constructed by John T. Shirley at Memphis, and were held up by the same difficulties and delays that plagued Murray and the Tifts down-river. In addition, bolts and spikes manufactured for Shirley were seized by Confederate officers for completion of a boat at Nashville, and General Leonidas Polk refused to grant Secretary Mallory's urgent request for detail of sorely needed ship carpenters. The loss of Island Number 10 in the Mississippi, just below the Kentucky-Tennessee boundary, on April 10, 1862, and the fall of New Orleans later in the month created such alarm as to the fate of Memphis that the *Tennessee* was destroyed in May before any iron was laid on her. The *Arkansas,* which had been partially ironed, was towed down the Mississippi to the Yazoo and up that river to Yazoo City. On May 26, 1862, a remarkably versatile and dynamic naval officer, Lieutenant Isaac N. Brown, was put in command of the vessel and directed to complete her as speedily as possible "without regard to expenditure of men or money."

Lieutenant Brown pitched into his work with a zeal that infused new life into the quiet little community on the Yazoo. He prevailed on local planters to furnish overseers and laborers and sent agents throughout the surrounding country to engage carpenters and blacksmiths. He set up sawmills, forges and power drills on the banks of the river and contracted with a firm in Canton, Mississippi, to build gun carriages. Night and day the countryside resounded with the pounding of hammers, the rasping of saws and the clanking of metal as bolts and brackets were fashioned, iron armor affixed to the shield, guns mounted and machinery installed. On July 13, six weeks after Brown took command, the *Arkansas* was ready for service. She was eased across the bar at Sartartia, and her complement of two hundred officers and men —among them sixty Missouri soldiers who never before had boarded a gunboat—were given final instructions for the impending dash to Vicksburg.

The *Arkansas* combined some of the features of the light-draft river boat and the sharp-keeled ocean steamer. She was broad and flat-bottomed amidships and tapered at both ends. She was 165 feet long and mounted ten guns. Her two propellers were driven by low-pressure steam engines built in Memphis. Her draft, when fully loaded, was more than fifteen feet and her speed in still water was about six knots. Her major defect was the thinness and looseness of the used railroad iron that covered her shield. Even so, she was a terror to her foes. In a historic encounter near Vicksburg on July 15, 1862, she pitted her ten guns and two hundred men against the combined fleets of Farragut, Davis and Ellet—"3,000 men and 300 heavy guns"—survived the ordeal and won for her crew the thanks of the Confederate Congress. A month later, while en route to Baton Rouge, her engines broke down and she had to be destroyed to prevent capture.

The ironclad ram *Albemarle,* built on the Roanoke River in 1863—

1864, was another notable achievement in naval construction. After two North Carolina citizens contracted to build the vessel, Secretary Mallory made available to them the services of Commander James W. Cooke, and this resourceful and energetic officer was put in charge of construction. Cooke and his associates set up shop in a cornfield, built the vessel's framework of unseasoned timber cut and sawed in the vicinity, and fashioned the machinery and armor of materials scrounged or wheedled from scrap piles and foundries. General R. F. Hoke detailed some soldier mechanics to help push the work to completion, but the ram had to be launched while construction was still in progress. As the vessel slowly cruised down the river in April, 1864, mechanics hammered away on deck and shield, shaping bolts at portable forges, attaching armor and mounting guns. Amidst the din and confusion, naval officers worked earnestly to convert their landlubberly crewmen into passable sailors.

The *Albemarle* was similar in design and construction to the *Arkansas*, though a little shorter and lighter. She carried only two guns—8-inch rifles—and the functioning of her engines and steering gear left much to be desired.

On the afternoon of April 18, as the *Albemarle* neared Plymouth, Commander Cooke sent the workers ashore and gave the gunners a final drill. Early the next morning the ship steamed toward Fort Williams, rammed and sank the U.S.S. *Southfield,* drove off the other Union vessels and then assisted the land forces in overpowering the fort and capturing Plymouth. Stung by the humiliating loss of this town, and the *Albemarle*'s threat to Union control of this portion of the North Carolina coast, Admiral Samuel P. Lee ordered that "at all hazards, the rebel ram must be destroyed." On May 5, 1864, a fleet of eight wooden gunboats attacked the *Albemarle* and came very near sinking her, but the plucky Cooke at the peak of crisis exhorted his men: "Stand to your guns! If we must sink, let us perform our duty and go down like brave men." The *Albemarle* survived this attack and inflicted severe damage on her antagonists. But on the night of October 14, 1864, while the gunboat was anchored at Plymouth, she was torpedoed and sunk by Lieutenant William B. Cushing of the Union navy in one of the most daring and thrilling exploits of the war.

Other ironclads built by or for the Navy Department included the rams *Manassas, Richmond* and *Texas;* the floating batteries *Huntsville, Phoenix* and *Tuscaloosa;* the steam sloops *Missouri, Neuse, North Carolina, Palmetto State, Raleigh* and *Savannah;* the twin-propeller steamer *Muscogee;* the side-wheel steamer *Nashville;* the *Virginia No. 2;* and a second *Tennessee.* Most of these vessels were built at Richmond, Wilmington, Charleston, Savannah and Mobile. The construction of all of them was impeded by shortage of mechanics and the difficulty of obtaining iron. Few of these vessels got into combat and most of them were destroyed to prevent capture by the Federals.

Lieutenant R. R. Stiles, C.S. Ironclad Richmond

The Confederate navy was made up largely of wooden craft. Some were converted trading vessels and others were designed and built for war purposes. They were of various kinds and classes, including schooners, sloops, tugs, rams, screw steamers and floating batteries, but the prevailing type was the side-wheel light-draft steamer, carrying from two to six guns. In some instances cotton was placed about the decks to protect the crews, hence the term "cottonclad." For both iron and wooden vessels the procurement of reliable engines and boilers was a considerable problem. Marine engines were manufactured at Confederate naval works in Charlotte, Richmond and Columbus. Those made at Columbus under the direction of Chief Engineer J. H. Warner were said to have been "of sufficient power to insure good speed."

In a category all to themselves were the fourteen steamboats comprising the "River Defence Fleet," fitted out at New Orleans early in 1862, under War Department auspices, to oppose the Union gunboats on the upper Mississippi. These boats were commercial craft seized by General Mansfield Lovell, partially shielded with rail iron and armed with one to four guns; some of them were fitted with rams. They were commanded by river boat captains, each of whom selected his own crew and fought pretty much on his own. Seven or eight of them engaged Captain C. H. Davis' Western Flotilla at Fort Pillow, some thirty miles north of Memphis, on May 10, 1862, and disabled two Union vessels. When they encountered the rams of Colonel Charles Ellet at Memphis on June 6, 1862, they were overwhelmed and six of them were lost. Six vessels of the "River Defence Fleet" were in the battle of April 24, 1862, below New Orleans, but their role was negligible.

Captain James Newland Maffit, C.S.S. Florida

The principal source of guns for the Confederacy's war vessels was the Norfolk navy yard where 1,198 cannon were obtained in April, 1861, as a result of Federal withdrawal from this locality. When Southerners evacuated Norfolk in May, 1862, they moved much of the machinery to the Charlotte navy yard and continued the manufacture of naval ordnance there. Guns of various calibers and types were also produced at the government naval works in Richmond, Pensacola, Atlanta, Augusta, Columbia, Mobile and Selma. Among private firms manufacturing cannon for the Navy Department were the Etowah Iron Works of Georgia and Tredegar of Richmond. In 1862 Commander John M. Brooke, who later became head of the Navy Department's Bureau of Ordnance and Hydrography, developed at Tredegar a 7-inch rifle known as the "Big Brooke." This rifle scored a notable triumph at Charleston in April, 1863, when one of its 140-pound shells penetrated and sank the monitor *Keokuk.*

Tredegar and the government naval works listed above also manufactured most of the machinery and appurtenances required to equip the South's war vessels. The Confederate rope works in Petersburg, Virginia, produced more than enough cotton cordage to meet the navy's needs. Coal was obtained from North Carolina, Alabama and Tennessee, but in the latter part of the war the rapidly deteriorating railroads frequently were unable to get the fuel to the places where it was needed. Sometimes vessels were compelled to fire their boilers with wood.

The biggest and most persistent problem encountered in equipping and maintaining ships, as in building them, was scarcity of skilled labor. The basic cause of this deficiency was the South's traditional commitment to agriculture. But the handicap was due in large part to the Confederacy's failure fully to utilize the mechanical talent that was available. Technicians possessed of skills urgently needed in armories and shops were required to carry muskets in the ranks, and this despite earnest and repeated efforts of naval authorities and civilians holding government contracts to pry them loose. Many of the South's artisans were foreigners who were willing enough to help manufacture the materials of war, but who were strongly opposed to entering the armed services. Threats of conscription, first by Confederate authorities and later by state governors, caused many alien artisans to flee to the North and impeded attempts to import technicians from Europe.

In view of the number and magnitude of the difficulties encountered by Mallory and his collaborators, it seems remarkable that they accomplished as much as they did in acquiring and operating the Confederate navy.

IX. *Confederate Women: The Staunchest Rebels*

The outbreak of hostilities in 1861 produced mixed reactions among Southern women. They were saddened by the departure of their menfolk for the war. But most of them accepted without question the oft-repeated statements of fire-eating orators that cotton was king, that Yankees were cowards, and that Southern armies would promptly rout their foes and come home in triumph to enjoy peace and prosperity in an independent Confederacy.

Sincere devotion to the Southern cause and confidence that independence would be quickly and easily won caused Confederate women to enter heartily into martial activities. They adorned themselves with miniature Confederate flags, lifted their voices in patriotic songs and urged men and boys to join the companies forming to repel the Northern invaders. They smiled and feted the "brave volunteers" and turned the coldest of shoulders to those males who showed any hesitancy about signing up for army service. "I wish he could stay home," wrote a young Tarheel girl whose beau was about to depart for the Virginia front, "but I would not have a sweetheart unless he was in the army."

The martial ardor of some women reached such a high pitch that they formed volunteer units of their own and took to drilling and shooting. A Georgia woman wrote in May, 1861: "We have formed a Female Company in Bascom for the purpose of learning to shoot, so that if all the men go to war we can protect our homes and selves. . . . The name of our Company is the Bascom Home Guards. You know how nervous and timid Mollie was. Well, now she can load and fire and hit a spot at a good distance. . . . We are all delighted with the idea of learning to shoot. Father says he thinks our uniform is prettier than the boys although ours are made of common calico."

A few women disguised themselves as men, donned the Confederate uniform and accompanied husbands or sweethearts to camp. Their army service was usually of short duration, though two—Mrs. L. M. Blalock and Mrs. Amy Clarke—are said to have been with their soldier

*Rose O'Neal Greenhow
and daughter at Old
Capitol Prison,
Washington, D.C.*

husbands in several battles. Many women chafed at their inability to join the fighting forces. One of the would-be-Amazons was twenty-year-old Sarah Morgan of Louisiana, who wrote in her diary the day the Federals entered Baton Rouge: "O! if I was only a man! Then I could don breeches and slay them with a will! If some few women were in the ranks, they could set the men an example they would not blush to follow!"

Some women rendered effective service as informers, scouts and spies. When General Nathan B. Forrest was blocked by a burning bridge in his pursuit of Colonel A. D. Streight through Alabama in May, 1863, sixteen-year-old Emma Sansom climbed up behind the general on his horse and guided him to a ford across Black Creek. Forrest wrote the girl a note commending her for gallant assistance and went on to capture his foe. Rose O'Neal Greenhow gave Beauregard timely and valuable information concerning McDowell's advance on Manassas in July, 1861. She was imprisoned by the Federals, then deported to the South, and was drowned in 1864 while running the blockade with money that she had raised in Europe for the Confederacy. Other women spies were Nancy Hart of West Virginia, who aided Jackson in his Valley campaigns and who killed a Federal guard to effect her escape after being

EMBATTLED
CONFEDERATES

Belle Boyd

Mrs. John Slidell, wife of the Confederate commissioner to France. Her husband's seizure by the Federal Navy from the British steamer, Trent, known as the "Trent Affair," angered Great Britain and helped promote the Southern cause in England

captured in 1862; Antonia Ford of Fairfax Courthouse, Virginia, who gathered information for Stuart and Mosby; Norah McCartney of Missouri; the Lomax sisters, Anne and Julia, of Maryland; and three ladies of the New Bern, North Carolina, area, Elizabeth Harland, Mrs. A. M. Meekins and Emmeline Piggott.

The most famous feminine spy of all was Belle Boyd of Martinsburg, West Virginia, a daring girl only seventeen years old in 1861, who repeatedly risked her life to provide Ashby, Stuart and Jackson with helpful information. Miss Boyd ran a gantlet of Federal fire at Front Royal, Virginia, in May, 1862, to tell Jackson that the town was lightly held and to urge a swift advance. She was twice imprisoned in Washington for collaborating with Confederates. After her second release she embarked in May, 1864, for England carrying papers for Jefferson Davis. She was captured en route and taken to Boston but was held for only a short time. She then went to Europe, where on August 24, 1864, she married Sam Wylde Hardings, an officer on the Federal ship that had taken her in custody earlier in the year.

Most Confederate women had to confine themselves to less spectacular activities than spying, such as making clothing and banners, cheering soldiers en route to war, and dispensing food and drink to the volunteers. As the war lengthened, much of the exuberance and light-heartedness disappeared, but activities were better organized and pointed more definitely to real needs. Instead of wasting effort on havelocks, gaiters and other useless accessories, the women formed soldier aid societies to make socks, shirts, drawers, trousers, coats and blankets.

Work of the societies was supplemented by a vast amount of individual activity. In some instances planters' wives outfitted entire companies with complete uniforms; and hardly any woman, however poor, failed to provide soldier members of her family with some article of clothing. The contribution of the Southern women is the more notable in view of the amount of labor that it required. Southern mills were able to meet only a small portion of the Confederacy's textile needs. Cut off as they soon were by the blockade, the women of Dixie had to retrieve cotton cards, spinning wheels and looms from attics and basements and do their own carding, spinning and weaving. Fortunately many of the older women still knew how to use this antiquated equipment and they shared their knowledge with younger associates. In some instances venerable slave women were the teachers.

Some women took their homespun thread to mills to be made up into cloth, but most of them had to do their own weaving. The home manufacturers took great pride in their handiwork. An upper-class South Carolina woman wrote to an acquaintance in 1861: "I am cutting coats & pantaloons with all the assurance of a professional tailor. Such is my occupation & such is the occupation of every lady in this parish. The amount of *work* we have accomplished is a wonder to ourselves, to say nothing of the world. I think if times continue hard I have learnt enough to make myself independent of the world. I have gone through a regular apprenticeship & can do journeyman work as well as anybody."

Many women entered war industries and government service, working in ordnance plants to help make Minié balls, paper cartridges, percussion caps, fuses and shells. Others labored in textile mills and garment plants, and some worked for the Confederate Treasury and Post Office Departments. In June, 1864, two hundred women were employed in the Treasury Note Bureau at Columbia, South Carolina, numbering and signing paper currency issued by the government. When the head of the Note Bureau made his report in October, 1864, he stated: "The experiment of employing ladies in the public offices, first instituted by Mr. Memminger, has not only proved a perfect success, but has been the means of relieving the necessities of many who have been driven from their homes and have lost all by the cruelty of our inhuman foe."

Wages apparently were lower than those paid to men performing the same tasks. Adult women engaged in government ammunition factories in Memphis early in the war received $4.50 a week; and girls, $3.00. An Augusta, Georgia, textile factory in 1863 paid girls who operated the spindles and looms $8.00 to $10.00 a week, but in view of the inflated condition of currency, this was a pittance. At that time a pound

Southern woman making clothes for Confederate soldiers

of butter cost $4.00; a head of cabbage, $1.00; a pound of bacon, $2.75; a bushel of sweet potatoes, $21.00; a gallon of molasses, $15.00; a pound of salt, $0.50; and a cord of wood, $40.00. Married women working for the Confederate States Laboratory in Richmond in the fall of 1864 received $7.00 a day, and single women, $5.00, but the depreciated currency in which they were paid had very little purchasing power.

In June, 1861, Sallie Reneau of Mississippi sought the aid of Governor Pettus in raising a company of "Mississippi Nightingales," armed, uniformed and paid like soldiers, to help care for the wounded. These ambitious plans did not materialize, but throughout the war many women, especially those living near battlefields and hospitals, working individually or in small groups, gave aid and comfort to sick and wounded soldiers. After the battle of Shiloh, ladies from far and near went to Corinth to help care for the casualties brought to the hotels, churches, schools and dwellings of that city. During and after the Seven Days' campaign of 1862, Richmond women went to the battlefield in their carriages, distributed food, and bandaged wounds; some took casualties to their homes and cared for them until they recovered or could be transferred to hospitals.

Some ladies became administrators and nurses in Confederate hospitals, and despite an enormous amount of opposition to their entry

Chimborazo Hospital, Richmond, Virginia, April, 1865

into what was generally regarded as a man's world, they rendered notable service. Sally L. Tompkins proved so efficient in managing a hospital which she improvised from an old Richmond mansion after the First Battle of Manassas that President Davis made her a captain of cavalry to regularize her status as she continued her work under government auspices. He thereby gave her the distinction of being the only woman ever to hold an official military commission in the Confederate service. She remained on duty until the end of the war and her hospital treated a total of 1,300 soldiers. Mrs. Arthur Francis Hopkins, wife of the Chief Justice of Alabama, took the lead in establishing the Alabama section of the Chimborazo Hospital in Richmond, and contributed about $200,000 for the treatment and relief of sick and wounded Confederates. She was twice wounded while assisting casualties at Seven Pines and ever afterward had a slight limp from the effect of her injuries. The state of Alabama gave her a vote of thanks and placed her likeness on two of its bank bills.

Another "Florence Nightingale of the Confederacy" was Ella King Newsom, an affluent widow of Arkansas. Mrs. Newsom very wisely prepared herself for her medical duties by serving an apprenticeship in the Memphis City Hospital. She began her army work at Bowling Green, Kentucky, in December, 1861, among the wounded soldiers of Albert Sidney Johnston's command, and acquitted herself so well that she was made superintendent of hospitals in that town. She later supervised hospitals in various other Southern cities including Nashville, Chat-

EMBATTLED
CONFEDERATES

tanooga and Atlanta. Throughout her Confederate career she displayed exceptional capacity for work and outstanding ability as an administrator.

Other women who made notable contributions as nurses or hospital executives were Kate Cumming of Mobile, who left a full and interesting record of her service in *Hospital Life in the Confederate Army of Tennessee;* Kate Mason Rowland; Louisa McCord; Sallie Law; Fannie Beers; Annie Johns; Emily Mason; Mary Joyner; and Margaret Weber. Conspicuous service was rendered by the various orders of Catholic nuns, including the Sisters of Charity, who attended sick and wounded soldiers at Harpers Ferry, Richmond, Lynchburg, Gettysburg and elsewhere; the Sisters of Mercy, who won warm praise for their selfless and efficient work at Vicksburg and other Mississippi towns; the Sisters of St. Dominic, who rendered efficient service at the Memphis City Hospital; the Sisters of Charity of Nazareth, who established a chain of hospitals in Kentucky; and the Sisters of Our Lady of Mercy, who administered to sick and wounded Rebs hospitalized in Charleston, South Carolina. All told, the nuns engaged in Confederate hospital service numbered less than two hundred, but because of the prior training of many of them as nurses, their exceptional devotion and the respect which they commanded, they made a contribution that would have been a credit to a much larger group.

One of the most remarkable of all the women engaged in the care of sick and wounded soldiers was Phoebe Yates Pember. Her book, *A Southern Woman's Story,* is the most engaging and revealing account of Confederate hospital service. Mrs. Pember, a young Jewish widow belonging to one of Savannah's leading families, was, from December, 1862, to April, 1865, the chief matron of "Hospital No. 2," one of the five principal divisions of Chimborazo Hospital in Richmond. Chimborazo, which treated a total of 76,000 patients during the Civil War, was reputed to be the largest military hospital that the world had ever known. When Mrs. Pember reported for duty, male members of the staff gave unmistakable evidence that they resented her presence. She won some of them over by her efficiency and charm, but others kept up a running fight with her for the duration of the war.

Chimborazo had its quota of complainers and malingerers but these Mrs. Pember handled with firmness and tact. As she made her rounds, she was called on to write letters for illiterates, prepare special dishes for those of poor appetite, comfort the homesick, bathe the brows of the feverish and offer spiritual comfort to the dying. She observed repeated instances of patients who, at first hearty and hopeful, suffered a reverse, slipped into decline, turned their faces to the wall and died. Misery and tragedy passed daily in review before her eyes; but she developed a strength which enabled her to maintain composure under the most trying circumstances. Fortunately the atmosphere was brightened now and then by flashes of soldier humor. One of the consequences of the hospital experience of this cultured aristocrat was the development of a deep

*Miss Emily Mason,
Confederate nurse*

admiration of the patience, cheerfulness and character of the common folk who filled her wards.

The great majority of Confederate women had to stay at home and devote themselves to sustaining their families. Upper-class women living in uninvaded areas felt the pinch of war least of all. Most of them had slaves to perform menial chores and heavy labor. Those whose menfolk were away in the army sometimes had to take over the supervision of slave labor. Some met their increased responsibilities magnificently and displayed superior managerial abilities. "I am a planter for the first time," wrote Caroline Pettigrew of South Carolina in 1862. "I insist upon myself being very energetic and making an appearance of knowing more than I really do." Anne Gorman Justice administered with notable success a small plantation in North Carolina, while her husband was away in the army. "Measuring corn, weighing shucks, and soaking wheat is a new business to me," she wrote on March 1, 1862. "But," she added, "we think of carrying on the farm ourselves next year without employing an overseer." With occasional help from relatives and neighbors, she supervised a great diversity of activities including the raising and slaughtering of hogs, cutting wood for home use and for sale, planting, cultivating, harvesting and storing food crops, and spinning, weaving and fabricating clothing for herself, her two small sons and her slaves. She also sent clothing and food to her husband. Her war letters reveal an abundance of resourcefulness and self-confidence, and she never complained about the extra burdens imposed upon her by her husband's absence. Not all women found the running of plantations to their liking or talents. In the spring of 1864, after long harassment by trifling overseers and loafing slaves, a Texas woman wrote her soldier husband: "With the prospect of another 4 years war, you may give your negroes away . . . and I'll move into a white settlement and work with my hands."

Both town and country ladies led much busier lives during the war than before. The blockade required the conversion of homes and plantations into industrial establishments, and women had to enter into and supervise the manufacture of cotton and woolen goods, making of clothing, tanning of leather, extraction of salt from dirt dug from beneath smokehouses, and the preparation of substitutes for many standard household items. All these activities, combined as they frequently were with soldier relief projects, church work and community responsibilities, made very full days. Mrs. Howell Cobb of Athens, Georgia, after outlining to her husband (then in process of raising a regiment) her schedule for one day, August 5, 1861, stated: "My head is *sore* and addled. . . . If you will not admit that I have a few annoyances, enough to addle a man's brain, then I will admit that organizing a regiment is more annoying than keeping house, raising children and being a Directress of a Volunteer aid society."

Despite their burdens and harassments many of the upper-class

A Texas wife with her Confederate husband

women were able to achieve a fair degree of happiness; some had a better time during the conflict than they had ever had before. Southern women were never the ethereal, male-dominated, helpless creatures portrayed in romantic writings about antebellum times. Smart, vivacious and articulate women like Varina Howell Davis, Mary Boykin Chesnut, Constance Cary, Phoebe Yates Pember and Sara Agnes Pryor always took a lively interest in politics and public affairs, and what they had to say on these subjects was listened to with respect by their husbands and masculine friends. But the war loosened conventions and enhanced women's status and freedom. Letters, diaries and newspapers of the time reveal a vast amount of travel by ladies at every stage of the war, to visit soldier and civilian relatives, to aid the sick and wounded, to seek employment or to elude the Federal invaders.

Social activities flourished throughout the war. Departure of units for camp was preceded by a whirl of parties, balls and religious services. Once the volunteers were in camp, the ladies busied themselves with bazaars, suppers, dances and various other projects to raise funds for their "brave defenders." Soldiers returning home on furlough were nearly always treated to a round of social events. Women living near camps often attended reviews, camp theatricals and musical concerts, and soldiers in turn called at private homes to talk, sing and play parlor games. In October, 1862, Cordelia Scales, a girl living near Holly Springs, Mississippi, wrote a former schoolmate: "Our army is in camp almost in sight of us. . . . Lou I do wish you were here. We would have so much fun. . . . I think we have about fifty soldiers with us every day. They are as thick as flies used to be in the dining room of the old College."

Mary Boykin Chesnut

Glamorous and gregarious generals like Stuart, Beauregard and Morgan were showered with feminine attention wherever they went, and often were honored guests at dinners and parties. A Tennessee woman described thus a party held at McMinnville, Tennessee, in February, 1863, for General Morgan and his staff: "We went late—11 o'clock, and returned early at 3. Everything was in full blast when we arrived and the young folks seemed to be enjoying themselves vastly. Everything looked more brilliant than I had supposed possible from the meagre resources at our command. The music was good—they had a brass band from Tullahoma and the dancing was very spirited. . . . Mrs. Morgan wore a crimson silk, trimmed with black lace, and a full set of pearl ornaments, head-dress, comb and all. She looked very well and was a conspicuous figure in the dance."

In the cities, and especially in Richmond, social life of upper-class ladies included dances, charades, tableaux, theatricals, musical concerts, receptions, and dinners where until the later months fine wines, run through the blockade, and elegant food were served. In the last years of the conflict, parties, dancing and merrymaking increased as people sought escape from the tragedy which surrounded them and the specter of ruin which hung over their heads.

The overwhelming majority of Southern women belonged to the yeoman class, and for them life was much harder than for the privileged minority. Often left at home with large families of children to support —for Confederate draft laws did not exempt fathers—these women planted, cultivated and harvested crops, looked after the livestock, killed the hogs, cut and hauled firewood and kept dwellings and premises in repair. At night they sat up late to run spinning wheels and looms. This crushing routine benumbed them with weariness. A Georgia woman left with the running of a farm and the care of four small children wrote her soldier husband in September, 1862: "I am so tired for I never get any rest night or day, and I don't think I will last much longer." When children became ill, the mothers had to resort to home treatment, with herbs, poultices and other folk remedies. When death came the mother usually had to bury the child and endure the grief alone, for furloughs were difficult to obtain and soldiers often did not learn that their children were sick until too late.

Croquet game at Patellus House, Virginia

States, counties and communities attempted to ease the lot of the needy with relief programs, but these were woefully inadequate, and the suffering of the poor in both rural areas and towns during the last two years of the war was tremendous. Little wonder that soldiers deserted by the scores and that "bread riots" occurred in Richmond, Salisbury, Mobile and other Confederate cities.

Poor women had less opportunity for diversion than those of the upper classes, but some were able to brighten their lives occasionally by attending corn shuckings, quilting parties, spinning bees, picnics, barbecues, candy pullings and religious services. Girls of yeoman families entertained their beaus with singing parties and dances, and summer revivals and camp meetings were always occasions for considerable "sparking." A Virginia Reb wrote to a male acquaintance at home: "right to me a bout the big meating and how you in joyed your self and how menny girls you sqese." Shortage of eligible males was a deterrent to social activities of all kinds. Teen-age boys did the best they could to fill in for the absent soldiers. "I am still flying around with the girls," wrote one youngster to his soldier uncle; "I tell you they keep me sterred up. . . . I went to meting . . . at Union and coming home I had to keep company with about a dozen girls. . . . I want you to make haste and kill these old Yankies by Christmas and come home and help me out for I tell you that I have my hands full."

When unattached Rebs went home on leave they tried to make up for time lost from courting. A Georgia boy whose brother was home on furlough wrote to a relative in July, 1862: "Me and Bud have been down

Wedding picture of Private John Scott Pickle, who served with Company B, Eighteenth Texas Cavalry

CONFEDERATE WOMEN: THE STAUNCHEST REBELS

Southern women and their servants

in Piney Woods to see mine & his little *intended*. I saw Miss Sallie and she looked as bewitching as ever. . . . She told me enough to make any one man happy through all coming times. I think if the war was ended I could be happy now with but three things, Miss Sallie, a *cradle* & Broom. . . . I got acquainted with a couple of nice young ladies last Saturday, one of them is Bud's June Bug, probably he will post you on that."

Among all classes the war brought a flood of marriages. In November, 1863, Judith McGuire of Virginia, in recording the marriage of a crippled soldier, stated: "I believe that neither war, pestilence nor famine could put an end to the marrying and giving in marriage which is constantly going on. Strange that these sons of Mars can so assiduously devote themselves to Cupid and Hymen; but every respite, every furlough must be thus employed." Courtships frequently were very brief and weddings usually were much less elaborate than in antebellum times, but everyone pitched in to make the best of existing circumstances, and feminine ingenuity sometimes triumphed over all difficulties.

The war and the blockade led to numerous adjustments in women's fashions and clothing. In 1861 patriotic fervor resulted in many discarding Yankee-made cloth in favor of Confederate homespun, but what at first was a fad after the opening years of the war became a widespread necessity. Expert use of homemade dyes and ingenious arrangement of threads in weaving resulted in a colorful variety of checks, plaids and stripes. Many women transformed old garments, draperies, curtains, sheets, pillowcases, mattress covers and even carpets into new clothing. Pride of the women in their resourcefulness and independence in providing their own apparel was reflected in a popular Confederate song. "The Homespun Dress," sung to the tune of the "Bonnie Blue Flag."

> My homespun dress is plain, I know;
> My hat's palmetto, too.
> But then it shows what Southern girls
> For Southern rights will do.
> We send the bravest of our land
> To battle with the foe;
> And we will lend a helping hand
> We love the South, you know.
>
> Chorus
>
> Hurrah! Hurrah!
> For the sunny South so dear
> Three cheers for the homespun dress
> That Southern ladies wear.

Hoop skirts continued to be a favorite vogue with upper-class ladies, though newspapers now and then cautiously criticized the extravagance and the waste of the long, billowing garments. In an article entitled "A Hint to the Ladies," a Columbia, South Carolina, editor pleaded for a simpler style on the grounds that it would reduce the ladies' laundry bills, please the gentlemen, and make more cloth available for soldiers' underclothing "and thus gratefully attach them more than ever to your skirts." The lack of cloth forced many ladies to comply. Homemade hats and bonnets were made of scraps of cloth, ribbon and lace, palmetto, and the straw of wheat, oats and rye. Some bonnets were of the "Quaker" or "Shaker" types, others were long-hooded sunbonnets, and still others were towering creations called "sky scrapers." Headpieces were trimmed with bits of lace or ribbon, feathers, shavings from cow horns, flowers, berries and leaves.

*A Southern belle in front
of Indian Rock, Lookout
Mountain, Tennessee*

Serviceable and even attractive shoes were made of leather tanned at home from the hides of cows, calves, horses, deer, sheep, dogs or other animals. Saddles, trunks and belts were cut up to provide the thick leather needed for soles. Lacking leather, many women fashioned shoes from canvas, duck and Osnaburg, made knitted footwear, or plaited shoes from strips of fiber or paper glued together with meal paste. Some resorted to wooden shoes. Among the very poor, entire families sometimes went barefooted the year round.

Hardship and deprivation was greatest for women of the piney woods and mountain sections. Those in invaded areas and the twilight zone lying between the hostile armies experienced far greater difficulty than those living in sections far removed from the conflict, for they were subjected to incursions by roving bands of scouts, rangers and brigands, often wearing Southern uniforms and nominally operating under state or Confederate authority, but actually controlled by no one. These groups

EMBATTLED
CONFEDERATES

stole and plundered at will, and subjected women to all sorts of indignities.

The coming of the Yankees was a time of terror for Southern women. The anticipation was sometimes worse than the fact, for most Federal generals tried to keep their men from entering homes or destroying private property. Orders usually required foraging to be done only by authorized groups operating under the jurisdiction of officers, but lower-ranking subordinates frequently ignored these instructions. A Michigan soldier wrote from Bolivar, Tennessee, on July 28, 1862, that the generals tried to protect the property of Southerners by posting guards, but added: "Our soldiers don't make very good guards in such cases. I know of some who *couldn't see* a Union soldier picking peaches in the orchard they were set to guard and others were kind enough to point out the best trees and turn their backs." Instances of physical harm to white women were relatively rare, but insulting language and threats of bodily harm were not uncommon. A Federal court-martial cited the following instance of plunder and insult by Union soldiers of Turchin's Brigade in Athens, Alabama, in May, 1862:

A party entered the dwelling of Milly Ann Clayton and opened all the trunks, drawers and boxes of every description, and taking out the contents thereof . . . destroyed, spoiled or carried away the same. They also insulted the said Milly Ann Clayton and threatened to shoot her, and then proceeding to the kitchen, they there attempted an indecent outrage on the person of her servant girl.

Women reacted to invasion in various ways. Nearly all maintained a show of calm and most of them had as little conversation with the Yankees as possible. But some manifested their disdain and hatred by stepping off the sidewalk or turning their heads when meeting Federal troops, refusing to return greetings or answer questions, displaying Confederate flags or defiantly singing Southern songs. A few greeted the invaders with insults and profanity, doused them with hot water or spat on them. A Vermont private wrote that as his regiment was passing through Culpeper, Virginia, "a window was raised and a thing that probably called itself [a] lady Spat Square in the face of Captain George D. Davenport, and screamed, 'Take that Yankee son-of-a-b——', and slammed the window down."

Hatred, expressed or restrained, was the prevailing attitude of the women in the invaded areas. But some greeted the Federals cordially, either because of genuine Union leanings, a desire to make the best of their plight, to protect their property, or to obtain some of the abundance brought by the men in blue. An Illinois sergeant, stationed at Vicksburg, wrote sarcastically: "I find these Southern nabobs and nabobesses who were going to die in the last ditch are quite willing to swear any amount of oaths in order to taste the sweets of Uncle Sam's pantry." Still other women, genuinely Southern in sentiment, were converted to friendliness by acts of kindness on the part of the invaders. Letters and diaries of

South Carolina lady

Union men in every occupied community reveal considerable social intercourse between Federals and "secesh" girls which in a good many instances led to romances and marriages. In Holly Springs, Mississippi, for example, where in 1862 the invaders encountered only cool and hostile attitudes, the situation gradually changed, and in August, 1864, a Union officer wrote from that town: "The citizens are very Friendly and Seem desirous of getting acquainted with as many Yankees as possible. . . . There are several . . . [young ladies] Engaged to Yankee officers."

Many women of the middle and upper classes who could afford it chose to flee the peril and humiliation of Yankee rule and seek new homes in other localities. Taking their children and as many of their possessions as possible, they headed for some place that seemed beyond the reach of the Yankees, sometimes moving more than once in spite of the hardships and expense of travel. Texas was a favorite resort for fugitives from Tennessee, Arkansas, Louisiana and Mississippi. Kentuckians frequently fled to Alabama and Georgia, and people from border and coastal sections of Alabama, Georgia, Virginia, the Carolinas and other invaded states often took refuge in towns, cities and rural areas of the interior. In the communities where the refugees settled, surroundings

John Minor Botts of Virginia, surrounded by members of his family

EMBATTLED
              CONFEDERATES

Departure from the old homestead

were strange, dwellings usually far less commodious and comfortable than those recently vacated, living costs high and people often unfriendly. The crowding of refugees into interior communities overtaxed facilities, increased the scarcity of food and other essentials and caused prices to soar. Old residents resented the disruption and inconvenience resulting from the intrusion of the newcomers and some of them made no effort to conceal their unhappiness. Hostility was by no means universal, but it was common enough to attract the notice of newspapers and to elicit considerable comment from the uprooted.

Kate Stone, who with her mother and brothers fled from the family plantation, "Brokenburn," in Louisiana to Texas in 1863, wrote in her journal after arriving in Tyler: "The more we see of people, the less we like them, and every refugee we have seen feels the same way. They call us *renegades* in Tyler. It is strange the prejudice that exists all through the state against refugees. We think it is envy, just pure envy. The refugees are nicer and more refined people than most of those we meet, and they see and resent the difference." With the passing of time the Stones formed friendships among the local people and life became tolerable and even pleasant for Kate. But her diary indicates continuing friction between other refugees and the natives until the end of the war.

Mrs. Warren Akin, wife of a Georgia Confederate congressman, moved with her children and a few slaves from her home in Cassville to Elberton, Georgia, where her husband had formerly lived. Despite the

Southern belles from North Carolina

fact that her husband had many acquaintances in the area, on January 15, 1865, she wrote her spouse: "Your friends here have rather slighted me this past Christmas. They had dining & teas among the married folks and never once gave me an invitation to any of their social gatherings. . . . I doubt not if you had been at home you would have been invited all about and perhaps I would too. But these folks here don't know what real true politeness is."

Those with less means suffered even more. Cornelia McDonald left her home in Winchester, Virginia, with seven young children to live the life of a refugee in Richmond, Lexington and elsewhere; and with little money and few close friends outside her home community, she had great difficulty maintaining herself and her large family during her long exile. She was able to keep her family together and to ward off starvation only by tutoring. "With all I could do we had barely enough food to keep from actual want," she wrote. Even so, what she earned "supplied little more than bread, beans and little fat bacon." Peace came after a while, but for Mrs. McDonald, as for many others, the first days of Reconstruction were even more miserable and more trying than the darkest period of the war.

The greatest tribulation for all Confederate women was the mental torture to which they were subjected. "I lie awake night after night, count each stroke of the clock, dread both night and day, tremble to open a letter," wrote the troubled mother of five soldier sons in 1864. She and

EMBATTLED CONFEDERATES

Going to the Union
commissary for rations
near Rappahannock
Station, Virginia,
February 18, 1864. Many
Southern families living
within Union lines were
fed by the United States
government during the
winter months

countless other Southern women worried about the progress of the war and the prospect of defeat; about the future of loved ones at home; and especially about the safety and welfare of husbands, sons and brothers in the army. Nearly every letter from camp brought news of death by disease of some acquaintance or relation, and this impressed on the whole community the perils of soldiering. The approach of a season of active campaigning caused tensions to mount, and reports that a battle was in progress created apprehensions that were almost intolerable. On being told by her Negroes that they heard cannonading in the distance, a Lexington, Virginia, woman cried out: "Oh! my husband! Could I but know that he was safe! I wonder that I do not lose my senses. My God! help me to stay my heart on thee!" Failure to hear from loved ones soon after a battle caused a further increase of anxiety, and when the first report told of wounds a new worry was created, for injuries which at first seemed trivial often were followed by fatal complications. A message of death caused some women to cry out in their anguish, while others shed their tears and endured their woe in silence. The latter were sometimes the least consolable. "Hearts do break in silence," wrote Mary Boykin Chesnut in 1864, and she cited two specific instances: "Mrs. Means and Mary Barnwell made no moan—simply turned their faces to the wall and died." The spirits of a good many women were broken by anxiety and suffering, and in their dejection some of them wrote pitiful letters to husbands and sons in the army urging them to come home. These pleas were in large measure responsible for the flood of desertions which swept through the Confederate ranks in the latter part of the war.

But the majority of Southern women remained staunch in spirit and strong in support of the Confederate cause. The contribution of some was enormous. Mrs. Enoch Hooper Cook of Alabama gave a husband, ten sons and two grandsons to Confederate military service; Flora Mac-Donald Jones and Lucy Faucett Simpson of North Carolina each gave eleven sons; and scores of other women contributed from five to ten sons. The patriotism of some of these women is reflected by an incident which occurred in Virginia. As Governor John Letcher was returning to Richmond from a visit to his home in Staunton, he stopped at the home of an old friend. The lady of the house told the Governor that she was by herself at the time because her husband and ten sons were all in the army. "You must be very lonely," the Governor said, "as you are accustomed to so large a family." "Yes," the noble matron replied, "[and] it is

Southern refugees encamping in the woods near Vicksburg

hard to be alone, but if I had ten more sons they should all be in the army." Mrs. John Banks of Georgia, whose nine sons were in the army, lost three of them in the Atlanta campaign. Mrs. Polly Ray, a widow of Cumberland County, North Carolina, lost all seven of her sons in the war. Mrs. Olive Tatum of Bladen County lost five sons, and Mrs. Oran Palmer of Chatham County had four sons killed in the battle of Gettysburg. A Tennessee lady, after losing three of her four boys in battle, said to General Leonidas Polk of the one still at home: "As soon as I can get a few things together, General, you shall have Harry too."

The patriotism of the Confederacy's stalwart women shines through the pages of the letters that they wrote to their menfolk in the army. A North Carolina woman wrote to her husband in 1862: "I would not have you leave your country's service as long as she needs you and you can serve. Do your duty to God and man . . . and you will have a clear conscience and your children the heritage of a good name." A lowly Virginia woman who by resourcefulness and ceaseless toil was able to sustain several children wrote her soldier husband late in the war: "Donte be uneasy about us. We will try and take care of [our]selves the best we can. I donte minde what I do [just] so you can get back safe."

Portrait found by the side of a dead
Confederate soldier on the battlefield
of Chancellorsville, May 3, 1863

A poor Georgia woman, burdened with the care of an infant, and so hard-pressed for funds that she was faced with the prospect of selling her small "patch" of land, received a letter from her spouse stating that he could not send her any money owing to the failure of the paymaster to make an expected appearance. This humble wife had a reserve of strength that enabled her to write in reply: "John dont disfurnish yourself on our account and dont be oneasy about us. We will get along somehow."

The spirit reflected by this simple statement inspired the tribute of a Rebel veteran: "Napoleon would have laurelled the Confederate Mother."

x. *Religion and Morals*

Estimates based on the United States census indicate that in 1860 one of every two Southerners had no church affiliation. Even so, evangelical religion was a tremendous force in the lives of the Southern people. By 1830 the skepticism and easy tolerance which characterized the age of Jefferson had been generally displaced by an orthodoxy stressing original sin, a burning hell, individual repentance, justification by faith and the control of human events by an omnipotent, personal God. This creed accorded well with frontier individualism and the political philosophy of Jacksonian democracy, and was effectively preached by the leaders of the Great Revival which swept over the South in the early 1800's and by successive generations of evangelists who swayed the masses in summer camp meetings. Baptists and Methodists were leading spirits in the evangelical movement and in 1860 nearly three-fourths of the South's church members were of these two denominations. The other one-fourth was comprised of Presbyterians, Episcopalians, Catholics, Jews, Lutherans, Cumberland Presbyterians, Quakers and sundry other sects.

The evangelical denominations, and other groups as well, had strengthened their hold on the Southern people by championing slavery. In the age of Jefferson most churchmen regarded slavery as an undesirable institution and looked forward to its demise. In the early nineteenth century, as slavery began to spread following invention of the cotton gin, churches inclined to the view that slavery, though an evil, was essential to racial harmony and economic progress. In the 1830's, with slavery still expanding and with Southerners smarting under the attack of the aggressive abolitionists, religious leaders began to proclaim slavery as a positive good and an institution ordained of God to Christianize the heathen Africans and to uplift the white folk who owned them and guided them into paths of righteousness and civilization. Southern ministers probably did more than any other group to formulate and articulate the proslavery doctrine.

In view of their close connection with slavery and the Southern way of life, it was only natural for Southern churches to identify themselves with secession and independence. Indeed, the political disruption that came in 1860–1861 was foreshadowed by the separation in 1845, over issues involving slavery, of Southern Methodists and Baptists from their

Blandford Church,
Petersburg, Virginia

Northern associates. But some Southern churchmen, and particularly those in the upper South, were slow in espousing secession; and a few chose to become exiles rather than support disunion. Attachment to the Union was especially strong among Presbyterian and Episcopal ministers, who frequently were of Whig background. "I am shocked at this disloyalty to the Union of our 'holy men,'" wrote a prominent Virginia Episcopalian in February, 1861, "but the fact is undeniable and their influence is now extensively debauching our people." About the same time a Presbyterian minister of the Old Dominion deplored the inclination of the people "to rush into division and civil war with nothing to be gained on either side." These and other moderates were very much annoyed by South Carolina's precipitate and singlehanded withdrawal from the Union. A Baptist preacher of Prince Edward County, Virginia, in December, 1860, noted with disgust that "the little sovereign filly erects her head & tosses her tail as if she were the acknowledged & sole mistress of the field."

By the end of 1860 the overwhelming majority of clergymen in the deep South were committed to secession. The outbreak of hostilities brought the ministry of the upper South into the fold of disunion. Except in eastern Tennessee, religious leaders throughout the eleven states com-

EMBATTLED
CONFEDERATES

prising the Confederacy were practically unanimous in their support of Southern independence when the new nation mobilized for war in the spring of 1861.

One of the most eloquent and influential champions of secession and independence was Benjamin M. Palmer, minister of the First Presbyterian Church of New Orleans. Palmer, a native of South Carolina and a protégé of the illustrious James H. Thornwell, was restrained in his expression of sectional views until after the election of Lincoln. He then came out openly and strongly in favor of disunion. On November 29, 1860, in a Thanksgiving Day sermon entitled "The South: Her Peril and Her Duty," Palmer stated that the divinely ordained institution of slavery was imperiled by the recent triumph of the Republican Party. He further declared that since God had entrusted to Southerners the responsibility of perpetuating slavery, it was their duty to withdraw from the Republican-dominated Union and set up their own government. The sermon was given wide circulation in newspapers and in pamphlet form. The influence was tremendous. A Baton Rouge minister who at that time counseled moderation, stated that his parishioners and a majority of Presbyterians throughout the state were converted to secession by Palmer's Thanksgiving discourse.

Reverend Benjamin M. Palmer of New Orleans

Though only forty-two years old in 1860, Palmer had already made an enviable reputation as a minister, editor and educator. He was a dynamic personality and a compelling speaker. His Thanksgiving sermon boosted his popularity and set him on the road to pre-eminence among ministerial advocates of the Confederate cause. In July, 1861, he took the lead in founding the Presbyterian Church in the Confederate States and served as moderator of its first General Assembly.

Palmer was called on to address New Orleans units departing for the war; he used these occasions to justify the Southern revolution. In a stirring message to the Washington Artillery on May 27, 1861, he declared: "It is fitting that religion herself should with gentle voice whisper her benediction upon your flag and your cause. Soldiers, history . . . records . . . [no war] that is holier than this in which you have embarked. It is a war of defense against wicked and cruel aggression— a war of civilization against a ruthless barbarism . . . a war of religion against a blind and bloody fanaticism. . . . May the Lord of Hosts be around you as a wall of fire, and shield your head in the day of battle."

Following the fall of New Orleans, Palmer traveled through Mississippi and Tennessee exhorting the troops. After the trip one general stated that the fiery minister was worth more to the Confederate cause than a thousand soldiers. In the fall of 1862 Palmer joined the faculty of Columbia Theological Seminary, but he continued to make many patriotic speeches. When the Federals approached Columbia, he again became a refugee. But to the very end he proclaimed the struggle of the South to be a holy war and urged the people to remain strong in their support of the righteous crusade.

Reverend Robert L. Dabney of Virginia, Stonewall Jackson's chief of staff

Reverend Charles T. Quintard, Chaplain of the First Tennessee Infantry

Another powerful advocate of slavery and secession was Palmer's mentor and fellow churchman, James H. Thornwell. From 1851 to 1855 Thornwell was president of South Carolina College, but he gave up this position to join the faculty of the Columbia Theological Seminary. This "Calhoun of the Church" preached a fast-day sermon shortly after Lincoln's election in which he advocated secession even though the "path to victory may be through a baptism of blood." A short time later he justified the South's position in a pamphlet, "The State of the Country," which had wide circulation and great influence. He also appealed to the Southern soldiers in a leaflet, "Our Danger and Our Duty," which presented a vivid picture of the degradation and humiliation in store for the South if the North should win. His efforts to bolster the spirits of his countrymen were brought to a premature end by his death from tuberculosis in August, 1862.

Among other prominent ministers who played leading roles in supporting the Southern revolution were Episcopal Bishop Stephen Elliott of Georgia; Thomas Smyth, minister of the Second Presbyterian Church in Charleston; Bishop Francis H. Rutledge of Florida; and Catholic Bishop Augustine Verot of Savannah. On November 21, 1860, Smyth preached a fiery sermon, later published in pamphlet form, extolling slavery, urging secession, and denouncing as atheistic the equality and democracy advocated by Northerners.

Most of the ministerial advocates of disunion believed that secession could be accomplished peaceably. Some of those who thought otherwise were deeply troubled by the thought of the church taking the lead in precipitating violence and bloodshed. In January, 1861, the Reverend Robert L. Dabney of Virginia wrote that "there were plenty of politicians to make the fire [of sectionalism] burn hot enough without my help to blow it," and several weeks later he deplored "the infamy which would attach to the Christianity of America . . . if it were found impotent to save the land from fratricidal war." But when war came Dabney joined other Southern clergymen in urging the people to take up arms in defense of the Confederacy's holy cause.

Ministers supported the war by writing articles for church periodicals justifying the South's course and predicting Confederate victory; by joining laymen to put synods, conferences and other church bodies on record as approving and sustaining the struggle for independence; and by exhorting and blessing volunteer companies departing for the fighting fronts.

Scores of ministers went to war, some as chaplains, some as soldiers, still others on a temporary basis, preaching, distributing tracts and otherwise bolstering the morale of the troops. Chaplains varied greatly in ability and influence, but comments of soldiers leave the impression that those of inferior devotion and talent outnumbered those possessed of superior zeal and eloquence. One of the most distinguished chaplains was Charles Todd Quintard of the First Tennessee Regiment, who was trained in both medicine and theology and hence able to provide both physical and spiritual succor to the troops whom he served.

In the heat of battle some chaplains could not resist the urge to join in the shooting. At Chancellorsville, Chaplain T. L. Duke of the Nineteenth Mississippi Regiment, according to an official report, "remained in the forefront of his regiment with his musket . . . and directed the movement of the skirmishers." Chaplain Brady, in an action near Columbus, Kentucky, was said to have shot two Yankees, slashed the throat of a third with his knife, and then rushed after the foe crying, "Go to hell, you damned sons of bitches." Several chaplains won official commendation for heroism on the battlefields and a few gave their lives in line of duty. Chaplain William H. Cone died of wounds received at Corinth; B. F. Ellison was fatally injured in the action at Monett's Ferry, and Father J. Emerson Blimeol was mortally wounded while ministering to a Catholic soldier during the Battle of Jonesboro, Georgia.

Ministers who left the pulpit for combat service found opportunity from time to time to perform religious duties. Bishop-General Polk

Bishop-General Leonidas Polk

*Religious services in "Stonewall" Jackson's camp: 1, Jackson;
2, Lt. Col. A. J. Pendleton; 3, A. P. Hill; 4, Lt. Col. William Allen;
5, Maj. H. K. Douglas; 6, Dr. Hunter McGuire; 7, Capt. J. Smith;
8, Maj. William J. Hawks*

*St. Paul's Church,
Richmond, Virginia*

*Reverend Charles
Minnegerode, Rector of
St. Paul's Episcopal
Church, Richmond,
Virginia*

EMBATTLED
CONFEDERATES

preached occasionally to his soldiers and baptized a number of his high-ranking associates, including Generals Hardee, Hood and Joseph E. Johnston. General William N. Pendleton, Lee's chief of artillery, and Major Robert L. Dabney, Stonewall Jackson's chief of staff, both ordained ministers, conducted religious services in camp. Among Confederate captains were a considerable number of clergymen, including the president of Howard College in Alabama, who raised an infantry company from his institution and led it to war. These minister-captains usually regarded religious instruction as a part of their command function.

On the home front the first two years of the war were a period of exceptional religious interest and activity. Entry of many males into military service changed the character of congregations, and sometimes deprived the members of their clergymen. But the women, the older men and the children made the necessary adjustments and carried on with renewed zeal. Most of the churches held special services on the days set apart by President Davis and state governors from time to time to fast and pray for Confederate success. Revivals and camp meetings flourished in most areas, and these helped to build up church membership. A Methodist minister of east Texas in September, 1862, reported that a camp meeting and several revivals had added more than two hundred members to congregations on his circuit. A few months earlier the editor of the *Southern Presbyterian* noted approvingly that "amidst all the excitement consequent upon the bloody war in which we are engaged God is nevertheless pouring out his Holy Spirit upon many portions of our Southern Zion." In Savannah and Columbus, Georgia, various denominations held joint meetings from time to time to promote the spiritual growth of their communities and pray for Confederate victory.

President Davis lent support to the religious quickening which spread over the South by invoking divine aid in his speeches and proclamations and becoming a communicant of the Episcopal Church. He frequently occupied the pew reserved for him in St. Paul's Church in Richmond and listened attentively to the sermons of the Reverend Charles Minnegerode. John M. Daniel, the sarcastic editor of the Richmond *Examiner*, belittled Davis for joining the church and "counting his beads" instead of marshaling the troops to repel the invaders threatening the Confederate capital. But the country at large approved the President's emphasis on religion.

From the beginning of the war the churches played an active role in providing relief for the families of soldiers. North Carolina Presbyterians raised funds to educate the children of deceased and disabled veterans. Jewish congregations in Vicksburg, Montgomery, Augusta and Richmond contributed money for the support of the families of Confederate volunteers. Georgia Baptists collected more than $200,000 to erect a home for war orphans. Numerous religious groups sponsored programs for the assistance of destitute families, many individual church members

pledged themselves to sell necessities to the poor at reduced prices, and some planters volunteered to share their produce with the needy.

Secession and war caused an intensification of religious activity on behalf of the slaves. This was due in part to a widespread feeling among church leaders that in antebellum times Southerners had neglected the spiritual indoctrination of their servants and hence had failed to live up to their responsibility for Christianizing and uplifting the people committed to their care. A more immediate and perhaps more compelling reason was a belief that religious instruction would have a wholesome effect on the conduct of the blacks and make them more submissive during the disruption and turmoil incident to war. The South Carolina Methodist Conference cited the value of the program "in securing the quiet and peaceful subordination of these people." A contributor to the *Religious Herald* stated: "May we not hope and pray that large numbers will be savingly converted to Christ thus becoming better earthly servants while they wear with meekness the yoke of their master in heaven." Ministers who preached to black congregations during the war leaned more heavily than ever on such texts as "Servants obey your masters for it is right in the sight of the Lord," "Render unto Caesar the things that are Caesar's and unto God the things that are God's," and "I have learned in whatsoever state I am therewith to be content."

During the war, as before, slaves commonly attended the churches of their masters, sitting in the front pews, in the balcony, or in some other section reserved for their occupancy; sometimes ministers preached to the Negroes alone in the afternoon. But as the number of clergymen

*Offering of church bells to
be cast into cannon*

diminished, it proved increasingly difficult to maintain slave missions in cities and on plantations, or to attend separately to the spiritual needs of both Negroes and whites. Because of this, the lack of funds and difficulty of travel, the responsibility of providing religious instruction fell more and more on slaveowners, and particularly on their wives, who conducted services in homes or private chapels. In remote areas, and especially on plantations where owners were indifferent to religion, slaves often were deprived of the opportunity to worship with their fellows under competent leaders.

Throughout the war the churches worked diligently to sustain public morale and promote the success of the Confederate cause. Many congregations donated their bells to be cast into cannon. St. Paul's Methodist Church of Columbus, Georgia, raised a special money offering and sent it to the Confederate Treasury, "with the earnest prayer that God may give us *peace, liberty* and *independence.*" Numerous other

EMBATTLED
CONFEDERATES

religious bodies throughout the South made similar contributions, and church leaders urged their followers to invest generously in Confederate bonds.

The churches used their influence to combat extortion, speculation and other reprehensible practices, occasionally dropped deserters from church rolls, and in a few instances forced ministers suspected of Union leanings to vacate their pulpits. In 1863 a Methodist conference in east Tennessee expelled five members for supporting the Federal cause, "a crime sufficient to exclude them from the kingdom of grace and glory." Slaves who abandoned their masters were sometimes shorn of their spiritual connections. The record book of a Virginia Baptist congregation contains this entry for September 17, 1864: "Forty-one excluded who have gone off to the enemy."

Churches aided the Confederacy in its efforts to win favor abroad. The Reverend Father John Bannon, a Confederate chaplain, went to Ireland in 1863 to cultivate the good will of the Catholic clergy and through them to promote Southern sympathy among the laymen. Early in 1864 President Davis appointed Catholic Bishop Patrick N. Lynch of South Carolina as special commissioner to the Vatican. The Bishop had several audiences with the Pope but was unable to obtain official recognition or to arrange a treaty. En route to Italy he visited Ireland, where he assisted Father Bannon in his attempt to dissuade the sons of Erin from joining the Federal forces. In April, 1863, ninety-six clergymen representing all faiths issued an "Address to Christians Throughout the World." This widely circulated pamphlet emphasized the piety of Southerners, represented slavery as a benign institution and emancipation as an evil, denounced Northerners as aggressors in a wicked conflict and predicted the eventual triumph of the Confederacy.

But the churches devoted most of their attention to promoting religion and patriotism among the Southern people. From their pulpits ministers denounced sin and the Yankees with equal earnestness and eloquently urged their listeners to put on the whole armor of God and do battle for righteousness and the Confederacy. In Richmond, Rabbi Michelbacher advised his flock to heed the words of the prophet Nehemiah: "Fight for your brethren, your sons, and your daughters, your wives and your houses." From the pulpit of St. Paul's nearby, the Reverend Charles Minnegerode declared that the hand of Providence was evident in all the events that had befallen the Confederacy. The irrepressible Thomas Smyth blended martial fervor and religious zeal to implore his parishioners: "Let all the people everywhere old and young, bond and free, *take up the war-cry* and say each to his neighbor 'Gather ye together and come against them, and rise to battle.'" The eloquent Benjamin M. Palmer roamed throughout the land urging eager audiences to stand firm in the faith and in the fight for independence; for, as he put it, "every blow struck by us is in defense of His supremacy." After listening to one of Palmer's exhortations, Mary Boykin Chesnut wrote in her diary:

Bishop John McGill of Richmond, Virginia

"What a sermon! The preacher stirred my blood. . . . A red hot glow of patriotism spread through me."

Pulpit pleas for support of the Confederate cause were ably seconded by pastoral letters and the church press. A total of fifty-five religious papers were published in the Confederacy at one time or another and their influence was tremendous. The editor of the Nashville *Christian Advocate* boasted in 1862 that religious periodicals had done more than secular papers "to shape the course and quicken the patriotism of the Southern Confederacy," and three years later the *Christian Observer* commended the church papers for the "remarkable unanimity" with which they had sustained the Southern cause.

Despite the best efforts of ministers, church periodicals and faithful laymen, both public morale and religious zeal suffered a marked decline in the last two years of the war. The spiritual retrogression was due to several influences. Prominent among these was the increasing impact of Federal invasion. Approach of the Federal armies disrupted church services and caused congregations to dwindle. "The ways of Zion languish and mourn," the Synod of Mississippi reported in the fall of 1863. "Pastors are parted from their flocks, God's worship interrupted or forbidden, while from many churches God's people are exiled sheep, scattered without their shepherds, the remnants left behind either worshipping in secret, or listening in their sanctuaries to strangers whose voices they do not know & whom they cannot follow." At Vicksburg, Fredericksburg, Atlanta and elsewhere churches were damaged by shells or destroyed by fire. In its minutes for 1864 the Dover Baptist Association of Virginia stated: "The commodious edifice of one of our largest churches is now a heap of ruins. Another building pierced by the cannon balls of our invaders shows ghastly rents . . . seven of our churches are within the enemy's line . . . their members refugees." In a few instances congregations were subjected to Federal fire in the midst of their worship. On June 23, 1863, Father Lawrence W. O'Bannon of Vicksburg, Mississippi, wrote in his diary: "Mr. Donovan's arm shot off this morning in front of the church by a Parrott shell from the Point. When I was about to go on the altar another shell passed through the church [but] no one hurt."

In July, 1864, General Robert E. Lee wrote his wife: "The shells have scattered the poor inhabitants in Petersburg so that many churches are closed, indeed they have been visited by the enemy's shells. . . . Mr. Platt, pastor of the principal E[piscopal] church . . . held service again today under the trees near my camp. We had quite a large congregation. . . . During the service I constantly heard the shells crashing among the houses in Petersburg."

Some ministers abandoned their flocks rather than submit to Federal control. Others experienced misfortunes which severely curtailed their spiritual activities. A Georgia woman noted in her journal during Sherman's invasion: "No church, our preacher's horse stolen by the Yankees."

Mrs. Susan P. Mills of Louisiana wrote her daughter in September, 1864: "Our preacher was taken prisoner above Clinton and was robbed of his fine mare, his buggy and clothes and even his ordination papers. There was a contribution made up yesterday for him and I hope he will soon be able to buy another horse."

Both Confederates and Federals converted churches into hospitals. Union soldiers occasionally were billeted in houses of worship; in some instances they mutilated furnishings, used benches for firewood and did other damage to the premises. The invaders took over the conduct of services in some churches. But usually they permitted the regular minister to continue preaching provided no "disloyal" sentiments were

Protestant Episcopal Theological Seminary, Alexandria, Virginia

Bishop Patrick Niesen Lynch of South Carolina

Reverend Maxmilian J. Michelbacher, rabbi of Beth Ahabah Congregation in Richmond, Virginia

injected into sermons or prayers. Worshipers, too, were expected to take cognizance of the new order. Five Vicksburg ladies who stalked out of an Episcopal church on Christmas Day, 1863, when the "loyal" minister prayed for the President of the United States were banished from the city and sent beyond the Union lines.

During 1863–1865 in both invaded and uninvaded areas the growing pinch of war took its toll of religious activities. Synods, conferences and other church gatherings met irregularly, if at all. Many church papers had to suspend publication. Numerous ministers had to seek other employment because their pay would not support their families. Clergymen vacating their positions for any reason were difficult to replace, for the Confederacy, while not subjecting ordained ministers to conscription,

THE COUNTERSIGN.

Brethren of the Southern Army,—Ye who have exchanged the quiet delights of home, the society of mother, sister, wife, the pleasant face of nature lit up with the sweet smiles of early spring, for the stormy music of the battle-field, the deep-mouthed cannon's heavy roar and the musket's sharp flash, ye who have flung freedom's banner to the winds, and appealed to the God of battles for strength and success, ye whose hearts, animated by an undying love of liberty, would willingly pour out their last and most precious drops to secure freedom and independence for your country, I address you this day.

I address you, the subjects of so many prayers—prayers offered in the holy sanctuary of the crowded city, where the church-going bells, summoning the worshippers, ring out sweetly on the balmy Sabbath's air, and the pealing organ's notes are heard; prayers offered in quiet little country churches, half hidden by the dense foliage of the encircling grove; prayers offered around the family altar, where the strong voice of the father grows tremulous as he prays for his absent sons; prayers offered in the retirement of the closet,

1

in the shady grove, in the solemn silence of the night, when God's ear alone could hear: I come this day to ask if, while arming yourselves for the defence of your country, you have also put on the armor of God? If, while you are careful to know the countersign of your camp, you have also learned that countersign which alone can procure you an entrance into the great camp above?

You are safe within the lines of your camp; you are surrounded by thousands of brave hearts willing to bleed in your defence; you are, as it were, in a city of refuge, from which no enemy will be able to drag you; and while thus shielded from your enemies, let me ask you if "the everlasting arms" are around you, to keep you from that worst of foes—sin?

You have identified yourself with the Southern cause; your cheeks flush with joy and pride as you read of Southern victories, as you hear the names of the gallant leaders of the South; have you made the cause of Christ your cause? and does your heart thrill at Zion's success, and with love for its great Captain?

Two armies are in the field; they speak the same language, frequently they wear the same uniform and the same badge. What, then, is to designate them? It is the COUNTERSIGN, breathed in a whisper only, by the officer, as he places the sentinel on his lonely post.

And thus, in a spiritual sense, two armies are in the field; on the one side the dark legions of sin and Satan, on the other, the army of the Lord of Hosts. To outward appearance they may be the same, but the

---

made no provision for exempting theological candidates. The result was a sharp decline in the number of persons seeking ordination. In 1858 new preachers admitted to the Georgia Methodist Conference totaled 27; in 1861 the number was 10; in 1862, 6; and in 1864, only 3.

Decline of religious interest manifested itself in a falling off of church membership and attendance. "How is it that not more than one-thirtieth part of the entire population are attendant upon any form of Christian worship on the Sabbath day?" wrote a Mobile editor in 1864. The Palmyra Baptist Church in Georgia, a large and active congregation in 1860, shrank during the conflict until in 1864 it had only eleven white members. Total white membership of Southern Methodist churches declined from 355,458 (reported by thirteen conferences) in 1861 to 251,849 (twelve conferences) in 1863 and to 191,240 (ten conferences) in 1864.

Prayer meetings and Sunday schools languished and the great wave of revivalism which swept over Confederate camps during the last two winters of the war had no counterpart on the home front. Church

great Captain, Jesus, has breathed His Countersign into the ears of His soldiers, and they have an inward witness known only to themselves that they are His.

Confederate soldier, have you this Countersign? Were you outside the lines of your camp, and had not the word which alone could secure your entrance, how would your heart sink with dismay and dread when challenged by the sentinel! And let me tell you, if you have not believed in Christ, that you are outside of the lines, that you have not the Countersign, and that you are exposed to the wrath of a sin-hating God.

But though this be your situation, yet you need not despair. You may yet learn the countersign from our great Captain, who says, "Him that cometh unto me I will in no wise cast out;" whose bowels yearn with tender compassion over the unhappy wanderer in the ways of sin, and who saves to the uttermost those that come unto God through Him, seeing He ever liveth to make intercession for them.

Let "the precious blood of Christ" be your countersign on earth, and your watchword at the gates of death, that the greeting of "All's well" may be yours, that you may be victor in a contest whose triumph shall never end.

To you who have this countersign, let me add a word of exhortation. When the powers of Satan and sin assault you to drive you from your duty, endure hardship like a good soldier, stand firm on your post until your Captain shall come to relieve you; for so strong and so wise is He, that so long as you stand firm, trust-

ing in Him, no force that the enemy shall be able to bring against you shall prevail over you.

You are, perhaps, surrounded by circumstances unfriendly to your growth in grace; but as if to show that nothing is too hard for the Lord, some of the brightest examples of the power of Divine grace have been raised up on the battle-field. The lives of Vicars, of Havelock, and of Gardiner, tell you of the high attainments in the Divine life to which a Christian soldier may arrive; and from Donelson's bloody sod, the voice of Dabney Carr Harrison calls you to follow to a death of glory and an immortal crown.

SOLDIERS of Christ, arise!
  And put your armor on,
Strong in the strength which God supplies,
  Through his eternal Son:
Strong in the Lord of hosts,
  And in his mighty power,
Who in the strength of Jesus trusts
  Is more than conqueror.

Stand, then, in his great might,
  With all his strength endued;
But take, to arm you for the fight,
  The panoply of God:
That having all things done,
  And all your conflicts past,
Ye may o'ercome through Christ alone,
  And stand entire at last.

Soldiers' Tract Society, Virginia Conference, M. E. Church, South.

---

periodicals frequently called attention to the contrast between the spiritual zeal of the soldiers and the indifference of the folks at home. In the fall of 1864 the editor of the Augusta, Georgia, *Baptist Banner* advised ministers to visit the camps so that they might "catch the inspiration of the army in religious things, and carry back to their cold flocks at home some of the fire." But such appeals were of little avail. Save for occasional manifestations of religious fervor in isolated areas, revivalism became virtually nonexistent among Confederate civilians as the shadow of defeat settled over the South.

As religion declined, the forces of evil increased. Letters, diaries, newspapers and other sources reveal a shocking spread of disorder, crime and immorality during the last two years of the conflict. Conditions were especially bad in the cities and in outlying areas frequented by deserters, guerillas and "independent scouts." In November, 1863, a citizen of Columbia County, Arkansas, wrote his congressman: "Nearly all of the Arkansas soldiers . . . from north of the Arkansas River have deserted & most of them turned highwaymen, making a

Grace Episcopal Church, Petersburg, Virginia

perfect reign of terror on that side of the river. They rob Union men and strangers in the daytime and Secessionists at night."

Southerners living near regions held by the Federals carried on a lively trade with the Yankees. Much of the cotton exchanged in this commerce was stolen by those who sold it. Throughout the Confederacy extortioners took advantage of inflation and scarcity to hoard essentials and capitalize on the misfortunes of the country and its people. After a trip through the deep South early in 1864 a Catholic chaplain of Lee's army wrote in his diary: "I found the stay-at-homes having but one great object in view, that is the making of money. Never had I seen such avariciousness as that displayed throughout my travels, but more particularly in Georgia. Money and their negroes appeared to be their gods."

In some of the cities and towns, assault and robbery became so common that respectable people were reluctant to leave their residences. In April, 1864, the Fulton County grand jury reported that "idle and vicious boys [are] roaming the streets of Atlanta at night, frequenting many places of vice, corrupting and being corrupted." In December, 1864, Congressman Warren Akin wrote his wife from Richmond that Congress had discontinued night sessions partly because of "the danger of assassination in the streets."

Drunkenness, brawling and gambling flourished in the cities. After a big party at Tyler, Texas, in April, 1865, Kate Stone wrote in her journal that "all the men present but two were said to be drunk," and that several were so intoxicated they could not escort the girls home. Florence Fleming Corley in *Confederate City, Augusta, Georgia, 1860–1865* thus describes conditions in that town early in 1865: "Shootings, stabbings, fights and fires occurred almost daily . . . stealing was the order of the day . . . the demoralized and desperate elements even sacked the churches. The communion table, chairs and cushions were taken from the Presbyterian Church and communion service and aisle carpets stolen from St. Paul's. Gambling, drinking and vice increased to such proportions that they became the subjects of town-wide comment."

Prostitution and illegitimacy increased in both town and country and decent people were shocked and disturbed by the general deterioration of morals. In May, 1863, a soldier in camp near Spring Hill, Tennessee, wrote his wife: "This is a most beautiful region of country here but I am sorry I cannot say much for the morals of it from the way I hear the boys speaking of going out to see the women. I fear the standard of virtue is not very high." A Mississippi lady in June, 1864, wrote her husband of the "shameful acts" committed by women of her community and added: "I am not astonished to hear of Gen. Sherman saying he could buy the chastity of any Southern woman for a few pounds of coffee . . . [though] there are still many virtuous women in the Confederacy."

EMBATTLED
CONFEDERATES

J. D. B. DeBow, a leading Southern journalist, was so depressed after a trip from Mississippi to Richmond and back in January, 1865, that he wrote to a friend: "You can have little idea of things in the heart of the Confederacy. Everything has been swept by a whirlwind. No public and little private virtue escaped the shipwreck."

This was an extreme statement. But there can be no doubt that immorality increased enormously in the latter part of the war. This does not mean that evil reigned supreme and unchallenged. At home and in the army many people remained firm in religion and staunch in character, and some were refined and strengthened by sorrow and suffering, and by triumphing over the evil that surrounded them.

XI. *Journalism and Literature*

WAR! WAR!! WAR!!!

With this headline the Atlanta *Daily Intelligencer* of April 13, 1861, jubilantly announced to its readers the initiation of hostilities at Fort Sumter. From Virginia to Texas similar notices adorned the pages of the public press. The tone of the accompanying editorials was with very few exceptions both exuberant and optimistic. The *Intelligencer* editor, John H. Steele, expressed the sentiments of most Southern journalists when he wrote:

> The aggressive policy of the Black Republican Party of the North has culminated in war. . . . The first gun has been fired in the war of Southern independence. . . . In the whole history of the world no people has entered into a conflict with higher spirits and brighter hopes than the people of this Government. We are determined not only to achieve our independence at whatever cost but we will teach these Northern Goths and Vandals a lesson before this war is over which they will never forget. . . . We will show them how superior is the valor of free men fighting on their own soil, for their altars and firesides, their wives, their children, and their dearest rights, to the hireling skill of treacherous and perfidious invaders.

The hurrahing of Southern editors for war is not difficult to explain. For years many of them had been denouncing Northerners as a godless, grasping, meddlesome people whose aim was to reshape the national government to their own selfish ends, emancipate the slaves and destroy the South's way of life. Fire-eating journalists had played a leading role in initiating secession. They welcomed war as a swift and sure means of bringing the upper South into the Confederacy, squelching Southern Unionists and molding the land of Dixie into a strong nation. While the conflict lasted news would be exciting and journalism would thrive.

Events of the war's first months seemed to confirm this rosy outlook. Eagerness for information built up subscription lists, military activities provided news, and the establishment of war industries stepped up the volume of advertising. Big Bethel on June 10, First Manassas on July 21 and Wilson's Creek on August 10, inspired a succession of thrilling reports and extravagant editorials headed by the exultant words "Glorious Victory." These successes were cited as convincing proof of the superiority of Southern valor and the certainty of Confederate triumph.

But things were far less auspicious than they seemed, both for the journalists and for the cause that they supported. Even while the initial flush of victory was at its peak, the newspapers were having their troubles, and difficulties were to increase with the passing of time.

One of the first wartime problems was the flood of martial fervor that almost cleaned out some journalistic establishments. The Macon, Georgia, *Telegraph* lost nine of its twenty employees before the end of April, 1861; and by March, 1862, this paper had contributed eighteen printers to the armed services. Shortly after the shooting started, James P. Hambleton, patriotic editor of the Atlanta *Southern Confederacy,* sold his paper and joined the army. Obadiah J. Wise, editor of the Richmond *Enquirer* and son of ex-Governor Henry A. Wise, became a Confederate captain; and John M. Daniel, brilliant but eccentric editor of the Richmond *Examiner,* also went to war.

Ironically, as the war continued, journalists became less eager to enter military service, and when the exemption act of April 21, 1862, failed to include editors, they raised a howl. When the law was revised on October 11, 1862, a provision was made for the exemption of "one editor and the necessary printers for each paper." On November 7, 1864, President Davis asked Congress to conscript all able-bodied men of military age, but his proposal aroused such tremendous opposition, especially from the newspapers, that it never became a law.

Statutory exemption and reduction of the number of papers eased the personnel situation after the first year of conflict, but shortage of equipment and supplies became an increasingly difficult problem. Presses and type were not manufactured in the Confederacy. In 1864 the Richmond *Dispatch* imported "a new suit of type" from England, but other newspapers had to get along with what they had on hand or what they could obtain from journals forced out of business by the fortunes of war. In some instances type became so worn that the print was indistinct; and fonts were so depleted that readers had to accustom themselves to occasional blank spaces. Southern firms began to produce printer's ink early in the war, and some users praised its quality. But ink became paler, scarcer and dearer with the passing of time, and at least one paper, the Memphis *Appeal,* had to resort to shoe polish to blacken the type.

The most critical problem of all was scarcity of newsprint. In 1860 the South had only about one-twentieth of the nation's paper mills, and their output fell far short of meeting the region's peacetime needs. The unusual demands created by war led to intense competition for available supplies. A New Orleans dealer reported in June, 1861, that Georgia paper manufacturers had taken orders for all the paper they could furnish for the next two years. In January, 1862, the Richmond

Enquirer complained that "thousands upon thousands of dollars invested in printing materials are now lying idle . . . for want of paper." But the situation worsened a short time later when the Federals took Nashville and deprived the Confederacy of one of its principal sources of newsprint. Already some papers had been compelled to reduce their dimensions, cut the number of pages and use smaller type. Others had shifted from a daily basis to biweekly or weekly issues. Despite resorting to these and various other expedients, many journals were unable to keep going. On May 31, 1862, a Virginia paper gave the following notice of its demise: "The proprietor has been reluctantly compelled to come to this decision in consequence of the lack of paper, ink, editors and printers and all other material necessary to issue the paper. He furthermore begs to state that in consequence of the editor, the compositors and the printers having gone to war, the devil only is left in the office."

Such notices became increasingly frequent in 1863 and 1864, especially among newspapers of invaded areas and the small-town weeklies. Before the end of 1864 more than half of Georgia's wartime newspapers had ceased publication and Mississippi's journals had shrunk from a prewar total of seventy-three to eight—one daily (the Meridian *Clarion*), one triweekly and six weeklies.

Papers that survived the war's first year found it increasingly hard to obtain newsprint. In April, 1863, a shipment of English newsprint reached Charleston through the blockade, much to the joy of the Savannah *Morning News* and the other papers that shared the windfall. But this fortunate event was more than offset by the burning a short time later of the Bath Paper Mills located in South Carolina. On April 15, 1863, the Montgomery *Advertiser* advised its readers to collect "rag bags" of cloth scraps, rope, thread and cotton and to sell the contents to paper manufacturers.

Wrapping paper and wallpaper were occasionally used for newsprint. Probably the best-known of the wallpaper issues was the one-page Vicksburg *Citizen* of July 2–4, 1863, which was ready for printing when the city surrendered. The Federals knocked out the bottom lines of the last column, inserted a paragraph announcing the Union occupation and ran off a small edition, copies of which Billy Yanks sent to their homefolk as souvenirs.

The odd appearance of papers issued during the latter years of the war was the source of considerable comment. The *Confederate States Almanac* for 1863 stated: "Our newspapers have felt the martial influence. They are of all types and colors. They are short enough for a pocket handkerchief one day and big enough for a table cloth another. They assume as many hues as Niagara in the sunshine and are by turns, blue, yellow, green, red, purple, gray and common brown."

Inevitably, advertising and subscription rates soared. On December 4, 1863, editor Dickinson of the Shreveport *News* informed his patrons: "Our charge for advertising is only double the old rate while all the materials we use are . . . not less than a thousand percent of former prices. We paid last week $2,500 for printing paper which in old times we would not have given $75 for. . . . A keg of ink which formerly cost $25 cannot be had for less than $150." Subscription rates of the *News* rose from $8 a year for the daily at the outbreak of the war to $20 a year for the semiweekly in November, 1863, and to $50 a year for the weekly in August, 1864. On September 8, 1863, Dickinson notified his readers: "The price of single copies of this paper is fifty cents and no grumbling." But his customers must have complained, for he occasionally published statements justifying his rates. "There is nothing made," he wrote on December 4, 1864, "even at our present extortionate rates." Apparently Dickinson was telling the truth and he probably could not have kept his paper alive throughout the war had he not received a considerable amount of business from civil and military authorities in the form of public notices and job printing.

During the war monthly subscription rates of the Atlanta *Daily Intelligencer* rose from fifty cents to five dollars, and rates shot up everywhere except in Richmond, and Columbia, South Carolina. In 1863 when Shreveport papers were selling at twenty cents a copy, the price of Richmond dailies was only ten cents. In July, 1864, subscription to the Columbia *South Carolinian* was only thirty dollars, though the editor stated that "the publication of a paper barely keeps soul and body together."

The high rates prescribed by the publishers were sometimes further inflated by the greed and chicanery of newsboys, who would double the price or tear papers in half and charge the full price for each piece.

Newspapers in invaded areas either ceased publication or, like the Louisville *Daily Courier*, the Memphis *Daily Argus*, and the *Bee*, the *Delta* and the *Crescent* of New Orleans, were suppressed by the occupying forces. Still others shifted their allegiance, made other adjustments as required and continued operations under the new regime. When invasion was in the nature of a raid, newspapers usually closed shop only temporarily. On the approach of Sherman's forces to Milledgeville, Georgia, the press and type of the *Southern Union* were taken to a nearby forest and covered with pine straw. After the Federals moved on, the paper came out of hiding and resumed operations. The *Southern Recorder* of the same city closed its doors a few days before the Yankees came; it escaped destruction but had to remain inactive for more than a month owing to circumstances stated on December 20, 1864: "The Yankee visitation has prevented publication of this paper for several weeks. We resume publication today under unusual embarrassments, arising from the absence of the junior editor who shouldered his gun on the advance of the enemy and is still in the militia . . . and also of the Yankee impressment of our pressmen. In addition to this we have scarcely any mail facilities."

Frank Vizetelly, whose drawings appeared in the press.

Capen's Sunday Evening Bulletin.

BY TELEGRAPH.

Sunday, April 14, 1861

Fort Sumpter Surrendered!

MAJ. ANDERSON
A PRISONER OF WAR

&c.　　&c.　　&c.

In order that our citizens may have the exciting news now passing to every city in our country, we have been at the expense to keep open the Telegraph Office to-day (Sunday) and take the following Telegrams, and issue them in a printed form as a "Sunday Evening Bulletin," hoping that the readers of it will acknowledge the enterprize by handing over enough of the 'filty lucre' to pay us for the expense.

We give the different dispatches as we received them, and do not hold ourselves accountable for the accuracy of any of them.

FIRST DISPATCH.

Charleston, April 13th.

Two of Anderson's Magazines have exploded, it is thought the magazines which have exploded are small ones. The cupalos, sfeeples, and every available place are packed with people. Three ships are now in the offing too late to come over the bar, as the tide is now ebbing. The ships are in offing quietly at anchor, and have not fired a gun. Anderson's barracks are in a sheet of flames. Shells from Cummings Point and Fort Moultre are bursting in and over Fort Sumter in quick succession. The flag is still waving over the Fort. Anderson's forces seem to be occupied in extinguishing the fire. Every shot seems to tell. The striking of Anderson's flag is anxiously looked for.

SECOND DISPATCH.

Montgomery, April 13th.

Gen'l Beauregard telegraphed to the Sec. of War, of the confederate states as follows :—

There was heavy firing all day Friday, four guns dismounted, four steamers are off the bar, sea rough.

The following dispatch has just been received, but believed to be false.

Fort Sumter has been surrendered, and the confederate flag now waves over its walls.

None of the government or confederate troops were injured.

THIRD DISPATCH.

N. Y., April 13th.

A special dispatch from Montgomery to the Herald says :

Sec. Walker also said in his speech last night, " let them try the southern confederacy, and test the strength of southern resources, and the confederate flag might eventually wave over Fanuiel Hall.

FOURTH DISPATCH.

Fort Sumpter has been unconditionally surrendered.

Ex Senator Chestnut, Ex Gov. Manning, and W. P. Miles, have just landed and marched to Gov. Pickins residence followed by a dense crowd, with great joy. It is reported that ten men of Fort Sumpter are killed, and that the Federal Flag was shot away by the Palmetto Guards at Morris Island.

In all two thousand shots have been fired.

Maj. Anderson and his men were conveyed to Morris Island

The bells are ringing merry peals and the people are engaged in every demonstration of joy.

It is estimated that there are 9000 men under arms on the Islands and in the neighborhood.

LATER.

We have seen W. P. Miles, who has just returned from Fort S., and assures me that NO one was killed at the Fort. This is reliable and puts at rest all previous reports about Sumpter.

Maj. Anderson has reached the city and is the guest of General Beauregard. Our people sympathize with Maj. Anderson, but ABHOR those who were in the steamers off our bar, and in sight of our people, and did not even ATTEMPT to reinforce him.

The Fairfield Regiment, one thousand strong, has just passed the Courier office on their way to Morris Island.

Judge Magruth, who has just returned, reports that the wood work and officers quarters are all burned.

The Fort will be taken possession of to-night by the confederate troops.

Charleston, April 13th.
Another Dispatch says :

Maj. Anderson hauled down the stars and stripes and hoisted the white flag, it was answered from the city and a boat left immediately for the Fort.

The Federal Flag was again hoisted over Fort Sumter, when Porcher Miles with a white flag went to the Fort, and in a few minutes the federal flag was again hauled down by Maj. Anderson and a white one unfurled.

Gen'l Beauregard with two aids have left for Fort Sumter.

LATEST.

Montgomery, 13th.

Lieut Reed of the Federal Navy has been taken prisoner of war, and his dispatches from Lieut. Slimmers to the Government at Washington, have been seized.

Fort Pickens was reinforced last night.

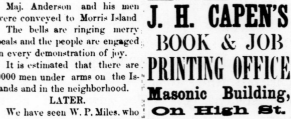

Some papers fled before the invaders to new homes in the interior and a few had to change residence more than once. The most renowned of the refugees was the Memphis *Appeal*. On June 6, 1862, the very day that Memphis fell, the *Appeal*'s editors, John R. McClanahan and Benjamin F. Dill, loaded their staff and equipment on a boxcar and headed south. Three days later they resumed publication at Grenada, Mississippi. But Grant's push into north Mississippi that autumn forced the *Appeal* on November 29 to flee to Jackson, where it remained until the persistent Grant, this time approaching from the southwest, again drove it into exile. The escape from the Mississippi capital on May 14 was too close for comfort. In the words of Andy Harmon, the *Appeal*'s pressman: "We got all packed up and ready to go. . . . We crossed Pearl River on a flat with our mules and had just made the trip when the Bluecoats reached the other bank. They had nothing to cross on so they took it out in cussing us and we gave 'em back as good as they sent. . . . We mounted our mules and rode to Brandon, Miss. where all our truck had been carried."

The *Appeal* moved eastward; stopped briefly at Meridian, where its one-cylinder, steam-driven press rolled out one-sheet extras for a week; and then proceeded to Atlanta. There it remained for a little more than a year—June 6, 1863, to July 20, 1864. Its main clientele during this period, as earlier, was the Army of Tennessee, in whose ranks were to be found many residents of the Memphis area. In Atlanta the *Appeal* had the good fortune to obtain the services of two men formerly associated with the Chattanooga *Rebel* and destined to achieve distinction in the world of journalism: Albert Roberts and Henry Watterson.

When Sherman's approach to Atlanta in July, 1864, brought to an end its happy residence in that city, the *Appeal* moved to Montgomery, where it continued in operation from September, 1864, until April, 1865. It then made another, final move to Columbus, Georgia. There General James H. Wilson's blue cavalrymen on April 16 destroyed the paper's remaining equipment and scattered the type in the streets. One important item escaped the raiders and survived the three years of exile. This was the "moving *Appeal*'s" worn and battered press, which had been hidden in Macon. In November, 1865, the *Appeal* went home to Memphis and resumed a career that has continued on down to the present.

Refugee newspapers and those unmolested by invasion both had considerable difficulty in obtaining ample and reliable news. Telegraphic service was poor and expensive. Neither Confederate nor state governments had any organization for the preparation and dissemination of press releases. The Confederate President refused to countenance any suggestion of newspaper suppression, even in instances where he and his administration were subjected to the severest criticism. But, as previously noted, he failed to appreciate the importance of keeping the people informed and he did little to assist newspapers in their work. The Confederate Congress excluded reporters from legislative halls when matters of any importance were under discussion. The War Department rarely attempted to impose censorship beyond prohibiting revelation of the strength, disposition or projected movements of military forces. But some of the army commanders followed a much more restrictive course. General Bragg became annoyed with a correspondent who wrote critically of him in June, 1862, and for a while barred reporters from his headquarters. His action was by no means unique.

In some instances editors toured cities and camps to gather news for their papers. More often reporting was done by special correspondents, most of whom represented several papers. Correspondents signed their dispatches with such pen names as "Hermes," "Zeta," "La Palma," "Sallust," "O.K.," and "Adsum." Some of these cannot be identified. Among the better-known and more talented correspondents were Gustave Meyer and W. G. Shepperson ("Bohemian") of the Richmond *Dispatch;* P. W. Alexander of the Savannah *Republican,* whose account of Gettysburg is something of a classic; Samuel C. Reid, Jr., who represented the New Orleans *Picayune* and the Memphis *Appeal* as "Sparta," the Mobile *Advertiser* as "Ora," and the Atlanta *Intelligencer* as "291"; and Felix G. de Fontaine, who was "Personne" of the Charleston *Courier* and who in the latter part of the war edited the *Carolinian* of Columbia. Fontaine, whose wartime notes and dispatches were compiled and published in 1864 in a book entitled *Marginalia,* was probably the most talented of all the Confederacy's war reporters, and his sketches of Lee, Jackson and other Confederate commanders were pithy and vivid.

Confederate correspondents were usually generous in their comments about the Southern rank and file. A striking exception was "Sallust's" report of Missionary Ridge to the Richmond *Dispatch* which began: "The Confederates have sustained today the most ignominious defeat of the whole war—a defeat for which there is little excuse or palliation. For the first time during our struggle for national independence our defeat is chargeable to the troops themselves and not to the blunders or incompetency of their leaders."

Some of the reporters were members of the fighting forces who collected and forwarded news as a side activity. The Charleston *Mercury* ran notices early in the conflict asking army officers and ship captains to forward "the news of the war at the earliest practicable moment" and promising that "important information when furnished to us exclusively will be liberally paid for." Editors also obtained and published private letters written by soldiers to their families, especially when these contained information about recent battles. Official dispatches and reports of commanding generals were usually passed on to the press, though frequently not until long after the events. For the smaller papers the richest and most frequently used news sources were the columns of other journals, especially those issuing from Richmond, Charleston and other advantageously situated cities. Northern papers, swapped on the picket line or run through the blockade, were quoted whenever they could be obtained, with or without comment. Editors usually made grateful acknowledgment of any papers brought to their offices by visitors, and they or their representatives often met incoming trains and boats to see what news they could glean from passengers and crews.

Early in the war Southern journalists realized the need of an organization for the collection and dissemination of news. Pioneer agencies were formed in Augusta, Georgia, and Richmond, Virginia, before the close of 1862 but their activities were too restricted to provide the desired services. After much preliminary discussion, Southern editors in February, 1863, launched the Press Association of the Confederate States of America. Dr. R. W. Gibbes of the Columbia *South Carolinian* was president; J. S. Thrasher was superintendent; and directors were Joseph Clisby of the Macon *Telegraph*, G. W. Adair of the Atlanta *Southern Confederacy*, W. G. Clark of the Mobile *Advertiser and Register*, James Gardner of the Augusta *Constitutionalist* and J. R. Sneed of the Savannah *Republican*.

Soon after his appointment, Superintendent Thrasher called on Beauregard, Bragg, Pemberton and Johnston, explained the objectives of his organization, and obtained from them assurances that the Association's correspondents would be received and given early access to intelligence compatible with the public interest. Thrasher pledged to the generals the Association's cooperation in preventing publication of information that might be helpful to the Federals.

Thrasher made arrangements for transmission of the Association's dispatches over the lines of the military telegraph, the Southern Telegraph Company and the South-Western Telegraph Company at half the regular rates. Papers to whom telegraph facilities were not available were served by couriers. Each Association member received a weekly news report for which the charge was twelve dollars if the length was not more than 3,500 words.

The Association sent correspondents to army headquarters and other key localities and gave them detailed instructions concerning their duties. They were told to be alert and aggressive in seeking information about military events, to weed out rumors, adhere to factual reporting, work closely with military authorities, avoid reference to troop movements, and keep the Press Association fully informed concerning censorship. The Association in 1863 paid its correspondents $25–$30 a week plus modest allowances for board and transportation, and permitted them to supplement their salaries by selling special reports and articles to individual newspapers.

The Press Association encountered many difficulties in its efforts to maintain the flow of news. In May, 1863, Thrasher complained to his superiors that the Secretary of War, the Postmaster General and military commanders all "claim the right to exercise censorship over the press reports and to dictate what shall and what shall not be transmitted by telegraph." Censorship was not uniformly interpreted and applied, he added, with the result that some officials had suppressed dispatches on the ground that they were "sensational" and others "without assigning any reason." In the autumn of 1863 both General Bragg and General Longstreet had to be appeased by changing the correspondents assigned to their headquarters. About the same time the South-Western Telegraph Company began stealing the news transmitted over its wires by the Press Association and selling it at reduced rates. Thrasher had to copyright the Association's dispatches to stop this baneful practice.

Despite all its difficulties, the Press Association closed the year 1863 in reasonably good condition. By that time all forty-three of the Confederacy's daily newspapers were subscribers to its services. Among its corps of correspondents were Smoot, who covered General Lee's headquarters; Woodson, who was assigned to the headquarters of the Army of Tennessee; Sanderson, who was stationed with Hardee; and Wagner, who had a special assignment in south Mississippi. The years 1864 and 1865 brought new and formidable problems growing out of inflation, extension of Federal occupation, and disruption of communication. But the Press Association maintained its organization and services until the Southern armies were defeated. Despite its late establishment and limited resources it was a valuable asset to Confederate journalism.

The news columns of Southern papers were devoted largely to military affairs, political activities, legislation and local events. Editorials frequently dealt with such matters as strategy, high command and state-Confederate relations. Jefferson Davis and his administration were the subjects of much editorial comment. During the early months of the war editors heaped praise on the President. Typical of the glowing tributes of this period was the Montgomery *Mail*'s editorial of March 8, 1861, which stated: "The President of the Southern Confederacy is a gentleman, a scholar, a soldier and a statesman. He has attained eminence in every department of life to which he has turned his attention and his name is the very synonym of purity and honor. Like the Chevalier Bayard, he is without fear and without reproach."

Almost the only early dissenters were the Robert Barnwell Rhetts, Junior and Senior, of the Charleston *Mercury*. This paper, one of the Confederacy's leading journals, was edited by the son, but the elder Rhett wrote many of the editorials. Rhett, Senior, aptly called "the Father of Secession," aspired to the Confederate Presidency, and his failure to obtain the office doubtless prejudiced him against Davis. In private letters to his son he characterized the President as "a dishonest man," "a liar" and "a great Rascal." As early as June, 1861, the *Mercury* began an indirect attack on the Chief Executive by urging a more aggressive conduct of the war, and after First Manassas it ran a series of editorials denouncing Davis for failure to follow up the Southern victory. The opposition thus begun increased with the passing of time and continued throughout the conflict. The *Mercury* accused the President of favoring reconstruction of the old Union, and when late in the war Davis advocated enlistment of Negroes, Rhett, Senior, stated that the President had never really believed in slavery.

There was a general decline of journalistic enthusiasm for Davis as the war and Confederate reverses continued, and a few newspapers came out openly against the administration. On April 4, 1862, the New Orleans *Daily True Delta*, edited by John Maginnis, stated: "Richmond has become in official depravity more loathsome than Washington was during the abominable career of the infamous Buchanan." Opposition to Davis was also voiced by three of the five daily papers published in Richmond—the *Examiner*, the *Whig* and the *Dispatch*. At first directing their fire largely at the government's defensive policy, John M. Daniel and Edward A. Pollard of the *Examiner* early in 1862 launched an aggressive attack on Davis which was to continue throughout the conflict and to make their paper the most vehement and powerful antiadministration journal in the entire South.

Davis' inaugural address of February 22, 1862, drew from Daniel the comment: "It throws no light on the real condition of the country. . . . It might, in fact, have been omitted from the ceremony, had not custom required that the President should say something on such an occasion." In subsequent editorials Daniel accused Davis of appointing nonentities to his cabinet so that he could control them and of demonstrating "puerile partiality" in promoting "little lieutenants and colonels" to major generals. "It would almost seem that the Government was afraid of genius and will," he added. Daniel attributed the loss of Vicksburg to Davis' egotism, blindness and obstinacy. "He prides himself in never changing his mind," Daniel wrote on August 5, 1863. ". . . [He] has alienated the hearts of the people by his stubborn follies, and the injustice he has heaped upon some whom they regarded as their ablest generals and truest friends. The people do not share in his chronic hallucination that he is a great military genius." The defeats at Chattanooga in November, 1863, drew from Daniel the statement: "Mr. Davis alone is responsible . . . [because it is his] pitiful perversity which has retained Bragg in command."

The *Examiner*'s sentiments were echoed by the Richmond *Whig*, which, like other journals identified with the defunct party of Henry Clay, bore a deep resentment against Democratic "ultras," whom they accused of recklessly leading the South into secession and war. The *Whig* charged Davis and his administration with favoring their own clique in making appointments, pushing anti-secessionists into the background, ignoring state rights and seeking to establish a dictatorship.

Robert Barnwell Rhett, Jr., editor of Charleston Mercury

Robert Ridgway of Virginia, who edited the Richmond Whig *until the outbreak of the war*

In February, 1862, the *Whig* editor stated: "If we are to live under a despotism . . . we would prefer a brute like Lincoln to a gentleman like Davis."

Another powerful and persistent opponent of the President was W. W. Holden, editor of the *North Carolina Standard,* published at Raleigh. Holden fought conscription, impressment, suspension of the writ of habeas corpus and other administration measures. "A military despotism is making rapid strides," he wrote in May, 1863; "North Carolina . . . will not submit to . . . investing Mr. Davis with dictatorial powers." Shortly afterward he became a leading advocate of peace. When General Henry L. Benning's troops passed through Raleigh in September, 1863, they raided the *Standard* office and scattered the type in the street.

The attitude of the Montgomery *Advertiser* toward the Davis administration is typical of that of many other papers as the Confederacy's fortunes deteriorated. Its initial warm and consistent support of the President and his policies declined markedly in 1862, and in 1863 changed to open criticism. It accused him of mistreating Beauregard and Joseph E. Johnston, neglecting the West, showing favoritism to incompetent leaders, and advocating measures calculated to undermine state prerogative and build up a centralized despotism. An editorial of October 2, 1863, stated: "We can only look with wonder and admiration at the patriotism of a country which can endure such imposition without publicly remonstrating with him to whom they have entrusted the chief direction of affairs."

By no means all the Southern papers turned against the President. Among those that supported him and his administration to the end was the venerable Richmond *Enquirer,* probably the Confederacy's best newspaper. When Davis became Chief Executive in February, 1861, the *Enquirer* endorsed him as "a brave and honest man," of "long, faithful and distinguished service." It did not approve all that Davis did during the next four years, but it never questioned his integrity, impugned his motives or challenged his fitness for the Presidency. The *Enquirer* was widely regarded as the President's mouthpiece and this impression, which apparently had no foundation other than the paper's consistent loyalty to the administration, sometimes worked to Davis' disadvantage. Shortly after the defeats at Gettysburg and Vicksburg, the *Enquirer* came out with an editorial which stated: "The whole country is in a state of siege; it ought to be all one camp. . . . All laws ought to be silent except military laws. We regard all Judges, Courts State and Confederate, all Congresses and Legislatures as a nuisance save in so far as they help us to strengthen the hands of the Commander-in-Chief of the Confederacy." This editorial was reprinted throughout the South and cited as evidence of a dangerous trend toward Presidential despotism.

Other papers that consistently supported the President were the

Charleston *Courier,* a daily with an illustrious career dating back to 1803; and in the hinterland, the Washington, Arkansas, *Telegraph.* Aaron S. Willington was owner and editor of the *Courier* in the early part of the war, and after his death in February, 1862, Richard Yeadon and Thomas Y. Simons ran the paper and wrote most of the editorials. The *Courier* repeatedly defended the President against the *Mercury's* tirades, and it showed no waning of admiration after the South's military fortunes began to decline. During the last year of the war it apparently was the only paper in South Carolina that consistently supported the President. John R. Eakin, editor of the Washington, Arkansas, *Telegraph,* was an ex-Whig and before Fort Sumter an opponent of secession. Eakin conceded the fallibility of Davis' judgment, but from the beginning to the end of the conflict he defended the President as a high-minded, courageous and devoted leader, thoroughly deserving of the unqualified support of every patriotic Confederate.

Editorial comments about the cabinet and Congress pursued the same general pattern of initial support followed by declining enthusiasm. Benjamin was the most maligned of all the cabinet; but Mallory, Memminger and Seddon were subjected to much disparaging comment. As a group Congress inspired more editorial malediction than the cabinet. Typical of numerous blasts hurled at the lawmakers was that delivered in December, 1863, by the Montgomery *Mail:* "The history of Christendom does not present such an instance of timid, halting, doubting, narrow and time-serving legislation . . . as have been furnished by our successive Confederate Congresses." Now and then a paper lifted a voice in defense of the congressmen by calling attention to the complexity of their problems and pointing out the fact that they consistently gave the President the laws which he requested. But such comments were conspicuous for their rarity.

Editors had their say from time to time about the various generals. Opinion was divided as to the merits of most high-ranking leaders. Bragg received more criticism than any other full general, and Lee, despite some adverse comment early in the war and in the wake of Gettysburg, elicited the most praise. The Richmond *Whig* expressed a sentiment which few if any papers would have challenged when it stated of Lee on December 7, 1863: "It is well for the Confederacy, and especially for Virginia, that this straightforward soldier came to our side. We know not what we should have done without him."

The Yankees were another topic on which the journals like to dwell. Occasionally an editor would concede some virtue to the opposition, particularly to the Northern fighting men. The Florida *Sentinel,* for example, observed shortly after Fort Donelson: "It is time that the evanescent chivalry in the South which has boasted that we could whip the Yankees ten to one subsided. . . . We have had enough of the contempt of the power of the North." But such statements were exceptional. Far more representative was the editorial comment published in the New Orleans *Crescent* of April 25, 1861: "The Yankee mode of fighting is like that of the Chinese—plenty of noise and fuss, but no execution. . . . [They are] a people whose most bloodthirsty achievements consist of harpooning whales and eviscerating codfish."

The influence of Confederate newspapers is difficult to assess. Their shortcomings were numerous and flagrant. In the early days they created false hopes in the minds of the people by exaggerating Southern assets and disparaging the strength of the North. Subsequently they belittled Northern achievements and glossed over Southern failures. After the Federals captured Vicksburg, and Port Hudson, Louisiana, the editors of the *South Carolinian* told their readers that the victory cost the Union 100,000 men and then posed the question: "What good does the opening of the Mississippi do the Yankees?" The New Orleans *Bee* and *True Delta* never recognized Shiloh as a Confederate defeat, and some papers continued to treat Gettysburg as a great Southern victory three weeks after Lee retreated into Virginia. The *Arkansas Telegraph* went so far as to hail the fall of Richmond as a blessing to the South.

Fantastic rumors of all sorts were circulated by the press. Mrs. Howell Cobb became so disgusted with false reports in September, 1861, that she wrote her husband: "The newspapers . . . are loaned to the Devil to assist him in enticing unworthy souls from their allegiance to the Soul of Truth." A Mississippi lieutenant wrote his fiancée in September, 1863: "I place no reliance on newspaper reports and hardly ever read one. I have been deceived so often by them that I have lost confidence in our press."

Publication of news helpful to the Federals was another fault of which all too many journals were guilty. On January 19, 1865, General Lee wrote Congressman Miles in response to a request for transfer of troops from Richmond to Charleston: "Nor in my opinion would it be possible to conceal the movement from the enemy. If he did not learn it through spies and traitors, it would be published in the papers & thus reach him. . . . It was through the Savannah papers that he ascertained the movement of Bragg to Georgia, and was induced to precipitate the attack upon Wilmington." Far more damaging to the Southern cause than the revelation of military secrets was the editors' widespread denunciation of the Confederacy's generals and statesmen, for this ill-considered criticism engendered crippling strife and undermined the confidence of the people in their leaders.

On the other hand, the newspapers' tardiness and inaccuracy in reporting the news were due in many instances to circumstances beyond their control. Their lack of realism in treating military events was attributable to inadequate information in some cases, and in others to a fear of depressing the public mind. Their enthusiastic and practically unanimous support of the war effort in 1861 did much to inspirit the people and promote volunteering. The best papers refused to join in the destructive criticism leveled at the South's leaders after the tide turned against the Confederacy, but instead continued to urge unity and persistence, to emphasize the South's strength and achievement without minimizing the North's resources and determination, and to hold out hope for victory in spite of setbacks and suffering. The weaknesses of the others were inherent in the Confederacy of which they were a part.

The experiences of Southern magazines during the war were very similar to those of the newspapers. Of the one hundred periodicals in existence at the outbreak of hostilities only a few survived the conflict. The *Southern Literary Messenger*, the antebellum South's most outstanding literary periodical, was edited during the war by George W. Bagby. It died in 1864 from a complication of difficulties including shortage of paper, decline of subscriptions and deterioration of the quality of its articles. The old South's leading commercial magazine, *DeBow's Review*, suspended publication in September, 1862, and except for one number issued in midsummer, 1864, did not resume until after the war. The *Southern Field and Fireside*, a farm and home journal published in Augusta, Georgia, and the *Southern Literary Companion* of Newnan, Georgia, both founded in 1859, went out of existence in 1864.

Several new magazines came into being during the war, but they fared no better than the old ones. Freligh's *Southern Monthly*, which began publication in Memphis in September, 1861, aspired to be a Southern *Harper's*. But the Federal invasion of west Tennessee forced the magazine to flee to Grenada, Mississippi, in March, 1862, where it issued two numbers and then expired. Another literary periodical founded in 1861 which had the hardihood to survive the conflict was the *Countryman*, edited and published at "Turnwold," the plantation of J. A. Turner near Eatonton, Georgia. Among the paper's employees during the war was a boy named Joel Chandler Harris who set type, helped operate the press, wrote articles for the magazine and soaked up material for the "Uncle Remus" stories that were to bring him fame in later years. Turner was a remarkably versatile man whose plantation enterprises included a hat factory, tannery and distillery as well as a printing plant.

The year 1862 saw the birth of two periodicals in Richmond: the *Southern Illustrated News*, edited for a short time by John R. Thompson, and the *Magnolia*, a literary magazine, edited by James D. McCabe. Both had auspicious beginnings and attracted such illustrious contributors as Paul Hamilton Hayne, Henry Timrod, John R. Thompson and George William Bagby. But in 1863 each of these magazines had to raise its subscription to twenty dollars a year, and neither survived the conflict. The *Southern Illustrated News*, like most other wartime periodicals, devoted considerable space to denouncing the Yankees. On one occasion the editor went so far as to state: "The more outrages they commit, the more we will hate them, and the more a people hate the Yankees, the wiser and better they will be." Other magazines that began during the war and rapidly failed were: *Southern Punch,* a collection of army jokes (some of them stale and strained), poems, reviews of books and plays, and drawings by John A. Elder; *Bohemian,* the life span of which was the Christmas, 1863, issue; *The Age* (January, 1864, to January, 1865), an eclectic magazine; and a promising professional organ, the *Confederate States Medical and Surgical Journal* (January, 1864, to February, 1865).

The literary efforts of Confederates were devoted largely to verse; despite shortage of paper, nearly all periodicals and newspapers set aside space for the poetic effusions of their patrons. Unfortunately, the quantity of verse was not equaled by the quality; most of it revealed far more of patriotic spirit than of poetic talent. Despite the urging of Henry Timrod for the production of an anthem worthy of the young nation's stirring history, none of the efforts "touched the heart of the people so deeply as to become one of its representative songs." "Dixie" was written before the war by a Northerner.

The best poetry produced in the Confederacy came from the pen of Henry Timrod. This young South Carolinian had already demonstrated considerable talent in the antebellum years, but as Professor Jay Hubbell has noted, Timrod's army service and his other war experiences stirred his emotions and helped develop his exceptional literary potential. Among his most outstanding wartime poems were "A Cry to Arms," "Carolina," "The Unknown Dead," "Charleston" and "Spring." Timrod's fellow South Carolinian and friend, Paul Hamilton Hayne, contributed a number of poems to Confederate newspapers and magazines, but his wartime verse fell below the level of that written in the antebellum years. In March, 1864, he remarked to a friend: "The war seems to me like a gloomy & terrible episode in existence. One cannot think calmly; the sympathies, fears, passions of the heart being abnormally excited, there is hardly any chance left for that cool, consistent mental action, essential to artistic success."

The war also disrupted the literary activities of another distinguished Southern poet, John R. Thompson, of Richmond. During the first years of the conflict Thompson served as assistant secretary of the Commonwealth and state librarian. He also helped edit the *Record*, an eclectic magazine, and the *Southern Illustrated News*. In July, 1864, he went to England where he became principal writer for the *Index*, a propaganda newspaper edited by the brilliant young Alabama journalist, Henry Hotze. In the midst of these varied activities, Thompson found time to write a few poems, the best of which were "The Burial of Latane," "Ashby," "Music in Camp," and "Lee to the Rear."

Francis O. Ticknor of Georgia wrote poetic tributes to several Southern generals, but his best war poem, not published until 1867, was "Little Giffen," a moving piece based on the experiences of a Tennessee boy soldier who was a patient for several months in the poet's home. Margaret Junkin Preston, wife of a Virginia colonel, was the author of a long poem, *Beechenbrook: A Rhyme of the War*, which treated of the suffering and pathos of the conflict. James Ryder Randall, a Marylander resident in Louisiana, was inspired by the report of the fight on April 19, 1861, between citizens of Baltimore and Massachusetts soldiers en route to Washington, to write "Maryland, My Maryland," rated by Professor Hubbell as "one of the two or three finest lyrics that came out of the Civil War." The Cary sisters of Baltimore

RIDING A RAID

"OLD STONEWALL"

BALTIMORE
Published by GEORGE WILLIG, No 1 N Charles St

matched Randall's words to the tune "Tannenbaum, O Tannenbaum" and introduced it to Beauregard's soldiers soon after First Manassas. This song immediately became a great favorite in the Confederacy, but it lost some of its appeal in 1862 when Marylanders failed to flock to the Confederate ranks during the Antietam campaign. Randall wrote some other war lyrics including "Pelham," "The Lone Sentry," and "There's Life in the Old Land Yet."

John Williamson Palmer, also of Maryland, provided both the words and the melody for the popular Confederate song "Stonewall Jackson's Way." Palmer was a soldier and his poetic tribute to Jackson was inspired by the sound of the guns at Antietam.

No account of Confederate war poetry would be complete without reference to "The Conquered Banner," written by a chaplain from Virginia, Father Abram Joseph Ryan. This beautiful lyric, recited and revered by thousands of Southern school children in the fifty years following Appomattox, closed with the verse:

Father Abram Joseph Ryan

> Furl that Banner, softly, slowly,
> Treat it gently—it is holy—
>   For it droops above the dead.
> Touch it not—unfold it never,
> Let it droop there, furled forever,
>   For its people's hopes are dead!

Father Ryan also wrote a beautiful poem entitled "The Sword of Robert E. Lee."

Southerners produced little fiction during the period 1861–1865. The turbulence and tragedy of the conflict virtually stilled the pen of William Gilmore Simms, the most prolific Southern novelist of the antebellum period. John Pendleton Kennedy, literary luminary of Maryland in prewar times, sided with the Union. Johnson Jones Hooper, celebrated author of *Some Adventures of Captain Simon Suggs*, abandoned literary pursuits to become Secretary of the Confederate Congress. He died on June 7, 1862.

Sidney Lanier

One of the few novels written and published in the Confederacy was Augusta Jane Evans' *Macaria: or, Altars of Sacrifice*. Miss Evans, who was to become world-famous after the war as the author of *St. Elmo,* had published two books, *Inez* and *Beulah,* before the conflict began. She was an ardent secessionist, and one of her reasons for writing *Macaria* was to bolster Southern morale. The book was published in two editions in 1864 by West and Johnston of Richmond. Late in the conflict Constance Cary completed a novel entitled *Skirmishing* but the manuscript was burned in the fire that swept over Richmond at the end of the war. The young Sidney Lanier began his first novel, *Tiger-Lilies,* in 1863 while serving as a Georgia volunteer, but this work was not completed until after the war. John Esten Cooke produced no book of fiction during the war. But he drew on his experiences as a member of "Jeb" Stuart's staff to prepare some sketches of army life

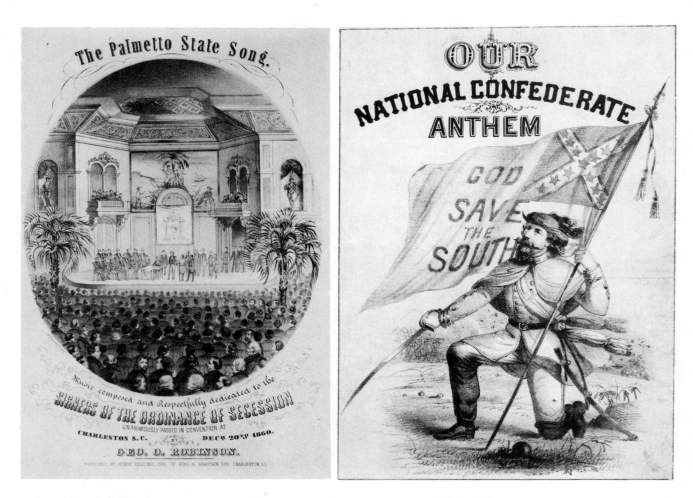

for *Southern Illustrated News* and kept a notebook which provided rich material for his postwar novels, *Surry of Eagle's Nest* and the *Wearing of the Gray*. His most outstanding literary achievement of the war years was a biography of Stonewall Jackson published in 1863.

During the war, as before, some of the best fictional writing was done by the humorists. Charles Henry Smith of Georgia provided amusement and diversion for many readers with his famous "Bill Arp" letters to "Abe Linkhorn" which had their beginning in the Rome *Confederation* in April, 1861. These engaging pieces appeared in various other newspapers but were not published in book form until after the war. Kittrell J. Warren, another accomplished Georgia humorist, wrote an amusing booklet on courtship entitled *Ups and Downs of Wife Hunting* for circulation among Confederate soldiers. Shortly after the war Warren published a more substantial humor book, *Life and Public Services of an Army Private,* based on his experiences in the army. Joke books prepared primarily for soldier readers included *Fun for the Camp, The Camp Follower,* and *The Camp Jester.* During the war George William Bagby, an outstanding humorist of the 1850's, was too deeply involved with his editorial duties to devote much attention to comedy. But his earlier "Letters of Mozis Addums to Billy Ivvins" were compiled and published in book form in 1862.

Historical writing during the war years was confined largely to personal narratives and unit histories, most of which were not published until after the conflict. One notable exception was Edward A. Pollard's *Southern History of the War*, which appeared in annual installments beginning in 1862. Pollard's strongly anti-Davis bias led Alexander St. Clair-Abrams to write a volume in defense of the Chief Executive entitled *President Davis and His Administration*.

Confederate publishers issued new editions of Victor Hugo's *Les Misérables*, Clara Mundt's books on Henry VIII and Joseph II and their courts, Bulwer-Lytton's *A Strange Story*, Dickens' *Great Expectations*, Beverley Tucker's *Partisan Leader*, J. B. Jones' *Wild Western Scenes*, A. B. Longstreet's *Master William Mitten* and various other works of foreign and American authors. They also printed a large assortment

Lieutenant Colonel Arthur J. L. Fremantle, H. M. Coldstream Guards, and William H. "Bull Run" Russell, two distinguished English visitors who wrote about the war.

of almanacs, songsters, sheet music, religious tracts and military manuals, some of which were reprints and some original productions. The total output, according to Richard B. Harwell, was "more than seven thousand bibliographical items." This vast array of Confederate imprints is an eloquent testimonial to the resourcefulness and persistence of Southern publishers, but it cannot be cited as evidence of outstanding literary achievement on the part of a people at war. Early in the conflict there were glowing predictions that the severance of the South's unhappy association with the materialistic North would result in the quick flowering of the region's superior but latent literary talents. But these promises were not fulfilled. In February, 1864, *Southern Punch* posed the question, "Are we a literary people?" and stated, "More in sorrow than in anger we answer: it is to be feared we are not." The editor's pessimism may have been due in part to unenthusiastic reception accorded his magazine. But the fact remains that the Confederacy failed to produce a great literature. It did not have the background for a quick cultural awakening and it was too deeply involved in the fight for survival to focus on literary pursuits. The influences of the war were not wholly negative, however, for the thrill, shock and suffering of these tragic times provided a heritage which native writers in future years were to utilize to bring about a Southern renaissance that some Confederates lived to see.

XII. *Education*

"There is nothing doing in college on account of the great excitement," wrote Duncan McCollum, a University of Mississippi senior, shortly after the capture of Fort Sumter. Previous entries in this student's diary tell of fiery speeches by faculty and townsmen, torchlight parades, and organization on the campus of a volunteer company known as the University Greys. The captain of the company soon accumulated fifty absences from class and was expelled from the university, but he remained on the campus drilling the company. Parents and teachers tried repeatedly to curb the martial fervor of the students, but to no avail. Seniors pressured the faculty into advancing the date of final examinations, and on May 1 the University Greys, after listening to a speech from Professor (soon to be Colonel) L. Q. C. Lamar, boarded a train "in great glee" and headed for camp. The next day Chancellor F. A. P. Barnard reported to the faculty that the student body had dwindled to five boys and that these would doubtless take their leave in a few hours. In June the trustees awarded degrees to the absent seniors and the university ceased operation for the duration of hostilities.

Many of the South's 260 institutions of higher learning had experiences similar to those of the University of Mississippi. When the faculty of Centenary College met to open the fall session on October 7, 1861, no students appeared, and the teachers had to go home; the faculty secretary concluded the minutes of the futile meeting with the notation: "Students have all gone to war. College suspended: and God help the right." The cadets at South Carolina College brushed aside requests of President A. B. Longstreet and the faculty that they remain on the campus and instead went in a body to participate in the attack on Fort Sumter. They returned after a few weeks and resumed their studies, though with notable lack of enthusiasm. The Federal attack on Port Royal in November, 1861, led to another general exodus from the campus. Classes were resumed after a brief interval, but not for long. At breakfast on March 8, 1862, a bulletin was read announcing a prospective state draft to meet a request for 18,000 Confederate troops. To students already chafing for service in the field the thought of conscription was intolerable; by evening nearly all of them had volunteered. Professors went to their classrooms as usual on Monday morning, March 10, but no pupils appeared. School was suspended for a week and an active campaign was initiated to recruit new students. On March 17, classes resumed with a total of nine pupils—five freshmen and four sophomores. The college limped along with about as many teachers as pupils until June, 1862, when it ceased operation for the remainder of the war. The buildings were taken over by Confederate medical authorities for use as hospitals.

Emory College closed its doors in November, 1861; Cumberland University, in March, 1862; Louisiana State Seminary, in April, 1863; Oglethorpe, in June, 1863; the University of Georgia, then known as Franklin College, in February, 1864; and the College of Charleston, in December, 1864. Davidson, Mercer, Randolph-Macon, Trinity, the University of Alabama, the University of North Carolina and a few other male institutions kept going throughout the war, though all experienced enormous difficulties.

The men's colleges were handicapped by declining enrollment. The University of Virginia, the old South's largest institution of higher learning, in 1860–1861 had 630 students. In 1861–1862 enrollment was 66; in 1862–1863, 46; in 1863–1864, 50; and in 1864–1865, 55. The University of North Carolina opened in the fall of 1860 with 376 students; in the last year of the war the student body had shrunk to about 50. It was the same everywhere; and in addition, student bodies became more youthful as they declined in size. Some institutions had no seniors and juniors at all during the latter part of the war.

College administrators resorted to various expedients in an effort to keep their institutions going. Randolph-Macon added military subjects to its curriculum. At the University of North Carolina and some other institutions, military companies were formed on the campus to provide training, satisfy the martial urge and forestall conscription. The "Trinity Guard," composed of faculty and students of Trinity College, was taken into state service for a while in 1861–1862 and was put to guarding Federal prisoners at Salisbury and helping to quell local disturbances. In the early days of the war, the College of Charleston rearranged its schedule so that students could perform military duty in the area without missing classes.

Many of the colleges added preparatory departments, or enlarged those already in existence, to attract students too young for military service. Trinity opened its doors to women in 1864, and about a score of girls enrolled. President W. T. Gannaway, in reporting to the trustees the effects of admitting women, stated: "Their presence was like an oasis in the Sahara of war and their instruction was an antidote from the hardness, roughness and inhumanity of the conflict."

Disabled veterans were welcomed to the near-empty classrooms and in some instances were exempted from tuition. Late in the war George Christian, who had lost a foot in combat, and W. C. Holmes, who had been severely wounded in the right arm, matriculated in the law school of the University of Virginia. Christian had great difficulty moving about the campus and Holmes was unable to take notes. So the two made an agreement whereby Holmes helped Christian to walk and Christian assisted Holmes with his writing.

Declining enrollment and increasing inflation necessitated raising of tuition and other fees. Faculty salaries were raised by some institutions, but nowhere did increments keep pace with the mounting cost of living. In most cases salaries had to be reduced, and institutions struggling along with token enrollments adopted the practice of dividing tuition receipts among faculty and staff. Many college teachers entered military service and some found other employment. Those who remained in the profession sometimes supplemented their salaries by tutoring, acting as custodians of buildings and performing other odd jobs. Most of them had a hard time sustaining themselves and their families.

Charges for board, both on and off the campus, soared as provisions became scarcer and money decreased in value. At Trinity College in September, 1863, board on campus was $25 a month; in 1865 it had soared to $200. After January, 1864, the college permitted students to pay their board in provisions at a rate of $7.50 to $8.00 per month on the basis of peacetime prices. John B. Yarborough, a crippled veteran, paid two and one-half months' board at Trinity early in 1865 with 7 bushels of wheat and 250 pounds of salt hauled from his home in Rockingham County.

The food served in college dining halls left much to be desired. The college treasurer at Davidson wrote of the wartime fare of that institution: "Flour bread was very scarce, corn dodgers all right, turnip

Beaufort College, Beaufort, South Carolina, built in 1852 and used as a hospital for contrabands during the war

pudding and dried apple pies acceptable, ginger cake a cherished luxury, and rye coffee and sorghum molasses (called long sweetening) were as inseparable as the Siamese twins. . . . A number of country bred boys had rabbit gums [traps] which they visited every morning and the catch of game gave a variety to our frugal meals."

The unsettled conditions of the times, boredom and restlessness led to neglect of study, remissness in attending class and a general deterioration of order and discipline. Cadets at the Louisiana State Seminary were unusually troublesome throughout the 1862–1863 session. On the morning of April 1, 1863, they engaged in a general riot during which "they took dishes, knives, and forks from the mess hall and threw them into the well and then destroyed the kitchen furniture." A student at Davidson wrote that in 1862 "a good deal of drinking went on." Literary societies and other extracurricular activities languished as enrollment declined and in some instances ceased altogether. The paramount desire of most of the boys was to take leave of the halls of learning and head for the battle front, and that is what most of them did as soon as they were old enough, or big enough, to enlist. They gave a good account of themselves. Davidson College, with an estimated total matriculation of 1,039 from 1840 to 1865, had at least 302 men in Confederate uniform, of whom 80 died in the service. Nearly all of the 31 members of Mercer's class of 1861 entered the army and 9 of them died on the battlefield. Of the 630 students enrolled at the University of Virginia in the school year 1860–1861, it is estimated that 515 donned the Confederate gray and that 86 died of hostile bullets or disease. During the period from 1825 to 1865 about 9,000 men were enrolled at Virginia; of these about 2,481 entered Confederate service, and the names of some 500 appear on the rolls of Confederate dead.

Women's colleges generally maintained their usual enrollment during the early period of the conflict, but some were closed by invasion, others by appropriation of their facilities for Confederate military use, and still others by the evils of inflation, scarcity, and the financial burden on parents. Among the few institutions that remained in operation throughout the war were Judson at Marion, Alabama; the Methodist Women's College at Tuskegee; the Female College at Port Gibson, Mississippi; the Central Female Institute at Clinton, Mississippi; and Wesleyan College at Macon, Georgia.

Betty Lou Curry's unpublished history of Wesleyan affords a good picture of the impact of war on a women's college of the deep South. The secession of Georgia on January 19 caused a wave of excitement to sweep over the campus. When Macon militiamen paraded past the campus that evening the girls displayed the flags of several Southern states and leaned from dormitory windows to cheer the marching soldiers. The troops responded with enthusiastic shouts for the ladies of Wesleyan and the independent state of Georgia. The attack on Fort Sumter set off another and more spirited round of marching, hurrahing

*Literary Department,
University of Nashville,
later Lindsley Hall,
Peabody Normal College*

and celebrating. But a few days later rejoicing gave way to weeping as the students' relatives and sweethearts departed for the fighting front. On April 20, 1861, Louisiana Burge wrote in her diary: "Em Bellamy spent nearly the whole evening in my room crying about the war and John T. Burr who leaves tonight. She and Fannie Perkins went down to Mr. Saulsbury's to tell him Goodbye. Between her and Cousin Emma Ward crying about Ed Guinn, I have had a time of it. The girls are almost all of them crying. Ginnie Gothing's feelings have overcome her; she has gone to bed, sick with crying about Bush Lumsden who don't care a snap for her. Ridiculous! I can hear Susie Clayton screaming way down in her room. I am glad I am not in love, if that is the way I would have to do if my sweetheart should leave for the wars." At the close of the term in June, seventeen seniors received their diplomas.

Wesleyan, like other colleges located in the interior, became a haven for refugees from the invaded areas, and these newcomers helped build up enrollment during the second and third years of conflict to more than two hundred. The students maintained their morale and aided the soldiers by giving occasional plays and musical programs, rolling bandages, knitting socks and sweaters, and making clothing and tobacco pouches. Each spring they had a grand May-day celebration and from time to time they enjoyed informal song fests featured by hearty renditions of "Dixie." They organized two mock military companies, the Bonnell Blues, named for the college president, and the Freeman Guards. A member of the Blues wrote shortly after the war: "We had dress parades, all arrayed in paper hats with tassels and paper epaulets and did a wonderful amount of marching and drum beating. The teachers seemed to encourage our military fervor in drills. Exciting, war-like speeches were made. . . . Some ingenious person furnished us with handmade wooden guns. We couldn't aspire to special dresses

—we just wore the ones we had—mostly homespun and homemade, not much for looks but great for wear. . . . Up and down the rocky hills we would tramp in our homemade cowhide shoes."

The effects of war soon became apparent in the scarcity of meat and flour biscuits, a delicacy reserved for Sundays—replaced by a regular diet of cornbread, hominy, sweet potatoes and field peas—and in an increase of tuition and board. But since the institution's only source of income during the war was student fees and since the policy was adopted early in the conflict of granting free tuition to daughters of Confederate servicemen, college authorities had to resort to sundry expedients to keep the school going. Operational and maintenance activities were greatly reduced. Faculty members agreed to accept whatever compensation the state of the treasury allowed, which meant a progressive lowering of salaries. Students were encouraged to pay their fees in kind. Late in the war a circular was issued fixing the monthly charge for board at "either 70 pounds of bacon, 210 pounds of flour, 21 bushels of meal or 30 gallons of syrup." This announcement also stated that "with non-producers the board is arranged by special contract." In the spring of 1864 Confederate medical authorities tried to convert Wesleyan into an army hospital, but the courts intervened to thwart this attempt. The capture of Atlanta on September 2, 1864, created great uneasiness in the minds of both college officials and patrons, and when school opened a short time later only 42 students enrolled. As Sherman's plans for the march to the sea developed, some parents withdrew their daughters, and school was suspended for three weeks. But when the invaders failed to show up at Macon, classes were resumed and enrollment eventually rose to 112. The approach of General Wilson's forces on April 25, 1865, led to another interruption of three days, but when the Federals took over the city they did not molest the college; school activities were again renewed and the session of 1864–1865 completed. Shortly after the Yankees arrived three students were haled before the provost marshal for refusing to walk beneath a United States flag, but they were not punished. Some of the girls put their fingers in their ears when the men in blue tried to serenade them, but the musicians held a parley with their audience and won them over by agreeing to include "Dixie" in their repertoire.

Beneath the colleges in the old South's educational system was a large assortment of private academies. In 1850 these institutions numbered 3,000 and their enrollment aggregated over 200,000. They have been aptly called "the distinctive schools of the South." Many were church-connected, a few were endowed and some received state aid. But most of them relied mainly on student fees for their support.

During the war the academies experienced the problems common to the colleges. In most institutions enrollment declined, the quality of work deteriorated, fees soared as currency depreciated, maintenance fell below prewar standards and dining-hall fare was the source of

Rotunda, University of Virginia

chronic complaint. Some institutions were able, in spite of all difficulties, to keep going throughout the conflict but a far greater number were compelled to suspend operations.

One of the institutions that succeeded in keeping its doors open throughout the war was Augusta Female Seminary, of Staunton, Virginia, the forerunner of Mary Baldwin College. In the summer of 1864 this school announced the following terms for the half-session beginning September 15 and ending February 1, 1865: "Board $1400 or $67.50 if paid in produce at the market prices of 1860; viz, extra flour, $6; corn, 75 cents; butter, 20 cents; bacon, 12½ cents; lard, 12½ cents; potatoes, 75 cents; molasses, 75 cents; wood, $2.50 per cord. Currency will not be received from those who can pay in produce. Tuition in English branches, $100; Latin, Greek, French and German, $50; primary department, $75; music and use of instruments, $200. Boarders furnish lights, candlesticks, towels, washing, one pair of sheets, one pair of pillow cases, half enough covering for the bed and one cup."

Whenever Federal soldiers visited the Seminary's premises the girls assisted in hiding precious provisions. Once they saved the school's supply of flour by rolling the barrels into their rooms and draping them with crinoline skirts to give them the appearance of dressing tables. On another occasion they hid hams in their study desks. A male intruder discovered on the grounds one night during the war was put to flight by the headmistress, Mary Baldwin, brandishing a poker at him and shouting: "If you don't go away I'll shoot you."

In the latter part of the war scarcity of food was perhaps the most formidable of all the difficulties faced by the academies. The headmaster of Bingham School in North Carolina moved his institution from a community where provisions were scant to a locality where edibles were more abundant and thus was able to nourish his students and keep the academy open. The May 29, 1863, entry in the diary of a sixteen-year-old girl enrolled at a Plantersville, South Carolina, academy states: "Our supper consists of a huge tray of corn dodgers which is brought into the school room and placed on the table, that we may help ourselves and the tray goes back empty." Most of the students endured their privations with reasonable equanimity and fortitude.

In the decade preceding the Civil War some of the Southern states, especially North Carolina, Kentucky, Tennessee and Alabama, had made notable progress toward the establishment of state-supported public schools. Attendance in the South's public schools increased 43.2 percent between 1850 and 1860. But, except in the border areas, state systems of public education had little more than a paper existence in 1860, support was largely permissive and control was local. Educational leaders such as Calvin H. Wiley of North Carolina strove mightily during the war to hold on to the gains made in the 1850's and to keep the common schools going. Some auspicious steps were taken, including the holding of a convention of Southern teachers in Columbia, South

St. Mary's Convent, St. Augustine, Florida

Female Seminary, Petersburg, Virginia, 1865

Carolina, April 27–30, 1863, at which the Educational Association of the Confederate States of America was formed to promote the educational interests of the South. The Confederate Congress took cognizance of educational needs by exempting from conscription teachers of twenty or more pupils in both private and public schools.

Figures on public school enrollment during the war years are fragmentary, but random comments in letters, diaries and newspapers indicate that the common schools suffered even more than private institutions. Those in rural communities were hardest hit of all. The public schools of Baldwin County, Alabama, ceased operation as early as 1861. In January, 1865, a resident of Albemarle County, Virginia, wrote the Governor: "I live in a neighborhood where there are many children . . . growing up in ignorance, there having been no school in this part of our district since the winter of 1860 & 61. . . . The few persons able to school their children have sent them out of the district & thereby left it entirely in ignorance."

The typical elementary school in the Confederacy seems to have been a one-room institution operating about six months of the year with time out for the autumn harvest, and run on a subscription basis for a few families who had the means to maintain it. Sometimes the classes were held at the home of the teacher or one of the patrons. Occasionally two or three pupils from outside the community would be accepted as boarding students. Tuition was payable in kind or in money. A Grayson

EDUCATION   227

Mary Sharpe College, Winchester, Tennessee. On May 1, 1861, 1,200 volunteers assembled on the campus. "They marched two miles to Decherd—their path was literally strewn with flowers from the hands of ladies and children, while girls sobbed quietly—and there they entrained for Montgomery to join Jeff Davis and the Southern Confederacy!" (History of Tennessee, by S. J. Folmsbee, R. E. Corlew and E. L. Mitchell)

County, Virginia, woman wrote her husband in May, 1864: "School is out now [and] Celia at home. She has went six weeks and learned the fastest for the time I ever saw her. Board came to three bushels of corn, the Tuition to 7 lbs. Bacon."

Both public and private schools were handicapped by poor teachers, and salaries as low as twenty dollars a month. Most of the regular male teachers of military age went to war and many of the Northern women who taught in the South in antebellum times returned to their homes. Some of the draft-exempt men and young refugee women who entered the teaching profession were ill-equipped for their positions. A young Louisiana woman, compelled by the fortunes of war to take up teaching, wrote her husband at the end of the session in July, 1863: "Teaching is the most unthankful business on the earth. A great many persons are angry with me and dissatisfied with the school because their daughters did not receive the honors."

The prolongation of hostilities compelled many mothers to take over the teaching of their children. An upper-class middle Tennessee woman wrote in her journal for May 26, 1862: "I have the children with me constantly. . . . I have commenced teaching them to write. Reading, spelling, writing, notation, speeches, drawing and music occupy a large portion of our time. I must endeavor to do them justice if everything else should be left by the board."

Teaching in both institutions and homes was made more difficult by scarcity of textbooks. In the late antebellum period many Southerners advocated replacement of Northern books by volumes written and published in Dixie and friendly to the South's people and institutions. Only in a few instances did this movement get beyond the talking stage. But the outbreak of hostilities virtually stopped importation of Northern publications and compelled Southerners to produce their own textbooks. Publishing houses in Richmond, Mobile, Raleigh, Greensboro, Charleston, Augusta, Macon and other Southern cities issued schoolbooks in considerable variety and quantity. Some of the publications were adaptations of old stand-bys such as Noah Webster's famous blue-back speller, but others were original works prepared especially for Southern pupils. Mrs. A. D. Chaudron, Mrs. Marinda B. Moore and Mrs. S. A. Poindexter each prepared a series of readers. L. M. Johnson, S. Lander and Charles E. Leverett compiled arithmetics. Washington Baird, John Neely and Richard M. Smith were authors of Confederate spelling books. Richard Sterling compiled a series of "Our Own" reading and spelling books and Charles Winslow Smythe was the author of a progression of "Our Own" grammars. William Bingham, head of the Bingham School, Mebane, North Carolina, prepared a Latin grammar and an edition of Caesar's commentaries on the Gallic War; and R. H. Rivers, president of Wesleyan University, Florence, Alabama, was the author of textbooks on mental and moral philosophy. Mrs. Marinda B. Moore compiled a geographical reader "for the Dixie children." A number of texts were known by the states in which they were issued; among them were *The Louisiana English Grammar, The New Texas Primary Reader* and *The Virginia Primer*. Many authors sought to enhance the appeal of their volumes by including the word "Dixie," "Confederate," or "Southern" in the titles.

Some of the books had a distinctive Confederate slant. The second edition of Mrs. Marinda B. Moore's geography, published in Raleigh in 1864, contained these questions and answers:

Q. Has the Confederate states any commerce?
A. A fine inland commerce and bids fair, sometime, to have a grand commerce on the high seas.

Q. What is the present drawback to our trade?
A. An unlawful Blockade by the miserable and hellish Yankee Nation.

Johnson's *Elementary Arithmetic,* published in Raleigh in 1864, posed these problems:

1. "A Confederate soldier captured 8 Yankees each day for 9 successive days; how many did he capture in all?"
2. "If one Confederate soldier kills 90 Yankees, how many Yankees can 10 Confederate soldiers kill?"
3. "If one Confederate soldier can whip 7 Yankees, how many soldiers can whip 49 Yankees?"

1   2   3   4   5   1   2   3   1   2   3   1
note, not, move, dove, book, tube, tub, full, type, hymn, myrrh, dew.

No. 101.—CI

Words of two syllables, accented on the second.

1	1		
Com bine′	gan grene	de clare	com peer
de fine	ob scene	in snare	ca reer
re fine	in sane	de spare	bab oon
con fine	hu mane	pre pare	buf foon
sa bine	post pone	re pair	dra goon
de cline	de throne	im pair	rac coon
ca nine	en throne	com pare	bal loon
re fine	a tone	sin cere	pla toon
su pine	je june	ad here	gal loon
en shrine	tri une	co here	shal loon
di vine	com mune	aus tere	lam poon
en twine	at tune	re vere	har poon
con vene	es cape	se vere	mon soon

No. 102.—CII.

A HUMANE man is kind to the poor, and merciful to his beast.

When a man loses his mind he is said to be INSANE. A man without a mind is a sad sight ; and yet some bad boys like to make sport of such poor unfortunate creatures.

We must not REPINE at the evils common to all mankind.

A BABOON is a large kind of monkey. A monkey when dressed in coat and pants, looks very much like a little boy.

General Morgan made a miraculous ESCAPE from the Yankees.

ADHERE to what is good and just.

---

1   2   3   4   5   1   2   3   1   2   3   1
note, not, move, love, book—tube, tub. bush—type, hymn, myrrh—dew.

No. 37.—XXXVII.
WAR.

It makes us sad to hear the booming of cannon in time of war. We think of our dear friends who are in the army, and fear they may be killed.

War is a sad thing, and those who bring it about will have much to answer for.

Some people lay all the blame at the door of the rulers of the nation. In some countries this is true, but in our country it is not so. The people elect their own rulers, and they should not choose bad men. If the rulers in the United States had been good Christian men, the present war would not have come upon us.

The people sent bad men to Congress, and they were not willing to make just laws, but were selfish, and made laws to suit themselves.

The Bible says " When the wicked bear rule the nation mourneth, but when the righteous are in authority, the people rejoice."

People often do wrong, and when trouble comes upon them, they say God sent it.

God has made good laws for man, and if we do right we will be happy ; but sin will always bring trouble.

Let every boy learn this lesson, and when he is a man, let him not vote for a bad man to fill an office of trust.— Then the men who wish to be in office will strive to be good, and the nation will be happy.

Most of the textbooks issued in the Confederacy were printed on inferior paper and flimsily bound in cardboard covers. It is not surprising that they wore out faster than they could be replaced. In the latter part of the war the supply became so depleted that volumes discarded in prewar times had to be restored to service; students in the same class often were required to use many different texts.

When all of the difficulties are considered, it seems remarkable that Confederate children received as much schooling as they did. The spark that kindled the educational awakening of the 1850's was dimmed by the costly and tragic conflict of the 1860's but it was not extinguished. When fanned by influences introduced by the victors during Reconstruction, it grew into a flame in which was molded a solid and enduring system of public education.

XIII. Negroes

The principal concern of the 3,500,000 slaves and 135,000 free Negroes living in the eleven Confederate states in 1861 was labor. The war caused some changes in the kind of work done by the Negroes but there was little reduction in the amount of toil. Some living in towns and cities were put to work in war industries. Many in various parts of the South were called on to build fortifications, maintain railroads, and serve with the armies as laborers, teamsters, musicians and hospital attendants. Slaves on farms and plantations were shifted from the cultivation of cotton and tobacco to the production of food crops. Some of them were engaged in such war-imposed activities as tanning leather, making soap, flailing and winnowing grain and boiling sea water to obtain salt. Colored women were trained to spin, weave and sew. The Negroes usually adapted themselves to their new duties with a facility that was gratifying to the whites.

The war also led to modification of the slaves' diet. The pork ration which in antebellum times normally was a half-pound a day had to be curtailed or eliminated, owing to shortage of salt for preserving meat. Many planters gave the slaves molasses in lieu of pork and others enriched the fare from time to time with sweet potatoes, turnips and field peas. Except in cities and in areas frequented by soldiers, slaves often were better fed during the war than before.

The same was not true with respect to clothing. After the first year or two of conflict most of the slaves had to wear homespun garments, and in winter many did not have enough clothing to keep them warm. In the latter part of the war some planters cut up mattresses and carpets to provide coats and blankets for their slaves. Many Negroes wore wooden-soled shoes and some had to go barefooted throughout the year.

Household servants were usually better clad than field hands, and their Sunday apparel sometimes was finer than that of their owners. The latter circumstance was due to the peacetime practice of whites passing on their little-used garments to colored attendants. When war came the whites by frequent use soon wore out their dressy habiliments while Negroes, who donned their fine clothes only on Sundays, made them last for several years. On a May Sabbath in 1863 Lieutenant

*Preparing cotton for the
gin on the Smith
plantation*

Colonel Arthur Fremantle reported seeing Negro women of Houston, Texas, parading about the streets in "silks, satins, crinolines . . . an absurd contrast to the simple dresses of their mistresses"; and J. B. Jones wrote in his diary on December 3, 1863, that on Sundays the Negroes were "the best-clad people in the South."

Most of the simple diversions enjoyed by the Negroes in peacetime were continued during the war. Saturday afternoons were usually spent in resting, visiting in the slave quarter, fishing and playing games. On the Fourth of July some planters allowed their Negroes to have barbecues or picnics and at Christmas they customarily dispensed presents to the slaves, though the latter practice was curtailed to some extent during the final years of the war. In the evening the slaves occasionally sang and danced in the quarter, though on weekday nights they were usually too exhausted from their labors to engage in such festivity. In fall and winter they sometimes hunted opossums and rabbits with dogs. Guns were denied them by state laws of long standing; in antebellum times these laws were sometimes ignored, but after the outbreak of hostilities they were rigidly enforced.

On Sunday the Negroes usually attended religious services, though they were not allowed to meet in groups of over four or five without the presence of a white person. The sermon, ordinarily, was delivered by a white minister, but the absence of many preachers in the army led to increasing reliance on white women and Negro laymen for religious instruction and exhortation. In summer Negroes participated in revival meetings. These were followed by baptizings which, in the instance of some sects, meant a special trip to a creek or pond for immersion of the converts. As previously noted, religious services for slaves received greater emphasis during the war than before, owing to the masters' desire to make full use of the scriptures in keeping the Negroes contented and submissive.

The behavior of the slaves during the war varied greatly with locale and circumstances. As a general rule the Negroes were most submissive and dutiful in areas farthest removed from the Federal lines and least subordinate and faithful in regions subjected to invasion. Other factors influencing their behavior were prior relations with their masters, the presence or absence of their accustomed supervisors, and the treatment accorded them after the outbreak of hostilities.

The most consistently faithful slaves were the house servants—the butlers, coachmen, waiters, housemaids, nurses, laundresses, seamstresses, gardeners and others comprising the domestic staff of the plantations. These Negroes were slavery's upper crust and they were proud of their status. Often they were bound to the ruling caste by strong ties

Negro family representing five generations, all born on the plantation of J. J. Smith, Beaufort, South Carolina

of affection based on long and intimate association. It was these slaves who during the trial of invasion buried the master's treasures, concealed his livestock, stood watch over his family and performed other acts of loyalty which moonlight and magnolia sentimentalists of the postwar period were repeatedly to cite as evidence that slavery was a benign institution and that Negroes were happy in bondage.

The colored aides or body servants who accompanied the planters to war were usually selected from the corps of household slaves. Body servants foraged and cooked for their masters, took care of their equipment, laundered their clothes, cleaned their quarters and performed

A scene on the plantation of James Hopkinson, Edisto Island, South Carolina

sundry other menial chores. In battle they were supposed to remain in the rear but now and then one of them would sneak up to the front, pick up a musket and join in the shooting. Early in the war many enlisted men enjoyed the luxury of colored aides, but shortage of rations, the demoralizing effects of camp life and economic pressure eventually caused most privates and subalterns to send their servants home.

Close association and exposure to common hardships tended to promote cordial and affectionate relations between soldier masters and their colored attendants. In battle some of the servants proved their fidelity and courage by risking their lives to seek out wounded masters and remove them to places of safety. When masters were killed, the servants wrote or dictated letters of condolence to the folks at home and requested instructions for disposition of the remains. After Lieutenant George Whitaker Wills of the Forty-third North Carolina Regiment was

EMBATTLED
CONFEDERATES

killed at Fisher's Hill on September 19, 1864, his servant "Wash" addressed the following note to a brother of the deceased:

Dear Master Richard

I will now try to give you an account of my feelings towards my young master who is now dead. I hope and trust he is saved. I have reason to believe so by the light which he gave me. . . . It seems that all fear had been banished from him through all. I am glad to tell you his coat was buttoned up in the prettiest style of uniform and in his breast pocket was his little Testament. Master Richard, I say to you it is good to be religious. . . .

We talked over everything, troubles sorrow and sicknesses. . . . He said he never went in any battle with the expectation of coming out safe, he seemed then to give himself up into the hands of Providence. . . . Master Richard, I believe it as much as I ever believed anything in my life, that he is at rest, my heart believes it. . . . Master Eddie says he wants me to go with him. I will go and do the best I can for him. I am willing to do anything I can do to help out our struggling country. I desire to see you and talk with you. . . . Master Richard I know something about trouble. . . .

> Your faithful servant
> Wash

General Stonewall Jackson's cook, Jeff Shields

Not all the colored aides and household servants were faithful to their masters. At the Battle of Sharpsburg a body servant who borrowed a horse to carry his wounded master beyond the range of Yankee bullets immediately afterward mounted the horse and headed for the Federal lines. Soon after the Yankees reached Culpeper, Virginia, a coachman dressed himself in his master's finery, appropriated his watch, told him that henceforth he could drive his own carriage and took off for the Union camps. But such behavior was exceptional among domestic servants.

The field hands, who comprised the overwhelming majority of the slave population, were far less faithful to their masters than were the domestics. Those residing in interior portions of the South sometimes took advantage of the absence of white men in military service to loaf, resist punishment and bargain for special privileges. "Idleness, half work . . . has to be winked at," wrote a deep-South planter in May, 1864. When an aged Texan tried to whip an unruly slave in 1863, the Negro cursed his master, took to the forest and sent word that he would not come back until the owner promised not to punish him. The pledge was given and the slave returned to his work. Women left in charge of plantations sometimes became afraid to discipline the slaves. "I shall say nothing if they stop work entirely . . . [and] will try to feel thankful if they let me alone," wrote a distraught Texas woman to her soldier husband in 1864. The wife of a South Carolina congressman wrote her spouse in 1862: "I can give orders first-rate, but when I am not obeyed, I can't keep my temper. . . . I am ever ready to give you a helping hand, but I must say I am heartily tired of trying to manage *free* negroes." Letters and diaries of the period leave the impression that in a good many isolated communities the Negroes rode about the country

Negroes mounting cannon at Morris Island for the attack on Fort Sumter, 1861

at night on their owner's horses, tarried in the quarter long after sun-up and worked as little as possible.

But owners living in interior localities had far less cause to complain than those residing in areas touched by invasion. When the Federal armies approached a community the slaves began to run away. The exodus increased as the invaders came closer and their actual arrival in many instances caused plantations to be stripped of their entire corps of laborers. A Mississippian who lived near Port Gibson wrote soon after Grant's troops captured that town in May, 1863: "When the advanced forces of the enemy reached Nitta Tola . . . the fetters of slavery were broken instantly, and the hoe and plow handle dropped from the hands of the negroes, and I ceased to be a planter forever. It is amazing with what intuitive familiarity the negroes recognized the moment of deliverance. Eleven of my young men were carried off at once, and thirty-two others—men, women and children—shortly afterward escaped to Grand Gulf where a Federal garrison was maintained. Two men, three women and eight children were all that remained with us and they were much demoralized."

In August, 1863, shortly after the Federals came to Yazoo City, Mississippi, a resident of that town wrote a friend: "The second day after the arrival of the vile creatures in Yazoo all our servants were missing. Allen, Father's *faithful* body servant was the first to make the move, and after that Dot or Alice, Nancy her daughter, Eliza and her daughter, Jacob, Sancho and Mary Ann, Janet and family, all took wings and disappeared in one night, and after that a good many from the plantation, amounting in all to thirty-two. . . . The second raid took forty-seven or eight."

Some of the Negroes who ran away eventually returned to their masters, but the system to which they came back was usually different, and so were the returnees. In June, 1862, a Mississippi planter wrote Governor Pettus that the Negroes in his county were getting "quite impudent" owing to "proximity to the enemy." A North Carolinian informed Governor Vance in August, 1864, that "our negroes are beginning to show that they understand the state of affairs, and insolence and insubordination are quite common." A South Carolina overseer who had difficulties with the hands wrote his employer in March, 1865: "The people the way they work will not make their Bread, go out at 10 o'clock, come in at 12 o'clock."

Slaves sometimes took advantage of invasion to compel owners to pay them wages, or drove off overseers and pillaged and robbed. They also gave the invaders helpful information about Confederate forces, roads, bridges, fords, and terrain; revealed the location of valuables hidden by their masters; and concealed and fed escaped Yankee prisoners and helped them on their way to freedom. Negroes on plantations

Jim Limber, colored boy adopted by Mrs. Jefferson Davis during the war

Negro family around the hearth near Spotsylvania Court House, Virginia

Above, a mule driver at Kelly's Ford, Virginia, in November, 1863; at right, slaves concealing their master from a Federal search party

in or near the Federal lines sometimes attacked overseers and masters, and a few whites met death at the hands of the slaves. Assaults on white women were rare but not unknown.

Letters and diaries of the period contain numerous references to planned insurrections, but few plots were brought to light and the only slave revolts that actually occurred were minor uprisings, none of which had as many as forty participants. In 1861 a small group of Negroes in Concordia Parish, Louisiana, discussed the possibility of killing their masters, ravishing the white women and organizing a general revolt, but the plot was discovered and the conspirators brought to trial.

Projected slave insurrections were detected and forestalled near New Orleans in September, 1862; in Hancock County, Georgia, in October, 1863; Brooks County, Georgia, in August, 1864; and Troy, Alabama, in December, 1864. Two minor outbreaks occurred among Mississippi slaves in July, 1862, and a third in 1864; all were quickly suppressed and the participants severely punished.

The slaves were kept down by tight laws, which included more frequent patrols, severe punishments for permitting slaves to assemble without white escort, and new safeguards to prevent Negroes from obtaining weapons and whiskey. Then, the Negroes lacked arms, and the opportunities to obtain them; they also lacked education; leadership; and effective means of communication. The best-educated and most talented slaves—and the only ones capable of planning and directing a large-scale revolt—were the house servants, who were inclined to be loyal. In addition, throughout the South there were sizable groups of partisan rangers, independent scouts and state militia, whose existence was a

Negroes leaving the plow as Federal troops march by

strong factor in keeping the Negroes under proper control. Their effectiveness in performing this role was demonstrated in south Mississippi in September, 1864. When thirty slaves of Amite County seized their masters' guns and horses and headed for the Yankee lines, they were overtaken a few miles short of their destination by a party of Confederate scouts and most of them killed on the spot.

Most of the slaves waited for deliverance at the hands of the hosts of men in blue who marched to the strains of "John Brown's Body" and the "Battle Cry of Freedom." The overwhelming majority of slaves earnestly desired emancipation. Many of them had vague and distorted ideas of the meaning of freedom; but some of their spirituals, such as "Bound to Go," "No Man Can Hinder Me," "Blow Your Trumpet, Gabriel," "Go Down, Moses," and "Let My People Go," reveal a deep-seated longing for liberation.

Throughout the war slaves met secretly in their quarters to pray for the Yankees and freedom. One of Booker T. Washington's most vivid memories was waking at night as a slave child, and seeing his mother kneeling by his bed, "fervently praying that Lincoln and his armies might be successful and that one day she and her children might be free." In his later years Washington expressed the view that "even the most ignorant members of my race on the remote plantations felt in their hearts that freedom of the slaves would be the one great result of the war, if the Northern armies conquered." He also declared that he had never seen a Negro "who did not want to be free, or one who would return to slavery."

The elation with which the Negroes greeted the invaders and the

"Dick, sketched on the 6th of May, the afternoon of General Hooker's retreat across the Rappahannock, on return to camp." Edwin Forbes

alacrity with which they shed their bonds attested their profound yearning for freedom. An Illinois soldier stated that when his regiment pitched camp east of Vicksburg in May, 1863, about twenty Negroes from a nearby plantation rushed out to welcome the Northerners "with all sorts of pious ejaculations . . . swinging their arms, clapping their hands and fairly shouting for joy." "The whole scene resembled a high pressure scene in a camp meeting," he added, "some exclaiming 'Praise de Lor' the Yankees come,' 'Lor bress the Yankees,' 'Nigger free now Yankees come,' . . . followed by a regular Hallelujah chorus from all hands." General Sherman wrote that as he passed through the Georgia countryside, cheering slaves hailed him as "Moses and Simon and other scriptural ones as well as Abraham Lincom, the Great Messiah of Dis Jubilee." When he led his troops into Covington, Georgia, with flags flying and bands playing, the blacks clustered about his horse shouting and praying, frantic with joy. "I have witnessed hundreds if not thousands of such scenes," he wrote after the war, "and can now see a poor girl in the very ecstasy of the 'Methodist shout' hugging the banner of one of the regiments and jumping up to the 'feet of Jesus.'"

Little wonder that slaves ignored the appeals of benevolent masters and brushed aside objections of Union soldiers to attach themselves to their deliverers and swell the marching columns. They knew not that

Negroes going to the commissary for rations, Culpeper Courthouse, Virginia, September 25, 1863

hunger, disease and death would be the lot of many. The sweet chariots had at last swung low and they were going to ride home to freedom while they could.

Well over 100,000 of the liberated blacks donned the Federal uniform to help vouchsafe their emancipation. When put to the test at Port Hudson, Louisiana, Milliken's Bend, Olustee and the Crater, they proved themselves worthy of the cause that they espoused, and many of them gave their lives for the freedom that they claimed.

EMBATTLED
CONFEDERATES

Negro laborers, City Point, Virginia

The white folks of the South ridiculed and denounced the Northern government for enlisting Negroes and professed utter contempt for the colored fighting men. But as Confederate forces dwindled in the latter part of the war, and the flow of replacements slowed to a trickle, sentiment changed and a number of prominent Southerners began to advocate recruiting of slaves. This proposal set off a heated and widespread controversy. Opponents of the proposal stated that Negroes were lacking in pride, courage, self-reliance and other qualities essential to effectiveness on the battlefield. They also argued that to entrust to the blacks the responsibility of bearing arms side by side with white men was to deprive the South of its principal justification of slavery. On January 8, 1865, Howell Cobb of Georgia wrote the Confederate Secretary of War: "The day you make soldiers of them is the beginning of the end of the revolution. If slaves will make good soldiers, our whole theory of slavery is wrong."

Advocates of the policy of arming the slaves based their case mainly on necessity. A Georgia planter who had lost two sons in Confederate service wrote President Davis on January 10, 1865: "The recruits must come from our negroes, nowhere else. . . . The negro must be put into the Army or we shall be subjugated." Secretary of State Benjamin and others argued that the North's recruitment of colored men reduced the South "to choosing whether the negroes shall fight for or against us." NEGROES 241

Above, November 8, 1863, refugees coming into the lines, near
Culpeper Court House, Virginia; below, fugitive Negroes
fording the Rappahannock, fleeing from Jackson's army, August,
1862

*Contrabands on Mr.
Foller's farm, Cumberland
Landing, Virginia, May
14, 1862*

One earnest supporter of enlisting the slaves wrote the Confederate President: "Some people say negroes will not fight. I say they will. They fought at Ocean Pond, Honey Hill and other places. The enemy fights us with the negroes and they will do very well to fight the Yankees." Many other Southerners held similar views. Indeed, some argued that slaves, accustomed as they were to obeying their masters, would fight better as Confederates under Southern leaders than as Yankees commanded by strangers.

Early in 1865 General Lee publicly indorsed the recruiting of slaves, on grounds both of expediency and necessity. Shortly afterward bills were introduced in both houses of Congress. On March 13, 1865, President Davis attached his signature to a law authorizing the enlistment of 300,000 Negroes. General Lee recommended that slaves who rendered faithful service as soldiers be given their freedom, but the law made no provision for emancipation.

Virginia took the lead in recruiting slaves; in late March, 1865, companies of Negro soldiers, clad in shining new uniforms, paraded on Capitol Square in Richmond. But the war ended before any of the

First African Church,
Richmond, Virginia, 1865

Negroes enrolled under the law of March 13, 1865, could be put into battle.

Early in the conflict a regiment of free Negroes was organized in New Orleans but this unit was never mustered into Confederate service. Throughout the conflict slaves and free Negroes were carried on company rolls of various states as musicians and accessories, but they were not soldiers. Some light-complexioned mulattoes doubtless wore the Confederate gray, but they were classified as whites. Federal sources occasionally make reference to the appearance of Negroes in Confederate ranks, but these probably were body servants or smoke-blackened whites. No evidence has been found of Negroes recognizable as such, participating in battle as full-fledged Confederate soldiers.

The law of March 13 was a last desperate measure of a nation standing on the brink of defeat. It came too late to be of any benefit, but it probably would have been of no avail had it been adopted earlier. It violated the fundamentals of slavery and it called on a people whose hearts were set on freedom to risk their lives for the perpetuation of bondage.

EMBATTLED
CONFEDERATES

XIV. *The Collapse of the Confederacy*

The painful decision to make soldiers of slaves was only one of many evidences of the South's impending collapse. For several months the plight of the embattled Confederacy had been rapidly worsening. Lincoln's re-election gave notice that the North was firmly committed to continuing the war, and only those who were ignorant or who closed their eyes to reality could seriously question the Union's ultimate triumph. The fall of Atlanta, Sheridan's victories in the Shenandoah Valley, Sherman's easy march through Georgia and Hood's disastrous defeat in Tennessee were convincing testimonials to the South's inability to cope with the North's overpowering strength. On October 2, 1864, one of Early's soldiers wrote his sister: "We have got two good whipings that the Yankes has give us. I tell you that we got a bad whiping on the 19th at Winchester and we fell back to Fisher's Hill and there we was run to the mountains. . . . There is a greate many Yankes in front of us. I am afraid we will not be able to whip them. . . . I fere the end . . . for I don't think the South can be able to stand up very much longer in men or Rashons for some days we almost starve. . . . I ot not to write this to you all as it will make you uneasy but it is the truth." In January, 1865, a Virginian serving with Lee wrote his wife: "All of us think we are whipped now. . . . We have no army worth a sent except ours & that can't whip the world. Some say we will have to go to Georgey, but the men will not go there & leave their friends and families hear behind; indeed, we have but little or no encouragement to fite atall. the men a great portion of them [are] raged & are getting half rashions . . . & no pay and that will not bye much."

Cold, hungry, ragged, weary, anxious about their families and dispirited by the military outlook, soldiers deserted in droves in the last winter of the war; among those who absconded were men who for more than three years had endured hardship and danger without murmur or faltering.

Early in 1865, General Lee repeatedly expressed concern about the increase of desertions. On March 9, 1865, General Beauregard wrote from Charlotte that soldiers of the Army of Tennessee en route to North Carolina had "deserted by hundreds," and that "desertion . . . is now an epidemic." General Bragg on March 26 wrote President Davis from Raleigh: "I passed poor Walthall . . . and inquired for his command. He pointed me to a small squad and said, 'My division now numbers two

The last of Lieutenant General Ewell's Corps, muskets raised hilt up in token of surrender, at Sayler's Creek, Virginia, April 6, 1865

brigadiers and sixty-three men for duty.' His is a sample of the whole, and nothing better may be expected."

Consolidated returns, covering most of the field forces and bearing various dates from December 31, 1864, to April 17, 1865, showed a total of 198,494 officers and men absent as against only 160,198 present for duty. According to General John S. Preston, superintendent of conscription, over 100,000 of the absentees were deserters.

Many of the deserters roved about the country plundering helpless citizens; the same was true of "home guards" and other local organizations whose avowed purpose was to maintain order and protect the people. Among both soldiers and civilians lawlessness and immorality increased notably during the early months of 1865 and this breakdown of traditional controls and standards gave further evidence of the Confederacy's approaching doom.

Other indications pointing to the same end were an upsurge of smuggling, tax evasion, inflation, hoarding and speculation; mounting resistance to impressment; and increasing deterioration of communication and transportation facilities. The result in terms of the masses of the people was an increase of loneliness, suffering and despair. Some in the army and at home had enough stamina and devotion to withstand

EMBATTLED CONFEDERATES

Ruins of the Northeastern Railroad Depot, Charleston, South Carolina, 1865

all the woes that beset them and urge continuing support of the cause that they had espoused four years before. But they were a rapidly dwindling minority.

General Bragg represented the South's tottering situation accurately when he wrote President Davis from North Carolina two weeks before Appomattox: "The sad spectacle [is] hourly presented of disorganization, demoralization and destruction. . . . [Deserters] are scattered over the States of North and South Carolina, Georgia, Alabama and Mississippi living at free quarters on the people. . . . Officers seem paralyzed, men indifferent to everything but plunder and the people, as well they may, appear disgusted and dismayed. This state of things cannot last and no one is so blind as not to see the inevitable result. . . . The people are disheartened and do not see what more can happen from the enemy."

Why did the Confederacy fail in the revolution that it so confidently launched in 1861? A primary cause of Confederate defeat was the North's tremendous superiority in human and material resources. The Northern states at the beginning of the conflict had a population of 22,000,000 as against the South's 9,000,000, of whom more than one-third were slaves. The North had far more of liquid wealth, banks, factories, mines and ships. Its communications and transportation facilities were vastly superior to those of the South. In 1861 the states adhering to the Union had nearly two and one-half times as many miles of railroad as the Confederacy and their rail lines were longer, better constructed and tied in more effectively with water transportation; Northern rolling stock was sturdier and more abundant; and facilities for extension, replacement and repair were far more adequate than those in the South. Industrial expansion and the influx of millions of immigrants in the three decades preceding the war had given to the North a richness and variety of managerial experience and technical skill unknown to the South; and in making the shift from littleness to bigness in trade and manufacturing, Northerners had become accustomed to working together. The North had more and better public schools, and its people were more literate. All of this was to be of tremendous moment in the conduct of what has been called "the first modern total war."

The South also possessed some important advantages. It had the interior position and the defensive role. All that the South had to do to win was to put up enough resistance to cause the North to desist from its effort to re-establish Federal control over the states that had seceded. The triumph of the Union, on the other hand, required that the North

The burnt district, Richmond, Virginia

invade and conquer the Confederacy and force the South into submission. The South also benefited from the greater familiarity of its youth with guns and horses and the greater popularity of the profession of arms among its people. Hundreds of military academies dotted the Southern countryside; in these institutions many boys who later were to lead companies, regiments and brigades in the Confederate army learned the rudiments of soldiering. For the most part they were planters' sons, and their identification with the ruling caste was an asset to their leadership. But the onslaught of epidemic disease, to which the rural Southerners were particularly vulnerable, and the early battles took a heavy toll of Confederate officers. In time the urban-bred men of the North learned to ride and shoot and in training camps and battle lines the Union forces developed a corps of able officers.

As previously noted, Southerners counted heavily on European recognition and assistance in their bid for independence. But this expectation was based on ignorance and wishful thinking. England held the key to European intervention and England's need of cotton was not nearly as great as Southerners believed. Huge surpluses already on hand sufficed to keep factories going during the first year of conflict and brought

The burnt district, Richmond, Virginia, April, 1865. Two women in mourning on the right

handsome profits. By the time the cotton famine began really to pinch, the North had avowed freedom as a war aim, and the strong antipathy to slavery among British factory laborers—and it was they who bore the brunt of the cotton shortage—worked strongly against recognition of the Confederacy. Other obstacles to recognition were the huge profits realized by English merchants who sold munitions and supplies to both belligerents, a natural inclination to caution and conservatism in British governmental circles, failure of Southern armies to win victories at times when the diplomatic situation seemed most propitious, and the unwillingness of Lord Palmerston and his associates to risk the war that William H. Seward and Charles Francis Adams told them would certainly ensue if they accorded recognition to the South.

While the North's superior resources and Europe's neutrality were unquestionably of prime importance in Confederate defeat, these were by no means the only reasons for the South's failure to achieve independence. Nor can it be said with certainty that they were the decisive factors. The South was severely handicapped by internal weaknesses. One of these, as previously noted, was ineffectual political leadership on levels high and low. Jefferson Davis lacked the vision, stamina, boldness, tact and glamour to head a revolution. Most of the cabinet were mediocrities, and there were remarkably few outstanding men among congressmen, governors and state legislators. Many of these men had made their reputations and risen to high positions as leaders of protest against "Northern aggression." They were habituated to negativism and obstruc-

Ruins in Columbia, South Carolina

EMBATTLED CONFEDERATES

tion. They had proved eloquent and impressive in denunciation but in 1861 they found it difficult, if not impossible, to turn about and assume a positive position and discharge the enormous responsibilities incident to building a new nation and fighting a big war. Nearly all of them, including Davis, were hamstrung by an outmoded state rights philosophy, and many were extremely provincial in their outlook and interest.

Another great handicap was dissension. Considerable strife was to be expected among a people caught in the strains and stresses of war. But the Confederacy had an inordinate amount of controversy, and much of it was unreasonable, abusive and personal. This excessive quarrelsomeness was due in part to habit. In the long and bitter slavery controversy with the North, Southerners had become accustomed to contention. When secession parted them from their traditional antagonists, they turned on each other. Habit was aided and abetted by frustration. Disappointed in their hopes of winning a quick and easy victory, and confronted as they were with the formidable task of conducting a long war with a nation that seemed to have unlimited resources, Southerners gave way to vehement accusations and emotional tirades. Contentiousness was aggravated by a feeling of guilt about slavery. While the South had ostensibly renounced the liberalism of the Jeffersonian

Flight of President Jefferson Davis and his ministers over the Georgia Ridge, five days before his capture

Brigadier General Joseph H. Lewis from Tennessee, who accompanied the presidential party on its flight

EMBATTLED CONFEDERATES

age and accepted slavery as a beneficent, divinely ordained institution, there lingered in many Southern minds a deep-seated uneasiness about holding fellow humans in bondage. When the war turned against the South, the feeling of guilt became more oppressive and some prominent churchmen tried unsuccessfully to inaugurate reforms that would rid slavery of its most patent evils. The gnawings of conscience and the growing conviction that in clinging to slavery they were shocking the moral sensibilities of the civilized world tended to make Southerners ill at ease with themselves and touchy in their relations with each other.

Much of the strife that beset the Confederacy had its roots in the exaggerated individualism nurtured by the plantation system. The planters who dominated Southern society were in effect petty sovereigns, proud, self-sufficient and unaccustomed to the give and take of joint enterprise. On February 5, 1861, just as the new government was coming into being, James H. Hammond wrote his friend, William Gilmore Simms: "Big-man-me-ism reigns supreme, and every one thinks every other a jealous fool or an aspiring knave." The characteristic noted by Hammond increased with the passing of time. The Confederacy was sorely crippled by the flood of ill-tempered and irresponsible criticism directed by individualistic malcontents at those charged with the difficult

Jefferson Davis and Mrs. Davis after his release from
Fort Monroe

task of directing public affairs. The injury was compounded by the inability of those under attack to accept the criticism in silence. Most of them talked back, heatedly and at great length.

Southern leaders might have avoided much criticism, and the Confederate cause might have been much benefited, had the people been better informed about public affairs. From the beginning the government followed a policy of secrecy. The minds of the people were not adequately prepared for such revolutionary and burdensome measures as conscription, impressment, suspension of habeas corpus, heavy taxation, crop control and the arming of slaves. Nor were they told what they had a right to know about important military operations. Before critical campaigns, false hopes were aroused by misinformation or silence. Many people did not learn the truth about disastrous reverses such as Fort Donelson, Vicksburg and Gettysburg until long after the events. As late as July 25, 1863, a prominent resident of Austin, Texas, wrote in his diary: "Went into town—Got extra and found it confirmed all about the taking of Washington, Harrisburg, etc. Also that Grant had attacked Johnston at Jackson and been utterly defeated. . . . The news glorious for our side." When the full extent of military defeats finally dawned on the unwary public, they were disillusioned and disgusted. James H. Hammond reflected a widespread sentiment when he wrote on April 16, 1864: "I wish they would fight a real battle somewhere & tell us the truth about it." Lacking dependable sources of information, the country was flooded with fantastic rumors and predictions, and all too frequently these were believed.

Another important reason for the South's defeat was its inability to adapt itself to changing situations and needs. This weakness was due in large measure to its history. During the decades immediately preceding the Civil War, the South had remained agricultural, rural and provincial, while the North was becoming industrial, urban and national. Earlier many Southern leaders had been favorably disposed toward industry and their outlook had been more national than sectional. But by 1830, largely as a result of the invention of the cotton gin, the South was thoroughly committed to agriculture and slavery. In the years that followed, as the outside world became increasingly hostile to slavery, the South drew back in a shell, planted cotton, lauded slavery, denounced its critics and fixed its gaze on the past.

In the spring of 1861 the South found itself involved in a big war. This was a new kind of war, requiring massive armies and enormous supplies. It had to be sustained by factories, skilled workers and trained managers. It called for varied talent, large-scale activity, close coordination and expert administration. The South made an enormous effort and demonstrated a valor unsurpassed in the annals of history. But the fact remains that its experience was too limited, its institutions too archaic, its outlook too restricted and its ways too inflexible to enable it to compete successfully in a modern war with a progressive and powerful nation.

EMBATTLED
CONFEDERATES

General Robert E. Lee,
photographed on the back
porch of his Richmond
home by Mathew B. Brady,
April, 1865

Appendices

A. CONFEDERATE CABINET *

Secretary of State	Robert Toombs, February 21, 1861
	Robert M. T. Hunter, July 25, 1861
	William M. Brown (ad interim, about February 1, 1862)
	Judah P. Benjamin, March 18, 1862
Attorney General	Judah P. Benjamin, February 25, 1861
	Wade Keyes (ad interim, September, 1861)
	Thomas Bragg, November 21, 1861
	Thomas H. Watts, March 18, 1862
	Wade Keyes (ad interim, October 1, 1863)
	George Davis, January 2, 1864
Secretary of the Treasury	Christopher G. Memminger, February 21, 1861
	George A. Trenholm, July 18, 1864
Secretary of the Navy	Stephen R. Mallory, March 4, 1861
Postmaster General	Henry T. Ellet, February 25, 1861 (declined appointment)
	John H. Reagan, March 6, 1861
Secretary of War	Leroy P. Walker, February 21, 1861
	Judah P. Benjamin, November 21, 1861 (was also Acting Secretary from September 17, 1861, to November 21, 1861, and from March 18, 1862, to March 23, 1862)
	Brig. Gen. George W. Randolph, March 18, 1862
	Maj. Gen. Gustavus Woodson Smith (ad interim, November 17, 1862)
	James A. Seddon, November 21, 1862
	Maj. Gen. John C. Breckinridge, February 6, 1865

* Dates indicate the time of confirmation by Provisional Congress or Senate.

B. CONFEDERATE CONGRESS *

1. CONGRESSES OF THE CONFEDERATE STATES

Provisional Congress

First Session	Assembled at Montgomery, Ala., February 4, 1861. Adjourned March 16, 1861, to meet second Monday in May.
Second Session	Met at Montgomery, Ala., April 29, 1861. Adjourned May 21, 1861.
Third Session	Met at Richmond, Va., July 20, 1861. Adjourned August 31, 1861.
Fourth Session (called)	Met at Richmond, Va., September 3, 1861. Adjourned same day.
Fifth Session	Met at Richmond, Va., November 18, 1861. Adjourned February 17, 1862.

First Congress

First Session	Met at Richmond, Va., February 18, 1862. Adjourned April 21, 1862.
Second Session	Met at Richmond, Va., August 18, 1862. Adjourned October 13, 1862.
Third Session	Met at Richmond, Va., January 12, 1863. Adjourned May 1, 1863.
Fourth Session	Met at Richmond, Va., December 7, 1863. Adjourned February 17, 1864.

Second Congress

First Session	Met at Richmond, Va., May 2, 1864. Adjourned June 14, 1864.
Second Session	Met at Richmond, Va., November 7, 1864. Adjourned March 18, 1865.

2. ALPHABETICAL LIST OF CONGRESSMEN

(Note: Unless otherwise indicated, service was for the entire period of the Congress to which legislator was elected.)

			Standing Committees
Akin, Warren	Georgia	House, Second Congress	Claims
Anderson, Clifford	Georgia	House, Second Congress	Ways and Means
Anderson, James Patton	Florida	Provisional (resigned May 2, 1861)	Military Affairs, Public Lands
Arrington, Archibald H.	North Carolina	House, First Congress (admitted February 20, 1862)	Indian Affairs
Ashe, Thomas S.	North Carolina	House, First Congress	Judiciary

* Compiled from the *Executive and Congressional Directory of the Confederate States, 1861–1865*, published by the U. S. Pension Bureau in 1899; *Journal of the Congress of the Confederate States of America, 1861–1865*, 7 Vols., U. S. Government Printing Office, 1904–1905; and "Proceedings of the Confederate Congress," Vols. 44–52, *Southern Historical Society Papers*, Richmond, Va., 1923–1959. The *Executive and Congressional Directory* contains many minor errors.

Atkins, John D. C.	Tennessee	Provisional (admitted August 13, 1861)	Military Affairs
		House, First Congress (admitted March 8, 1862)	Post Office and Post-Roads
		House, Second Congress	Commerce, Foreign Affairs, Ordnance and Ordnance Stores
Avery, William W.	North Carolina	Provisional (admitted July 20, 1861)	Military Affairs
Ayer, Lewis M.	South Carolina	House, First Congress (admitted March 6, 1862)	Quartermaster and Commissary Department and Military Transportation, Ordnance and Ordnance Stores
		House, Second Congress (admitted May 12, 1864)	Commerce, Ordnance and Ordnance Stores
Baker, James M.	Florida	Senate, First Congress	Public Lands, Claims, Commerce, Buildings, Engrossment and Enrollment, Naval Affairs, Post Office and Post-roads
		Senate, Second Congress	Claims, Naval Affairs, Post Office and Post-roads, Public Buildings, Public Lands
Baldwin, John B.	Virginia	House, First Congress (admitted February 27, 1862)	Ways and Means
		House, Second Congress	Ways and Means
Barksdale, Ethelbert	Mississippi	House, First Congress	Foreign Affairs, Printing
		House, Second Congress	Ordnance and Ordnance Stores, Ways and Means
Barnwell, Robert W.	South Carolina	Provisional	Finance
		Senate, First Congress	Finance
		Senate, Second Congress (admitted May 5, 1864)	Finance, Territories
Barry, William S.	Mississippi	Provisional	Finance
Bartow, Francis S.	Georgia	Provisional (killed, First Manassas, July 21, 1861)	Engrossment, Flag and Seal, Military Affairs
Bass, Nathan	Georgia	Provisional (admitted, January 14, 1862)	None
Batson, Felix I.	Arkansas	House, First Congress	Military Affairs, Territories and Public Lands
		House, Second Congress (admitted November 18, 1864)	Judiciary
Baylor, John R.	Texas	House, Second Congress (admitted May 25, 1864)	Indian Affairs, Patents
Bell, Caspar W.	Missouri	Provisional (admitted December 6, 1861)	Public Lands, Territories
		House, First Congress	Medical Department, Military Affairs, Patents
Bell, Hiram P.	Georgia	House, Second Congress	Elections, Patents, Post Office and Post-Roads
Blandford, Mark H.	Georgia	House, Second Congress	Judiciary, Pay and Mileage

Bocock, Thomas S.	Virginia	Provisional (admitted July 23, 1861)	None
		House, First Congress	None
		House, Second Congress	None
Bonham, Milledge L.	South Carolina	House, First Congress (resigned January 17, 1863)	Ways and Means
Boteler, Alexander R.	Virginia	Provisional (admitted November 27, 1861)	Public Buildings, Flag and Seal, Indian Affairs, Printing
		House, First Congress	Flag and Seal, Ordnance and Ordnance Stores, Rules and Officers of the House
Boudinot, Elias C.	Cherokee Nation	House, First Congress (admitted October 9, 1862)	Indian Affairs (corresponding)
		House, Second Congress	Indian Affairs (corresponding)
Boyce, William W.	South Carolina	Provisional	Postal Affairs, Executive Organization
		House, First Congress	Naval Affairs, Ways and Means
		House, Second Congress	Naval Affairs
Bradford, Alexander B.	Mississippi	Provisional (admitted December 5, 1861)	Public Lands
Bradley, Benjamin F.	Kentucky	House, Second Congress	Ordnance and Ordnance Stores, Post Office and Post-Roads
Branch, Anthony M.	Texas	House, Second Congress	Elections, Military Affairs, Territories and Public Lands
Breckinridge, Robert J., Jr.	Kentucky	House, First Congress	Foreign Affairs
Bridgers, Robert R.	North Carolina	House, First Congress	Military Affairs, Pay and Mileage
		House, Second Congress	Military Affairs
Brockenbrough, John W.	Virginia	Provisional (admitted May 7, 1861)	Judiciary
Brooke, Walker	Mississippi	Provisional	Executive Organization, Patents
Brown, Albert G.	Mississippi	Senate, First Congress	Naval Affairs, Territories
		Senate, Second Congress	Naval Affairs
Bruce, Eli M.	Kentucky	House, First Congress (admitted March 20, 1862)	Military Affairs
		House, Second Congress	Ways and Means
Bruce, Horatio W.	Kentucky	House, First Congress	Commerce, Enrolled Bills
		House, Second Congress	Foreign Affairs, Patents
Burnett, Henry C.	Kentucky	Provisional (admitted December 16, 1861)	Finance
		Senate, First Congress (admitted February 26, 1862)	Buildings, Claims, Commerce, Judiciary, Naval Affairs, Pay and Mileage, Military Affairs
		Senate, Second Congress	Claims, Engrossment and Enrollment, Military Affairs
Burnett, Theodore L.	Kentucky	Provisional (admitted December 16, 1861)	None
		House, First Congress (admitted February 19, 1862)	Claims, Pay and Mileage
		House, Second Congress	Commerce, Pay and Mileage

Callahan, S. B.	Creek and Seminole Nations	House, Second Congress (admitted May 30, 1864)	None
Campbell, J. A. P.	Mississippi	Provisional	Accounts, Pay and Mileage, Territories
Caperton, Allen T.	Virginia	Senate, First Congress (admitted January 26, 1863)	Accounts, Engrossment and Enrollment, Judiciary
		Senate, Second Congress	Accounts, Engrossment and Enrollment, Foreign Relations, Indian Affairs, Post Office and Post-Roads
Carroll, David W.	Arkansas	House, Second Congress (admitted January 11, 1865)	Commerce
Caruthers, Robert L.	Tennessee	Provisional (admitted August 12, 1861)	Judiciary
Chambers, Henry C.	Mississippi	House, First Congress (admitted February 19, 1862)	Commerce, Enrolled Bills, Military Affairs
		House, Second Congress	Flag and Seal, Military Affairs
Chambliss, John R.	Virginia	House, First Congress	Naval Affairs
Chesnut, James, Jr.	South Carolina	Provisional	Naval Affairs, Territories
Chilton, William P.	Alabama	Provisional	Buildings, Printing, Postal Affairs
		House, First Congress	Patents, Post Office and Post-Roads, Quartermaster and Commissary Department and Military Transportation
		House, Second Congress	Flag and Seal, Judiciary, Patents, Rules and Officers of House
Chrisman, James S.	Kentucky	House, First Congress (admitted March 3, 1862)	Medical Department
		House, Second Congress	Elections, Indian Affairs, Territories and Public Lands
Clapp, J. W.	Mississippi	House, First Congress	Claims, Elections, Ordnance and Ordnance Stores
Clark, John B.	Missouri	Provisional (admitted December 6, 1861)	Foreign Affairs, Indian Affairs
		Senate, First Congress	Foreign Affairs, Post Office and Post-Roads, Printing, Public Lands, Territories, Indian Affairs
		House, Second Congress (admitted June 10, 1864)	Elections, Military Affairs
Clark, William W.	Georgia	House, First Congress	Post Office and Post-Roads, Medical Department, Quartermaster and Commissary Department and Military Transportation
Clay, Clement C.	Alabama	Senate, First Congress (admitted February 19, 1862)	Commerce, Indian Affairs, Rules, Military Affairs
Clayton, Alex M.	Mississippi	Provisional (admitted February 8, 1861; resigned May 11, 1861)	Judiciary
Clopton, David	Alabama	House, First Congress	Claims, Naval Affairs, Ordnance and Ordnance Stores
		House, Second Congress	Medical Department, Naval Affairs

Cluskey, Michael W.	Tennessee	House, Second Congress (admitted November 7, 1864)	Naval Affairs
Cobb, Howell	Georgia	Provisional	None
Cobb, Thomas R. R.	Georgia	Provisional	Judiciary, Printing
Collier, Charles F.	Virginia	House, First Congress (admitted August 18, 1862)	Commerce, Naval Affairs
Colyar, Arthur S.	Tennessee	House, Second Congress	Ways and Means
Conrad, Charles M.	Louisiana	Provisional (admitted February 7, 1861)	Executive Organization, Naval Affairs
		House, First Congress	Naval Affairs, Ordnance and Ordnance Stores
		House, Second Congress	Public Buildings, Ways and Means
Conrow, Aaron H.	Missouri	Provisional (admitted December 2, 1861)	Finance
		House, First Congress	Post Office and Post-Roads
		House, Second Congress (admitted November 7, 1864)	Public Buildings, Quartermaster and Commissary Department
Cooke, William M.	Missouri	Provisional (admitted December 5, 1861)	Accounts, Commerce, Naval Affairs
		House, First Congress (died, April 14, 1863)	Commerce, Ordnance and Ordnance Stores
Craige, Burton	North Carolina	Provisional (admitted July 23, 1861)	None
Crawford, Martin J.	Georgia	Provisional	Accounts, Commercial Affairs
Crockett, John W.	Kentucky	House, First Congress	Elections
Cruikshank, M. H.	Alabama	House, Second Congress	Ordnance and Ordnance Stores, Printing, Enrolled Bills
Currin, David M.	Tennessee	Provisional (admitted August 16, 1861)	Commercial Affairs, Naval Affairs
		House, First Congress (elected to Second Congress but did not take his seat; died May 21, 1864)	Naval Affairs, Public Buildings
Curry, Jabez L. M.	Alabama	Provisional	Commercial Affairs, Flag and Seal, Postal Affairs, Rules
		House, First Congress	Commerce, Elections
Darden, Stephen H.	Texas	House, Second Congress (admitted November 21, 1864)	Naval Affairs
Dargan, Edward S.	Alabama	House, First Congress	Judiciary
Davidson, Allen T.	North Carolina	Provisional (admitted July 20, 1861)	None
		House, First Congress	Quartermaster and Commissary Department and Military Transportation, Post Office and Post-Roads
Davis, George	North Carolina	Provisional (admitted July 20, 1861)	None
		Senate, First Congress (resigned January, 1864)	Buildings, Claims, Finance, Naval Affairs

Davis, Nicholas, Jr.	Alabama	Provisional (admitted April 29, 1861)	Pay and Mileage, Public Lands, Territories
Davis, Reuben	Mississippi	House, First Congress (resigned, January 21, 1864)	Military Affairs
Dawkins, James B.	Florida	House, First Congress (resigned, December 8, 1862)	Elections, Naval Affairs, Quartermaster and Commissary Department and Military Transportation
De Clouet, Alexander	Louisiana	Provisional	Accounts, Commercial Affairs
De Jarnette, Daniel C.	Virginia	House, First Congress House, Second Congress	Foreign Affairs Foreign Affairs, Medical Department
DeWitt, W. H.	Tennessee	Provisional (admitted August 16, 1861)	Printing, Territories
Dickinson, James S.	Alabama	House, Second Congress	Claims, Commerce
Dortch, William T.	North Carolina	Senate, First Congress Senate, Second Congress	Accounts, Commerce, Naval Affairs, Engrossment and Enrollment Accounts, Commerce, Engrossment and Enrollment
Dupré, Lucius J.	Louisiana	House, First Congress House, Second Congress	Indian Affairs, Printing Judiciary, Printing
Echols, Joseph H.	Georgia	House, Second Congress	Indian Affairs, Medical Department, Pay and Mileage
Elliott, John M.	Kentucky	Provisional (admitted January 15, 1862) House, First Congress House, Second Congress (admitted May 24, 1864)	None Enrolled Bills, Indian Affairs Indian Affairs, Post Office and Post-Roads
Ewing, George W.	Kentucky	Provisional (admitted February 14, 1862) House, First Congress House, Second Congress	None Territories and Public Lands Claims, Territories and Public Lands
Farrow, James	South Carolina	House, First Congress House, Second Congress	Claims, Medical Department Accounts, Claims, Commerce, Medical Department
Fearn, Thomas	Alabama	Provisional (resigned April 29, 1861)	Territories, Public Lands
Foote, Henry S.	Tennessee	House, First Congress House, Second Congress (expelled February 27, 1865)	Foreign Affairs, Quartermaster and Commissary Department and Military Transportation Foreign Affairs, Quartermaster and Commissary Department
Ford, S. H.	Kentucky	Provisional (admitted January 4, 1862)	None
Foreman, Thomas M.	Georgia	Provisional (admitted August 7, 1861)	None
Foster, Thomas J.	Alabama	House, First Congress (admitted February 19, 1862) House, Second Congress (admitted May 6, 1864)	Accounts, Territories and Public Lands Indian Affairs, Post Office and Post-Roads, Territories and Public Lands

Freeman, Thomas W.	Missouri	Provisional (admitted December 5, 1861)	Postal Affairs
		House, First Congress	Territories and Public Lands, Enrolled Bills, Naval Affairs
Fuller, Thomas C.	North Carolina	House, Second Congress	Commerce, Enrolled Bills, Patents
Funsten, David	Virginia	House, First Congress (admitted December 7, 1863)	Printing
		House, Second Congress (admitted May 3, 1864)	Flag and Seal, Naval Affairs
Gaither, Burgess S.	North Carolina	House, First Congress	Naval Affairs
		House, Second Congress	Judiciary
Gardenshire, E. L.	Tennessee	House, First Congress	Claims, Elections, Enrolled Bills
Garland, Augustus H.	Arkansas	Provisional (admitted May 18, 1861)	Judiciary, Public Lands
		House, First Congress	Judiciary, Enrolled Bills, Medical Department
		House, Second Congress (resigned about November 8, 1864)	Judiciary, Territories and Public Lands
		Senate, Second Congress (admitted November 8, 1864)	Military Affairs, Post Office and Post-Roads
Garland, Rufus K.	Arkansas	House, Second Congress (admitted May 21, 1864)	Ways and Means
Garnett, Muscoe R. H.	Virginia	House, First Congress (died February 14, 1864)	Military Affairs, Ways and Means
Gartrell, Lucius J.	Georgia	House, First Congress	Judiciary
Gentry, Meredith P.	Tennessee	House, First Congress (admitted March 17, 1862)	None
Gholson, Thomas S.	Virginia	House, Second Congress	Judiciary
Gilmer, John A.	North Carolina	House, Second Congress	Elections, Ways and Means
Goode, John, Jr.	Virginia	House, First Congress	Enrolled Bills, Indian Affairs, Medical Department
		House, Second Congress	Commerce, Printing
Graham, M. D.	Texas	House, First Congress	Ways and Means
Graham, William A.	North Carolina	Senate, Second Congress	Naval Affairs, Finance
Gray, Henry	Louisiana	House, Second Congress (admitted December 28, 1864)	Judiciary
Gray, Peter W.	Texas	House, First Congress	Flag and Seal, Judiciary
Gregg, John	Texas	Provisional (admitted February 15, 1861)	Accounts, Claims, Military Affairs
Hale, Stephen F.	Alabama	Provisional	Indian Affairs, Judiciary, Military Affairs
Hanly, Thomas B.	Arkansas	House, First Congress	Accounts, Indian Affairs, Claims, Enrolled Bills, Post Office and Post-Roads,
		House, Second Congress	Indian Affairs, Military Affairs, Pay and Quartermaster and Commissary Department and Military Transportation, Mileage

Harris, Thomas A.	Missouri	Provisional (admitted December 6, 1861)	Military Affairs
		House, First Congress	Military Affairs
Harris, Wiley P.	Mississippi	Provisional	Judiciary, Military Affairs, Public Lands
Harrison, James T.	Mississippi	Provisional	Flag and Seal, Postal Affairs, Printing, Rules
Hartridge, Julian	Georgia	House, First Congress (admitted March 14, 1862)	Commerce, Ordnance and Ordnance Stores, Ways and Means
		House, Second Congress	Commerce
Hatcher, Robert A.	Missouri	House, Second Congress (admitted November 7, 1864)	Enrolled Bills, Ordnance and Ordnance Stores
Haynes, Landon C.	Tennessee	Senate, First Congress	Engrossment and Enrollment, Judiciary, Patents, Post Office and Post-Roads, Printing
		Senate, Second Congress	Commerce, Judiciary, Patents, Printing, Post Office and Post-Roads
Heiskell, Joseph B.	Tennessee	House, First Congress (resigned February 6, 1864)	Judiciary
		House, Second Congress	Claims, Elections, Patents
Hemphill, John	Texas	Provisional (admitted March 2, 1861; died January 4, 1862)	Finance, Judiciary
Henry, Gustavus A.	Tennessee	Senate, First Congress	Finance, Military Affairs, Pay and Mileage
		Senate, Second Congress	Military Affairs, Public Lands
Herbert, Caleb C.	Texas	House, First Congress	Ordnance and Ordnance Stores, Post Office and Post-Roads
		House, Second Congress (admitted November 21, 1864)	Claims, Commerce
Hill, Benjamin H.	Georgia	Provisional	Claims, Patents, Postal Affairs
		Senate, First Congress	Judiciary, Naval Affairs, Patents, Printing
		Senate, Second Congress	Judiciary, Patents
Hilton, Robert B.	Florida	House, First Congress	Military Affairs, Patents, Post Office and Post-Roads
		House, Second Congress	Elections, Military Affairs, Territories and Public Lands
Hodge, Benj. L.	Louisiana	House, Second Congress (admitted May 25, 1864; died August 12, 1864)	None
Hodge, Geo. B.	Kentucky	Provisional (admitted January 11, 1862)	None
		House, First Congress (admitted August 18, 1862)	Naval Affairs, Ordnance and Ordnance Stores
Holcombe, James P.	Virginia	House, First Congress (admitted February 20, 1862)	Judiciary
Holder, Wm. D.	Mississippi	House, First Congress (admitted January 21, 1864)	None
		House, Second Congress (admitted May 4, 1864)	Elections, Medical Department, Naval Affairs, Public Buildings

Holliday, Frederick W. M.	Virginia	House, Second Congress (admitted May 4, 1864)	Claims, Quartermaster and Commissary Department
Holt, Hines	Georgia	House, First Congress (did not attend last session; resigned between December 19, 1863, and January 12, 1864)	Ways and Means
House, John F.	Tennessee	Provisional (admitted August 12, 1861)	Finance
Hunter, Robert M. T.	Virginia	Provisional (admitted May 10, 1861)	Finance
		Senate, First Congress	Finance, Foreign Affairs
		Senate, Second Congress	Finance
Ingram, Porter	Georgia	House, First Congress (admitted January 12, 1864)	Medical Department
Jemison, Robt., Jr.	Alabama	Senate, First Congress (admitted December 28, 1863)	Claims, Finance, Naval Affairs
		Senate, Second Congress	Finance, Post Office and Post-Roads
Jenkins, Albert G.	Virginia	House, First Congress (resigned August 5, 1862)	Printing, Territories and Public Lands
Johnson, Herschel V.	Georgia	Senate, First Congress (admitted January 19, 1863)	Finance, Foreign Affairs, Naval Affairs, Post Office and Post-Roads
		Senate, Second Congress (admitted May 24, 1864)	Naval Affairs
Johnson, Robert W.	Arkansas	Provisional (admitted May 18, 1861)	Indian Affairs, Military Affairs
		Senate, First Congress	Indian Affairs, Military Affairs, Naval Affairs, Rules, Accounts
		Senate, Second Congress	Indian Affairs, Military Affairs, Public Lands, Rules
Johnson, Thomas	Kentucky	Provisional (admitted December 18, 1861)	Military Affairs
Johnson, Waldo P.	Missouri	Senate, First Congress (admitted December 24, 1863)	Claims
		Senate, Second Congress	Claims, Engrossment and Enrollment, Foreign Relations, Indian Affairs
Johnston, Robert	Virginia	Provisional (admitted July 20, 1861)	None
		House, First Congress	Post Office and Post-Roads
		House, Second Congress	Accounts, Quartermaster and Commissary Department
Jones, George W.	Tennessee	House, First Congress	Rules and Officers of House, Ways and Means
Jones, H. C.	Alabama	Provisional (admitted April 29, 1861)	Claims, Indian Affairs, Patents, Pay and Mileage
Jones, Robert M.	Choctaw Nation	House, First Congress (admitted January 17, 1863)	None
Jones, Thomas M.	Tennessee	Provisional (admitted August 12, 1861)	Flag and Seal, Naval Affairs
Keeble, Edwin A.	Tennessee	House, Second Congress	Judiciary

Keitt, Lawrence M.	South Carolina	Provisional	Foreign Affairs, Indian Affairs, Rules
Kenan, Augustus H.	Georgia	Provisional House, First Congress	Engrossment, Military Affairs Military Affairs
Kenan, Owen R.	North Carolina	House, First Congress	Accounts
Kenner, Duncan F.	Louisiana	Provisional House, First Congress House, Second Congress (admitted May 25, 1864)	Finance, Patents Ways and Means Ways and Means
Lamkin, John T.	Mississippi	House, Second Congress	Commerce, Patents, Post Office and Post-Roads
Lander, William	North Carolina	House, First Congress	Patents, Quartermaster and Commissary Department and Military Transportation
Leach, James M.	North Carolina	House, Second Congress	Quartermaster and Commissary Department
Leach, James T.	North Carolina	House, Second Congress	Post Office and Post-Roads, Territories and Public Lands
Lester, George N.	Georgia	House, Second Congress	Quartermaster and Commissary Department, Rules and Officers of House
Lewis, David P.	Alabama	Provisional (admitted February 8, 1861; resigned April 29, 1861)	Indian Affairs, Patents
Lewis, David W.	Georgia	House, First Congress	Rules and Officers of House, Territories and Public Lands, Printing
Lewis, John W.	Georgia	Senate, First Congress (admitted April 7, 1862)	Finance, Post Office and Post-Roads
Logan, George W.	North Carolina	House, Second Congress	Ordnance and Ordnance Stores, Printing
Lyon, Francis S.	Alabama	House, First Congress House, Second Congress	Ways and Means Ways and Means
Lyons, James	Virginia	House, First Congress	Public Buildings, Commerce
McCallum, James	Tennessee	House, Second Congress (admitted May 3, 1864)	Accounts, Medical Department, Post Office and Post-Roads
McDowell, Thomas D.	North Carolina	Provisional (admitted July 22, 1861) House, First Congress	None Commerce
Macfarland, William H.	Virginia	Provisional (admitted July 20, 1861)	Commercial Affairs
McLean, J. R.	North Carolina	House, First Congress	Claims, Foreign Affairs
McMullin, Fayette	Virginia	House, Second Congress	Post Office and Post-Roads, Public Buildings, Territories and Public Lands
McQueen, John	South Carolina	House, First Congress	Accounts, Foreign Affairs
McRae, Colin J.	Alabama	Provisional	Buildings, Engrossment, Finance, Naval Affairs
McRae, John J.	Mississippi	House, First Congress	Quartermaster and Commissary Department and Military Transportation, Ways and Means

Macwillie, Malcolm H.	Arizona Territory	House, First Congress (admitted March 11, 1862)	None
		House, Second Congress	None
Machen, Willis B.	Kentucky	House, First Congress	Ways and Means, Accounts
		House, Second Congress	Quartermaster and Commissary Department
Marshall, Henry	Louisiana	Provisional	Claims, Territories, Public Lands
		House, First Congress	Claims, Quartermaster and Commissary Department and Military Transportation, Territories and Public Lands, Patents
Marshall, Humphrey	Kentucky	House, Second Congress	Military Affairs
Martin, John M.	Florida	House, First Congress (admitted March 25, 1863)	Naval Affairs
Mason, James M.	Virginia	Provisional (admitted July 24, 1861)	Foreign Affairs
Maxwell, Augustus E.	Florida	Senate, First Congress	Commerce, Engrossment and Enrollment, Patents, Foreign Affairs, Naval Affairs
		Senate, Second Congress	Commerce, Engrossment and Enrollment, Indian Affairs, Patents
Memminger, Christopher G.	South Carolina	Provisional	Commercial Affairs
Menees, Thomas	Tennessee	House, First Congress	Medical Department, Printing, Territories and Public Lands
		House, Second Congress	Medical Department, Territories and Public Lands
Miles, William Porcher	South Carolina	Provisional	Commercial Affairs, Flag and Seal, Military Affairs, Printing
		House, First Congress	Military Affairs
		House, Second Congress	Military Affairs
Miller, Samuel A.	Virginia	House, First Congress (admitted February 24, 1863)	Territories and Public Lands
		House, Second Congress (admitted May 3, 1864)	Elections, Indian Affairs
Mitchel, Charles B.	Arkansas	Senate, First Congress	Accounts, Engrossment and Enrollment, Post Office and Post-Roads
		Senate, Second Congress (died September 20, 1864)	Post Office and Post-Roads, Territories
Monroe, Thomas B.	Kentucky	Provisional (admitted December 16, 1861)	Foreign Affairs, Judiciary, Military Affairs
Montague, Robert L.	Virginia	House, Second Congress	Ordnance and Ordnance Stores, Rules and Officers of House
Moore, James W.	Kentucky	House, First Congress	Judiciary
		House, Second Congress	Judiciary
Morehead, John M.	North Carolina	Provisional (admitted July 20, 1861)	None
Morgan, Simpson H.	Texas	House, Second Congress (admitted May 21, 1864; died January 16, 1865)	Judiciary

Morton, Jackson	Florida	Provisional (admitted February 6, 1861)	Commercial Affairs, Flag and Seal, Indian Affairs
Munnerlyn, Charles J.	Georgia	House, First Congress (admitted February 22, 1862)	Claims, Naval Affairs
Murray, John P.	Tennessee	House, Second Congress	Indian Affairs, Ordnance and Ordnance Stores
Nisbet, Eugenius A.	Georgia	Provisional (resigned December 10, 1861)	Foreign Affairs, Territories
Norton, Nimrod L.	Missouri	House, Second Congress (admitted November 21, 1864)	Claims, Territories and Public Lands
Ochiltree, William B., Sr.	Texas	Provisional (admitted, February 19, 1861)	Military Affairs, Pay and Mileage, Postal Affairs, Territories
Oldham, Williamson S.	Texas	Provisional (admitted March 2, 1861)	Engrossment, Judiciary, Naval Affairs, Territories
		Senate, First Congress	Indian Affairs, Naval Affairs, Post Office and Post-Roads, Commerce
		Senate, Second Congress	Claims, Commerce, Finance, Indian Affairs, Judiciary, Post Office and Post-Roads
Orr, James L.	South Carolina	Provisional (admitted February 17, 1862)	None
		Senate, First Congress	Flag and Seal, Foreign Affairs, Pay and Mileage, Rules, Commerce
		Senate, Second Congress	Finance, Foreign Relations, Printing, Rules
Orr, Jehu A.	Mississippi	Provisional (admitted April 29, 1861)	Claims, Engrossment, Patents
		House, Second Congress	Foreign Affairs, Quartermaster and Commissary Department
Oury, Granville H.	Arizona Territory	Provisional (admitted January 24, 1862)	None
Owens, James B.	Florida	Provisional	Accounts, Naval Affairs
Perkins, John, Jr.	Louisiana	Provisional	Foreign Affairs, Military Affairs, Printing, Rules
		House, First Congress	Foreign Affairs, Rules and Officers of House, Ways and Means
		House, Second Congress	Commerce, Foreign Affairs, Rules and Officers of House
Peyton, Robert L. Y.	Missouri	Provisional (admitted, January 22, 1862)	None
		Senate, First Congress (died December 19, 1863)	Claims, Commerce, Engrossment and Enrollment, Indian Affairs, Post Office and Post-Roads
Phelan, James	Mississippi	Senate, First Congress (Admitted February 19, 1862)	Engrossment and Enrollment, Judiciary, Post Office and Post-Roads, Printing, Indian Affairs
Preston, Walter	Virginia	Provisional (admitted July 22, 1861)	None
		House, First Congress	Foreign Affairs, Quartermaster and Commissary Department and Military Transportation

Preston, William B.	Virginia	Provisional (admitted July 20, 1861)	Military Affairs
		Senate, First Congress (died January 15, 1863)	Flag and Seal, Foreign Affairs, Military Affairs
Pryor, Roger A.	Virginia	Provisional (admitted July 24, 1861)	Military Affairs
		House, First Congress (resigned April 5, 1862)	Military Affairs
Pugh, James L.	Alabama	House, First Congress	Military Affairs, Public Buildings
		House, Second Congress	Public Buildings, Military Affairs
Puryear, Richard C.	North Carolina	Provisional (admitted July 20, 1861)	Naval Affairs
Ralls, John P.	Alabama	House, First Congress	Indian Affairs, Medical Department
Ramsay, James G.	North Carolina	House, Second Congress	Medical Department, Naval Affairs
Read, Henry E.	Kentucky	House, First Congress	Patents
		House, Second Congress	Medical Department, Quartermaster and Commissary Department
Reade, Edwin G.	North Carolina	Senate, First Congress (admitted January 22, 1864)	None
Reagan, John H.	Texas	Provisional (admitted March 2, 1861)	None
Rhett, Robert Barnwell, Sr.	South Carolina	Provisional	Foreign Affairs
Rives, William C.	Virginia	Provisional (admitted May 13, 1861)	Foreign Affairs
		House, First Congress	None
		House, Second Congress (resigned March 1, 1865)	Flag and Seal, Foreign Affairs
Robinson, Cornelius	Alabama	Provisional (admitted November 30, 1861; resigned January 24, 1862)	Postal Affairs
Rogers, Samuel St. George	Florida	House, Second Congress (admitted May 3, 1864)	Enrolled Bills, Indian Affairs, Naval Affairs
Royston, Grandison D.	Arkansas	House, First Congress	Medical Department, Post Office and Post-Roads, Quartermaster and Commissary Department and Military Transportation
Ruffin, Thomas	North Carolina	Provisional (admitted July 25, 1861)	None
Russell, Chas. W.	Virginia	Provisional (admitted July 20, 1861)	None
		House, First Congress	Judiciary, Naval Affairs
		House, Second Congress	Judiciary
Rust, Albert	Arkansas	Provisional (admitted May 18, 1861)	Postal Affairs
Sanderson, John P.	Florida	Provisional (admitted February 5, 1862)	Claims, Military Affairs, Public Lands
Scott, Robert E.	Virginia	Provisional (admitted July 22, 1861)	None

Seddon, James A.	Virginia	Provisional (admitted July 20, 1861)	None
Semmes, Thomas J.	Louisiana	Senate, First Congress (admitted February 19, 1862)	Finance, Flag and Seal, Judiciary
		Senate, Second Congress	Finance, Judiciary, Rules
Sexton, Franklin B.	Texas	House, First Congress	Quartermaster and Commissary Department and Military Transportation, Commerce
		House, Second Congress	Post Office and Post-Roads, Ways and Means
Shewmake, John T.	Georgia	House, Second Congress	Accounts, Naval Affairs
Shorter, John Gill	Alabama	Provisional	Accounts, Buildings, Engrossment, Executive Organization, Flag and Seal
Simms, William E.	Kentucky	Senate, First Congress	Accounts, Indian Affairs, Naval Affairs, Post Office and Post-Roads
		Senate, Second Congress	Accounts, Foreign Relations, Naval Affairs, Public Buildings
Simpson, William D.	South Carolina	House, First Congress (admitted February 5, 1863)	Claims
		House, Second Congress	Elections, Quartermaster and Commissary Department
Singleton, Otho R.	Mississippi	House, First Congress	Indian Affairs, Pay and Mileage
		House, Second Congress (admitted May 9, 1864)	Indian Affairs
Smith, James M.	Georgia	House, Second Congress	Military Affairs
Smith, Robert H.	Alabama	Provisional	Accounts, Judiciary, Naval Affairs
Smith, William	Virginia	House, First Congress (resigned April 6, 1863)	Claims, Naval Affairs
Smith, William E.	Georgia	House, Second Congress	Ordnance and Ordnance Stores, Territories and Public Lands
Smith, William N. H.	North Carolina	Provisional (admitted July 20, 1861)	None
		House, First Congress	Elections, Medical Department, Rules and Officers of House
		House, Second Congress (admitted February 19, 1862)	Claims, Rules and Officers of House
Smith, William R.	Alabama	House, First Congress (admitted February 21, 1862)	Flag and Seal, Foreign Affairs, Printing
		House, Second Congress (admitted May 21, 1864)	Foreign Affairs
Snead, Thomas L.	Missouri	House, Second Congress (admitted November 7, 1864)	Foreign Affairs
Sparrow, Edward	Louisiana	Provisional	Flag and Seal, Indian Affairs, Military Affairs
		Senate, First Congress	Military Affairs
		Senate, Second Congress	Military Affairs
Staples, Walter R.	Virginia	Provisional (admitted May 7, 1861)	Military Affairs
		House, First Congress	Elections, Patents
		House, Second Congress	Military Affairs

Stephens, Alexander H.	Georgia	Provisional	Executive Organization, Rules
Strickland, Hardy	Georgia	House, First Congress	Accounts, Patents
Swan, William G.	Tennessee	House, First Congress House, Second Congress	Military Affairs Military Affairs, Printing
Thomas, James H.	Tennessee	Provisional (admitted August 12, 1861)	Foreign Affairs
Thomas, John J.	Kentucky	Provisional (admitted December 30, 1861)	None
Thomason, Hugh F.	Arkansas	Provisional (admitted May 18, 1861)	Territories
Tibbs, William H.	Tennessee	House, First Congress	Enrolled Bills, Indian Affairs
Toombs, Robert	Georgia	Provisional	Finance
Triplett, George W.	Kentucky	House, Second Congress	Claims
Trippe, Robert P.	Georgia	House, First Congress	Commerce, Elections, Quartermaster and Commissary Department and Military Transportation
Turner, Josiah	North Carolina	House, Second Congress	Foreign Affairs, Indian Affairs
Tyler, John	Virginia	Provisional (admitted August 1, 1861; died January 18, 1862)	None
Venable, A. W.	North Carolina	Provisional (admitted July 20, 1861)	Foreign Affairs, Naval Affairs
Vest, George G.	Missouri	Provisional (admitted December 2, 1861) House, First Congress House, Second Congress (admitted November 7, 1864; resigned January 13, 1865) Senate, Second Congress (admitted January 12, 1865)	Judiciary Elections Judiciary None
Villeré, Charles J.	Louisiana	House, First Congress House, Second Congress	Claims, Commerce, Military Affairs Military Affairs
Walker, Richard W.	Alabama	Provisional Senate, Second Congress	Foreign Affairs Commerce, Engrossment and Enrollment, Judiciary, Post Office and Post-Roads, Public Builldings
Ward, George T.	Florida	Provisional (admitted May 2, 1861; resigned February 5, 1862)	Claims, Military Affairs, Public Lands
Watkins, W. W.	Arkansas	Provisional (admitted May 18, 1861)	Commerce
Watson, John W. C.	Mississippi	Senate, Second Congress	Claims, Engrossment and Enrollment, Judiciary, Printing
Waul, Thomas N.	Texas	Provisional (admitted February 19, 1861)	Commercial Affairs, Indian Affairs

Welsh, Israel	Mississippi	House, First Congress	Pay and Mileage, Post Office and Post-Roads, Quartermaster and Commissary Department and Military Transportation
		House, Second Congress	Accounts, Claims
White, Daniel P.	Kentucky	Provisional (admitted January 2, 1862)	None
Whitfield, Robert H.	Virginia	House, Second Congress (resigned January 13, 1865)	Naval Affairs, Patents
Wickham, William C.	Virginia	House, Second Congress (admitted November 7, 1864)	Military Affairs
Wigfall, Louis T.	Texas	Provisional (admitted April 29, 1861)	Foreign Affairs
		Senate, First Congress	Foreign Affairs, Military Affairs, Territories, Flag and Seal
		Senate, Second Congress	Foreign Affairs, Military Affairs, Territories
Wilcox, John A.	Texas	House, First Congress (died February 7, 1864)	Enrolled Bills, Military Affairs, Territories and Public Lands
Wilkes, Peter S.	Missouri	House, Second Congress (admitted November 8, 1864)	Indian Affairs, Post Office and Post-Roads
Wilson, William S.	Mississippi	Provisional (resigned April 29, 1861)	Engrossment, Patents
Withers, Thomas J.	South Carolina	Provisional	Judiciary
Witherspoon, James H.	South Carolina	House, Second Congress (admitted May 5, 1864)	Foreign Affairs, Ordnance and Ordnance Stores, Post Office and Post-Roads
Wright, Augustus R.	Georgia	Provisional	Naval Affairs, Public Lands
		House, First Congress	Medical Department, Naval Affairs, Pay and Mileage, Printing
Wright, John V.	Tennessee	House, First Congress (admitted about March 18, 1862)	Ordnance and Ordnance Stores
		House, Second Congress	Naval Affairs
Wright, William B.	Texas	House, First Congress	Indian Affairs, Patents, Claims, Enrolled Bills
Yancey, William L.	Alabama	Senate, First Congress (admitted March 27, 1862; died July 28, 1863)	Foreign Affairs, Public Lands, Rules, Territories, Naval Affairs

C. STATE GOVERNORS

Alabama
Andrew B. Moore, December, 1859–December, 1861
John Gill Shorter, December, 1861–December, 1863
Thomas Hill Watts, December, 1863–

Arkansas
Henry M. Rector, November, 1860–November, 1862
Thomas Fletcher (acting), November, 1862
Harris Flanagan, November, 1862–

Florida
M. S. Perry, November, 1857–November, 1861
John Milton, November, 1861–April, 1865
A. K. Allison, April, 1865–

Georgia
Joseph E. Brown, November, 1857–

Kentucky
George W. Johnson, November, 1861–April, 1862
Richard Hawes, October, 1862–

Louisiana
Thomas O. Moore, January, 1861–January, 1864
Henry W. Allen, January, 1864–

Mississippi
John J. Pettus, January, 1860–January, 1864
Charles Clark, January, 1864

Missouri
Claiborne F. Jackson, January, 1861–December, 1862
Thomas C. Reynolds, December, 1862–

North Carolina
John W. Ellis, September, 1858–July, 1861
Henry T. Clark (ad interim), July, 1861–September, 1862
Zebulon B. Vance, September, 1862–

South Carolina
Francis W. Pickens, December, 1860–December, 1862
M. L. Bonham, December, 1862–December, 1864
A. J. McGrath, December, 1864–

Tennessee
Isham G. Harris, November, 1857–

Texas
Edward Clark, November, 1859–November, 1861
F. R. Lubbock, November, 1861–November, 1863
Pendleton Murrah, November, 1863–

Virginia
John Letcher, January, 1860–December, 1863
William Smith, January, 1864–

D. GENERALS *

Generals

Beauregard, Pierre Gustave
   Toutant
Bragg, Braxton
Cooper, Samuel
Hood, John Bell

Johnston, Albert Sidney
Johnston, Joseph Eggleston
Lee, Robert Edward
Smith, Edmund Kirby

Lieutenant Generals

Anderson, Richard Heron
Buckner, Simon Bolivar
Early, Jubal Anderson
Ewell, Richard Stoddert
Forrest, Nathan Bedford
Hampton, Wade
Hardee, William Joseph
Hill, Ambrose Powell
Hill, Daniel Harvey

Holmes, Theophilus Hunter
Jackson, Thomas Jonathan
Lee, Stephen Dill
Longstreet, James
Pemberton, John Clifford
Polk, Leonidas
Stewart, Alexander Peter
Taylor, Richard

Major Generals

Allen, William Wirt
Anderson, James Patton
Bate, William Brimage
Bowen, John Stevens
Breckinridge, John Cabell
Brown, John Calvin
Butler, Matthew Calbraith
Cheatham, Benjamin Franklin
Churchill, Thomas James
Clayton, Henry DeLamar
Cleburne, Patrick Ronayne
Cobb, Howell
Crittenden, George Bibb
Donelson, Daniel Smith
Elzey, Arnold
Fagan, James Fleming
Field, Charles William
Forney, John Horace
French, Samuel Gibbs
Gardner, Franklin
Gilmer, Jeremy Francis
Gordon, John Brown
Grimes, Bryan
Heth, Henry
Hindman, Thomas Carmichael
Hoke, Robert Frederick
Huger, Benjamin
Johnson, Bushrod Rust
Johnson, Edward
Jones, David Rumph
Jones, Samuel
Kemper, James Lawson
Kershaw, Joseph Brevard
Lee, Fitzhugh

Lee, George Washington Custis
Lee, William Henry Fitzhugh
Lomax, Lunsford Lindsay
Loring, William Wing
Lovell, Mansfield
McCown, John Porter
McLaws, Lafayette
Magruder, John Bankhead
Mahone, William
Marmaduke, John Sappington
Martin, William Thompson
Maury, Dabney Herndon
Pender, William Dorsey
Pickett, George Edward
Polignac, Prince de, Camille
   Armand J. M.
Price, Sterling
Ramseur, Stephen Dodson
Ransom, Robert, Jr.
Rodes, Robert Emmett
Rosser, Thomas Lafayette
Smith, Gustavus Woodson
Smith, Martin Luther
Smith, William
Stevenson, Carter Littlepage
Stuart, James Ewell Brown
Trimble, Isaac Ridgeway
Twiggs, David Emanuel
Van Dorn, Earl
Walker, John George
Walker, William Henry Talbot
Walthall, Edward Cary
Wharton, John Austin
Wheeler, Joseph

* **Compiled from Ezra J. Warner,** *Generals in Gray.*

Major Generals (*cont.*)

Whiting, William Henry Chase
Wilcox, Cadmus Marcellus
Withers, Jones Mitchell

Wright, Ambrose Ransom
Young, Pierce Manning **Butler**

Brigadier Generals

Adams, Daniel Weisiger
Adams, John
Adams, William Wirt
Alexander, Edward Porter
Allen, Henry Watkins
Anderson, George Burgwyn
Anderson, George Thomas
Anderson, Joseph Reid
Anderson, Robert Houstoun
Anderson, Samuel Read
Archer, James Jay
Armistead, Lewis Addison
Armstrong, Frank Crawford
Ashby, Turner
Baker, Alpheus
Baker, Laurence Simmons
Baldwin, William Edwin
Barksdale, William
Barringer, Rufus
Barry, John Decatur
Barton, Seth Maxwell
Battle, Cullen Andrews
Beale, Richard Lee Turberville
Beall, William Nelson Rector
Bee, Barnard Elliott
Bee, Hamilton Prioleau
Bell, Tyree Harris
Benning, Henry Lewis
Benton, Samuel
Blanchard, Albert Gallatin
Boggs, William Robertson
Bonham, Milledge Luke
Branch, Lawrence O'Bryan
Brandon, William Lindsay
Brantley, William Felix
Bratton, John
Brevard, Theodore Washington
Browne, William Montague
Bryan, Goode
Buford, Abraham
Bullock, Robert
Cabell, William Lewis
Campbell, Alexander William
Cantey, James
Capers, Ellison
Carroll, William Henry
Carter, John Carpenter
Chalmers, James Ronald
Chambliss, John Randolph, Jr.

Chesnut, James, Jr.
Chilton, Robert Hall
Clanton, James Holt
Clark, Charles
Clark, John Bullock, Jr.
Clingman, Thomas Lanier
Cobb, Thomas Reade **Rootes**
Cocke, Philip St. George
Cockrell, Francis Marion
Colquitt, Alfred Holt
Colston, Raleigh Edward
Conner, James
Cook, Philip
Cooke, John Rogers
Cooper, Douglas Hancock
Corse, Montgomery Dent
Cosby, George Blake
Cox, William Ruffin
Cumming, Alfred
Daniel, Junius
Davidson, Henry Brevard
Davis, Joseph Robert
Davis, William George **Mackey**
Dearing, James
Deas, Zachariah Cantey
DeLagnel, Julius Adolph
Deshler, James
Dibrell, George Gibbs
Dockery, Thomas Pleasant
Doles, George Pierce
Drayton, Thomas Fenwick
DuBose, Dudley McIver
Duke, Basil Wilson
Duncan, Johnson Kelly
Dunovant, John
Echols, John
Ector, Matthew Duncan
Elliott, Stephen, Jr.
Evans, Clement Anselm
Evans, Nathan George
Featherston, Winfield Scott
Ferguson, Samuel Wragg
Finegan, Joseph
Finley, Jesse Johnson
Floyd, John Buchanan
Forney, William Henry
Frazer, John Wesley
Frost, Daniel Marsh
Fry, Birkett Davenport

276

Gano, Richard Montgomery
Gardner, William Montgomery
Garland, Samuel, Jr.
Garnett, Richard Brooke
Garnett, Robert Selden
Garrott, Isham Warren
Gartrell, Lucius Jeremiah
Gary, Martin Witherspoon
Gatlin, Richard Caswell
Gholson, Samuel Jameson
Gibson, Randall Lee
Girardey, Victor Jean Baptiste
Gist, States Rights
Gladden, Adley Hogan
Godwin, Archibald Campbell
Goggin, James Monroe
Gordon, George Washington
Gordon, James Byron
Gorgas, Josiah
Govan, Daniel Chevilette
Gracie, Archibald, Jr.
Granbury, Hiram Bronson
Gray, Henry
Grayson, John Breckinridge
Green, Martin Edwin
Green, Thomas
Greer, Elkanah Brackin
Gregg, John
Gregg, Maxcy
Griffith, Richard
Hagood, Johnson
Hanson, Roger Weightman
Hardeman, William Polk
Harris, Nathaniel Harrison
Harrison, James Edward
Harrison, Thomas
Hatton, Robert Hopkins
Hawes, James Morrison
Hawthorn, Alexander Travis
Hays, Harry Thompson
Hébert, Louis
Hébert, Paul Octave
Helm, Benjamin Hardin
Higgins, Edward
Hill, Benjamin Jefferson
Hodge, George Baird
Hogg, Joseph Lewis
Holtzclaw, James Thadeus
Humes, William Young Conn
Humphreys, Benjamin Grubb
Hunton, Eppa
Imboden, John Daniel
Iverson, Alfred, Jr.

Jackson, Alfred Eugene
Jackson, Henry Rootes
Jackson, John King
Jackson, William Hicks
Jackson, William Lowther
Jenkins, Albert Gallatin
Jenkins, Micah
Johnson, Adam Rankin
Johnson, Bradley Tyler
Johnston, George Doherty
Johnston, Robert Daniel
Jones, John Marshall
Jones, John Robert
Jones, William Edmondson
Jordan, Thomas
Kelly, John Herbert
Kennedy, John Doby
Kirkland, William Whedbee
Lane, James Henry
Lane, Walter Paye
Law, Evander McIvor
Lawton, Alexander Robert
Leadbetter, Danville
Lee, Edwin Gray
Leventhorpe, Collett
Lewis, Joseph Horace
Lewis, William Gaston
Liddell, St. John Richardson
Lilley, Robert Doak
Little, Lewis Henry
Logan, Thomas Muldrup
Long, Armistead Lindsay
Lowrey, Mark Perrin
Lowry, Robert
Lyon, Hylan Benton
McCausland, John
McComb, William
McCulloch, Ben
McCulloch, Henry Eustace
McGowan, Samuel
McIntosh, James McQueen
Mackall, William Whann
McNair, Evander
McRae, Dandridge
McRae, William
Major, James Patrick
Maney, George Earl
Manigault, Arthur Middleton
Marshall, Humphrey
Martin, James Green
Maxey, Samuel Bell
Mercer, Hugh Weedon
Miller, William

Moody, Young Marshall
Moore, John Creed
Moore, Patrick Theodore
Morgan, John Hunt
Morgan, John Tyler
Mouton, Jean Jacques Alfred
  Alexander
Nelson, Allison
Nicholls, Francis Redding Tillou
Northrop, Lucius Bellinger
O'Neal, Edward Asbury
Page, Richard Lucian
Palmer, Joseph Benjamin
Parsons, Mosby Monroe
Paxton, Elisha Franklin
Payne, William Henry Fitzhugh
Peck, William Raine
Pegram, John
Pendleton, William Nelson
Perrin, Abner Monroe
Perry, Edward Aylesworth
Perry, William Flank
Pettigrew, James Johnston
Pettus, Edmund Winston
Pike, Albert
Pillow, Gideon Johnson
Polk, Lucius Eugene
Posey, Carnot
Preston, John Smith
Preston, William
Pryor, Roger Atkinson
Quarles, William Andrew
Rains, Gabriel James
Rains, James Edwards
Randolph, George Wythe
Ransom, Matt Whitaker
Reynolds, Alexander Welch
Reynolds, Daniel Harris
Richardson, Robert Vinkler
Ripley, Roswell Sabine
Roane, John Selden
Roberts, William Paul
Robertson, Beverly Holcombe
Robertson, Felix Huston
Robertson, Jerome Bonaparte
Roddey, Philip Dale
Ross, Lawrence Sullivan
Ruggles, Daniel
Rust, Albert
St. John, Isaac Munroe
Sanders, John Caldwell Calhoun
Scales, Alfred Moore
Scott, Thomas Moore

Scurry, William Read
Sears, Claudius Wistar
Semmes, Paul Jones
Sharp, Jacob Hunter
Shelby, Joseph Orville
Shelley, Charles Miller
Shoup, Francis Asbury
Sibley, Henry Hopkins
Simms, James Phillip
Slack, William Yarnel
Slaughter, James Edwin
Smith, James Argyle
Smith, Preston
Smith, Thomas Benton
Smith, William Duncan
Sorrel, Gilbert Moxley
Stafford, Leroy Augustus
Starke, Peter Burwell
Starke, William Edwin
Steele, William
Steuart, George Hume
Stevens, Clement Hoffman
Stevens, Walter Husted
Stovall, Marcellus Augustus
Strahl, Otho French
Taliaferro, William Booth
Tappan, James Camp
Taylor, Thomas Hart
Terrill, James Barbour
Terry, William
Terry, William Richard
Thomas, Allen
Thomas, Bryan Morel
Thomas, Edward Lloyd
Tilghman, Lloyd
Toombs, Robert Augustus
Toon, Thomas Fentress
Tracy, Edward Dorr
Trapier, James Heyward
Tucker, William Feimster
Tyler, Robert Charles
Vance, Robert Brank
Vaughan, Alfred Jefferson, Jr.
Vaughn, John Crawford
Villepigue, John Bordenave
Walker, Henry Harrison
Walker, James Alexander
Walker, Leroy Pope
Walker, Lucius Marshall
Walker, Reuben Lindsay
Walker, William Stephen
Wallace, William Henry
Waterhouse, Richard

Brigadier Generals (cont.)		
	Watie, Stand	Winder, Charles Sidney
	Waul, Thomas Neville	Winder, John Henry
	Wayne, Henry Constantine	Wise, Henry Alexander
	Weisiger, David Addison	Wofford, William Tatum
	Wharton, Gabriel Colvin	Wood, Sterling Alexander Martin
	Whitfield, John Wilkins	Wright, Marcus Joseph
	Wickham, Williams Carter	York, Zebulon
	Wigfall, Louis Trezevant	Young, William Hugh
	Williams, John Stuart	Zollicoffer, Felix Kirk
	Wilson, Claudius Charles	

E. A REPRESENTATIVE INFANTRY COMPANY

Company A (125 enlisted men), Eighth Alabama Volunteers, organized in Perry County, Alabama, spring of 1861 *

Place of Birth	Number	Occupation	Number	Age	Number	Age	Number
Alabama	93	Farmer	92	15	1	34	2
Georgia	14	Mechanic	7	16	2	35	1
Ireland	4	Laborer	4	17	6	36	1
Massachusetts	3	Clerk	3	18	5	37	3
Maryland	2	Printer	2	19	3	38	1
North Carolina	2	Teacher	2	20	2	40	4
Canada	1	Dentist	1	21	11	44	1
Florida	1	Horse Dealer	1	22	12	45	2
Illinois	1	Mason	1	23	9	46	3
Louisiana	1	Machinist	1	24	8	47	2
South Carolina	1	Merchant	1	25	1	49	1
Tennessee	1	Peddler	1	26	10	51	1
Virginia	1	Preacher	1	27	3	52	1
		Physician	1	28	7	55	1
		Saddler	1	29	3	57	1
Marital Status	Number	Student	1	30	2	60	1
		Teamster	1	32	4	62	2
Single	78	Trimmer	1	33	4	Unknown	4
Married	43	Occupation					
Unknown	4	Unknown	3				

* Source: Manuscript Regimental Records, National Archives.

Picture Credits

TITLE PAGE, Great Seal of the Confederacy, photograph courtesy Library of Congress

CHAPTER 1 PAGE 2, top left, engraving by J. C. Buttre, courtesy Library of Congress; top center, photograph by Mathew B. Brady, courtesy Library of Congress; top right, engraving courtesy Library of Congress; bottom, photograph by Mathew B. Brady, courtesy National Archives, Washington, D.C. PAGE 3, top, courtesy of Library of Congress; bottom photograph by Mathew B. Brady, courtesy National Archives, Washington, D.C. PAGES 4 AND 5, top left, photograph by Mathew B. Brady, courtesy Library of Congress; bottom, wood engraving, Frank Leslie's Illustrated Newspaper, 1860, courtesy Library of Congress. PAGE 6, wood engraving, Frank Leslie's Illustrated Newspaper, January, 1861, courtesy Library of Congress. PAGE 7, top, photograph by George S. Cook, courtesy Library of Congress; bottom, photograph by Mathew B. Brady, courtesy National Archives, Washington, D.C. PAGES 8 AND 9, top left, photograph by Mathew B. Brady, courtesy National Archives, Washington, D.C.; center wood engraving courtesy Library of Congress; right, photograph courtesy Library of Congress. PAGES 10 AND 11, left, broadside courtesy Rare Book Room, Library of Congress; center, wood engraving, Frank Leslie's Illustrated Newspaper, 1861, courtesy Library of Congress; left, broadside courtesy Rare Book Room, Library of Congress. PAGE 12, relic, South Carolina Confederate Relic Room, Columbia, South Carolina.

CHAPTER 2 PAGE 13, Broadside courtesy Rare Book Room, Library of Congress. PAGE 15, photograph by Mathew B. Brady, courtesy National Archives. PAGE 16, photograph courtesy Library of Congress. PAGE 17, photograph by Mathew B. Brady, courtesy Brady-Handy Collection, Library of Congress. PAGE 18, wood engraving, Frank Leslie's Illustrated Newspaper, 1861, courtesy Library of Congress. PAGE 19, top, photograph by Mathew B. Brady, courtesy National Archives; bottom, photographer unknown, courtesy Library of Congress. PAGE 20, top, photograph by Mathew B. Brady, courtesy Library of Congress; center, photograph courtesy Southern Historical Collection, University of North Carolina, Chapel Hill; bottom, photograph by Mathew B. Brady, courtesy National Archives. PAGE 21, left, photograph by Brady, courtesy Library of Congress; right, photograph by Mathew B. Brady, courtesy Library of Congress. PAGE 22, top, photograph courtesy Brady-Handy Collection, Library of Congress; bottom, photograph courtesy Brady-Handy Collection, Library of Congress. PAGE 23, right, photograph by Mathew B. Brady, courtesy Library of Congress; bottom, photograph courtesy Library of Congress. PAGE 24, left, photographer unknown, courtesy Library of Congress; right, photograph courtesy Confederate Museum, Richmond, Virginia. PAGE 25, photograph by Mathew B. Brady, courtesy National Archives. PAGE 27, photograph by Mathew B. Brady, courtesy Brady-Handy Collection, Library of Congress. PAGE 29, photograph by Mathew B. Brady, courtesy Library of Congress. PAGE 31, left, photograph by Mathew B. Brady, courtesy Library of Congress; right, photograph by Mathew B. Brady, courtesy National Archives. PAGE 32, wood engraving courtesy Library of Congress. PAGE 34, photograph by Mathew B. Brady, courtesy Brady-Handy Collection, Library of Congress. PAGE 35, photograph courtesy Brady-Handy Collection, Library of Congress. PAGE 36, photograph by Mathew B. Brady, courtesy Brady-Handy Collection, Library of Congress. PAGE 37, photograph by Mathew B. Brady, courtesy National Archives. PAGE 40, photograph courtesy Library of Congress.

CHAPTER 3 PAGE 43, photograph courtesy Library of Congress. PAGE 44, top, photograph courtesy Library of Congress; bottom, photograph courtesy Library of Congress. PAGE 45, far left, photograph by Cook, courtesy Brady-Handy Collection, Library of Congress; left center, photograph by Minnes, courtesy Cook Collection, Valentine Museum, Richmond, Virginia; center right, photograph courtesy Brady-Handy Collection, Library of Congress; far left, photograph by Shipp or Gard, courtesy William H. Townsend, Lexington, Kentucky. PAGE 46, top left, photograph courtesy Cook Collection, Valentine Museum, Richmond, Virginia; top center, photograph courtesy Cook Collection, Valentine Museum, Richmond, Virginia; top right, photograph courtesy Library of Congress; bottom, photograph by Mathew B. Brady, courtesy National Archives. PAGE 47, photograph courtesy Cook Collection, Valentine Museum, Richmond, Virginia. PAGE 48, photograph courtesy Cook Collection, Valentine Museum, Richmond, Virginia. PAGE 49, photograph by Vannerson, courtesy Cook Collection, Valenttine Museum, Richmond, Virginia. PAGE 52, left, photograph courtesy Cook Collection, Valentine Museum, Richmond, Virginia; right, photograph cour-

tesy Brady-Handy Collection, Library of Congress. PAGE 55, photograph courtesy Cook Collection, Valentine Museum, Richmond, Virginia. PAGE 57, photograph courtesy Library of Congress. PAGE 58, photograph courtesy Cook Collection, Valentine Museum, Richmond, Virginia. PAGE 59, photograph courtesy Library of Congress. PAGE 60, photograph courtesy Cook Collection, Valentine Museum, Richmond, Virginia. PAGE 62, photograph by Mathew B. Brady, courtesy Library of Congress. PAGE 64, photograph courtesy Library of Congress. PAGE 65, photograph courtesy Library of Congress. PAGE 66, top, photograph courtesy Brady-Handy Collection, Library of Congress; bottom, photograph courtesy Library of Congress. PAGE 67, far left, photographer unknown, courtesy Confederate Museum, Richmond, Virginia; center, photograph courtesy Cook Collection, Valentine Museum, Richmond, Virginia; right, photograph courtesy Cook Collection, Valentine Museum, Richmond, Virginia. PAGE 68, photograph courtesy National Archives.

CHAPTER 4 PAGE 70, drawing by Thompson, courtesy Mr. Alexander McCook Craighead, Dayton, Ohio. PAGE 71, top, photograph courtesy Library of Congress; bottom, photograph courtesy Cook Collection, Valentine Museum, Richmond, Virginia. PAGE 72, left, ambrotype courtesy Mrs Contee Adams; right, courtesy V. Jordon Brown, Ashville, N.C. PAGE 73, top, photograph courtesy Library of Congress; bottom, courtesy Confederate Museum, Richmond, Virginia. PAGE 74, tintype courtesy Mrs. Walter B. Hill, Clarksville, Ga. PAGE 75, drawing by L. Miller, courtesy Historical Society of York County, York, Pa. PAGE 76, broadside courtesy Confederate Museum, Richmond, Virginia. PAGE 77, courtesy Mr. John Rawls, Vienna, Virginia. PAGE 78, courtesy Confederate Museum, Richmond, Va. PAGE 79, tintype courtesy Georgia Department of Archives and History, Atlanta, Georgia. PAGE 80, top, courtesy Confederate Museum, Charleston, South Carolina; bottom, photograph by Quinby, courtesy National Archives. PAGE 81, drawing by Alfred R. Waud, courtesy Library of Congress. PAGE 82, ambrotype, courtesy Memorial Hall, Louisiana Historical Association, New Orleans. PAGE 83, top, ambrotype courtesy Confederate Museum, Richmond, Va.; bottom, courtesy Confederate Museum, Richmond, Virginia. PAGE 84, drawing by Frank Vizetelly, courtesy The Houghton Library, Harvard College. PAGE 85, photograph by George S. Cook, courtesy Library of Congress. PAGE 86, courtesy Mr. John Rawls, Vienna, Virginia. PAGE 87, courtesy West Point Museum, U.S. Military Academy. PAGE 88, top left and right, courtesy Mr. John Rawls, Vienna, Virginia; bottom, broadside courtesy Rare Book Room, Library of Congress. PAGE 89, top left and right, courtesy Mr. John Rawls, Vienna, Virginia; bottom, ambrotype courtesy Washington and Lee University, Lexington, Virginia. PAGE 90, top, photograph courtesy Cook Collection, Valentine Museum, Richmond, Virginia; bottom, tintype courtesy Mrs. Bertha Waldrop, Alexandria, Virginia. PAGE 91, drawing by Frank Vizetelly, courtesy The Houghton Library, Harvard College. PAGE 92, photograph by George N. Barnard, 1862, courtesy Library of Congress. PAGE 93, ambrotype courtesy Col. Paul A. Rockwell, Ashville, N.C. PAGE 94, top, tintype courtesy Confederate Museum, Richmond, Virginia; center, courtesy Treasure Room, Emory University Library, Emory University, Georgia. PAGE 95, ambrotype courtesy Confederate Museum, Richmond, Virginia.

CHAPTER 5 PAGE 97, courtesy Smithsonian Institution. PAGE 98, top right, courtesy West Point Museum, U.S. Military Academy; center right, courtesy Mr. John Rawls, Vienna, Virginia; bottom right, courtesy West Point Museum, U.S. Military Academy; left, tintype courtesy Mr. William S. Powell, Chapel Hill, N.C. PAGE 99, top left, courtesy Confederate Museum, Richmond, Virginia; top center, courtesy John Hunt Morgan House, Lexington, Kentucky; top right, courtesy West Point Museum, U.S. Military Academy; bottom, photograph by J. D. Edwards, courtesy National Archives. PAGE 100, top, photograph by George N. Barnard, courtesy Library of Congress; far left center, photograph courtesy Library of Congress; far left bottom, photograph courtesy Library of Congress; center, photograph by J. D. Edwards, courtesy National Archives; right, photograph by George N. Barnard, courtesy Library of Congress. PAGE 101, left top, photograph courtesy Library of Congress; left center, photograph courtesy Library of Congress; center, photograph courtesy Library of Congress; right, tintype, Confederate Memorial Hall, Louisiana Historical Association, New Orleans. PAGE 102, center top, photograph by Samuel Cooley, courtesy Library of Congress; right top, photograph by T. H. O'Sullivan, courtesy Library of Congress; center, photograph courtesy Library of Congress; center right, photograph courtesy Library of Congress; bottom, photograph courtesy Library of Congress. PAGE 103, top, drawing by Alfred R. Waud, courtesy Library of Congress; bottom, photograph courtesy Cook Collection, Valentine Museum, Richmond, Virginia; top left, courtesy Confederate Museum, Richmond, Virginia; top right, ambrotype courtesy Miss Virginia S. Wheeler, Washington, D.C.; center left tintype courtesy Confederate Museum, Richmond, Virginia; center right, photograph courtesy Brady-Handy Collection, Library of Congress. PAGE 105, top, ambrotype courtesy Museum, Virginia Military Institute, Lexington, Virginia; bottom, photograph by Alexander Gardner, courtesy Library of Congress. PAGE 106, top, photograph courtesy Library of Congress; bottom, photograph by Alexander Gardner, courtesy Library of Congress. PAGE 107, top, photograph courtesy Library of Congress; bottom, photograph courtesy Library of Congress. PAGE 108, photograph courtesy Cook Collection, Valentine Museum, Richmond, Va. PAGE 109, photograph courtesy Library of Congress. PAGE 110, courtesy Rare Book Room, Library of Congress.

CHAPTER 6 PAGE 113, photograph, courtesy Library of Congress. PAGE 114, photograph by Alexander Gardner, courtesy Library of Congress. PAGE 115, top, drawing by Alfred R. Waud, courtesy Library of Congress. PAGE 115, bottom, photograph courtesy Library of Congress. PAGE 116, drawing by Edwin Forbes, courtesy Library of Congress. PAGE 117, top, photograph courtesy Library of Congress; bottom, drawing by Alfred R. Waud, courtesy Library of Congress. PAGE 118, photograph by T. H. O'Sullivan, courtesy Library of Congress. PAGE 119, photograph by T. H. O'Sullivan, courtesy Library of Congress. PAGE 120, photograph by T. H. O'Sullivan, courtesy Library of Congress. PAGE 121, photograph courtesy National Archives. PAGE 122, photograph by George N. Barnard, courtesy Library of Congress. PAGE 123, photograph courtesy Library of Congress. PAGE 124, top, drawing by Alfred R. Waud, courtesy Library of Congress; bottom, photograph courtesy Library of Congress. PAGE 125, photograph courtesy Library of Congress. PAGE 126, courtesy Library of Congress. PAGE 127, broadside courtesy Rare Book Room, Library of Congress.

CHAPTER 7 PAGES 130 and 131, map by William K. Hubbell from The Railroads in the Confederacy, by Robert C. Black, Chapel Hill, 1952; reproduced by permission of the University of North Carolina Press. PAGE 132, photograph by George N. Barnard, courtesy Library of Congress. PAGE 133, photograph by Mathew B. Brady, courtesy Brady-Handy Collection, Library of Congress. PAGE 134, photograph by J. D. Haywood, courtesy Library of Congress. PAGE 135, photograph courtesy Library of Congress. PAGE 136, broadside, December 26, 1862, courtesy Rare Book Room, Library of Congress. PAGE 139, photograph by George N. Barnard, courtesy Library of Congress. PAGE 140, photograph by George N. Barnard, courtesy Library of Congress. PAGE 141, photograph by George N. Barnard, courtesy Library of Congress. PAGE 142, drawing by Edwin Forbes, courtesy Library of Congress. PAGE 143, photograph courtesy Manassas National Battlefield Park, Manassas, Virginia.

CHAPTER 8 PAGE 145, top, painting by Conrad Wise Chapman, courtesy Confederate Museum, Richmond, Virginia; bottom, photograph courtesy Brady-Handy Collection, Library of Congress. PAGE 148, top, photograph courtesy National Archives; bottom, photograph courtesy Library of Congress. PAGE 149, top, photograph courtesy Lee Wallace, Arlington, Virginia; bottom, photograph by James F. Gibson, courtesy Library of Congress. PAGE 150, top, photograph by Bell Bros., courtesy Library of Congress; middle, photograph by A. Ken, Paris, France, courtesy Confederate Museum, Richmond, Virginia; bottom, photograph courtesy Chicago Historical Society, Chicago, Illinois. PAGE 151, drawing by Captain Ole Peter Hansen Balling, 1st Regt., N.Y. Infantry Volunteers, courtesy Library of Congress. PAGE 152, photograph courtesy Mr. John Howells, Houston, Texas. PAGE 153, top, photograph courtesy Library of Congress; bottom, photograph courtesy Library of Congress. PAGE 154, top, wash drawing by G. Perkins, courtesy Library of Congress; far left, photograph courtesy Confederate Museum, Richmond, Virginia; bottom left, photograph by E. Swift & Son, Liverpool, England, courtesy Confederate Museum, Richmond, Va.; bottom center, photograph by Mage Bros., Brest, France, courtesy Confederate Museum, Richmond, Virginia; center right, photograph by Mage Bros., Brest, France, courtesy Confederate Museum, Richmond, Virginia. PAGE 155, top, wood engraving, Illustrated London News, 1864, courtesy Library of Congress; bottom, photograph courtesy Cook Collection, Valentine Museum, Richmond, Virginia. PAGE 156, photograph by Mathew B. Brady, courtesy Library of Congress. PAGE 157, lithograph by E. Sachse, 1862, after drawing on the spot by Sgt. Charles Worret, 20th Regt., N.Y.V., courtesy Library of Congress. PAGE 160, photograph courtesy Cook Collection, Valentine Museum, Richmond, Virginia. PAGE 161, photograph by C. D. Fredericks, Havana, Cuba, courtesy Confederate Museum, Richmond, Virginia.

CHAPTER 9 PAGE 164, photograph by Mathew B. Brady, courtesy Brady-Handy Collection, Library of Congress. PAGE 165, left, photograph by Mathew B. Brady, courtesy Brady-Handy Collection, Library of Congress; right, photograph by Mathew B. Brady, courtesy Chicago Historical Society, Chicago, Illinois. PAGE 167, etching by Adalbert John Volck, courtesy Library of Congress. PAGE 168, photograph courtesy Library of Congress. PAGE 169, photograph courtesy Cook Collection, Valentine Museum, Richmond, Virginia.

PAGE 170, photograph courtesy Witte Memorial Museum, San Antonio, Texas. PAGE 171, painting by Osborne, courtesy Mrs. Hendrix B. Van Rensselaer, Summit, New Jersey. PAGE 172, photograph courtesy Library of Congress. PAGE 173, top, photograph by T. H. O'Sullivan, courtesy Library of Congress; bottom, photograph courtesy Mrs. Mabel Huckaby, Confederate Museum, Austin, Texas. PAGE 174, photograph courtesy Western Reserve Historical Society, Cleveland, Ohio. PAGE 176, photograph courtesy National Archives. PAGE 177, tintype courtesy South Carolina Confederate Relic Room, State Capitol, Columbia, South Carolina. PAGE 178, photograph by T. H. O'Sullivan, courtesy Library of Congress. PAGE 179, photograph courtesy Library of Congress. PAGE 180, tintype, courtesy Confederate Museum, Richmond, Virginia. PAGE 181, drawing by Edwin Forbes, courtesy Library of Congress. PAGE 182, wood engraving The London Illustrated News, August 29, 1863, courtesy Library of Congress. PAGE 183, ambrotype courtesy Confederate Museum, Richmond, Virginia.

CHAPTER 10 PAGE 186, photograph courtesy Library of Congress. PAGE 187, photograph courtesy Library of Congress. PAGE 188, photograph by Mathew B. Brady, courtesy Library of Congress; bottom, photograph courtesy Brady-Handy Collection, Library of Congress. PAGE 189, top, photograph by Mathew B. Brady, courtesy Library of Congress; bottom, etching by Adalbert John Volck, courtesy Library of Congress. PAGE 190, top, photograph courtesy Library of Congress; bottom, photograph courtesy Cook Collection, Valentine Museum, Richmond, Virginia. PAGE 191, photograph courtesy Library of Congress. PAGE 192, etching by Adalbert John Volck, courtesy Library of Congress. PAGE 194, photograph courtesy Brady-Handy Collection, Library of Congress. PAGE 195, left, photograph courtesy Library of Congress; center, photograph courtesy Library of Congress; right, photograph courtesy American Jewish Historical Society, New York, New York. PAGES 196 AND 197, broadside, Soldiers' Tract Society, Virginia Conference, M. E. Church, South, courtesy Rare Book Room, Library of Congress. PAGE 198, photograph courtesy Library of Congress.

CHAPTER 11 PAGE 203, photograph by Mathew B. Brady, courtesy Library of Congress. PAGE 204, broadside, April 14, 1861, courtesy Rare Book Room, Library of Congress. PAGE 209, photograph by Mathew B. Brady, courtesy Brady-Handy Collection, Library of Congress. PAGE 210, photograph by Mathew B. Brady, courtesy Brady-Handy Collection, Library of Congress. PAGE 214, wood engraving courtesy Library of Congress. PAGE 215, sheet music cover published by George Willig, Baltimore, Maryland, lithograph, 1863, courtesy Library of Congress. PAGE 216, top, painting by J. Massalon, courtesy Historic Mobile Preservation Society, Mobile, Alabama; bottom, photograph courtesy Library of Congress. PAGE 217, left, sheet music cover, published by Henry Siegling, Charleston, South Carolina, courtesy Library of Congress; right, lithograph by E. Crehen, Richmond, Virginia, courtesy Library of Congress. PAGE 218, left, photograph courtesy Library of Congress; right, photograph by Mathew B. Brady, courtesy Brady-Handy Collection, Library of Congress.

CHAPTER 12 PAGE 222, photograph by Samuel Cooley, November 1, 1864, courtesy National Archives. PAGE 224, photograph by George N. Barnard, courtesy Library of Congress. PAGE 225, photograph, Cook Collection, courtesy Valentine Museum, Richmond, Virginia. PAGE 227, left, photograph by Samuel Cooley, courtesy Library of Congress; right, photograph courtesy Library of Congress. PAGE 228, lithograph by Robertson, Seibert and Sherman, New York, New York, courtesy Library of Congress. PAGE 230, courtesy Rare Book Room, Library of Congress.

CHAPTER 13 PAGE 232, photograph by T. H. O'Sullivan, courtesy Library of Congress. PAGE 233, photograph by T. H. O'Sullivan, courtesy Library of Congress. PAGE 234, photograph by Henry P. Moore, courtesy Library of Congress. PAGE 235, photograph copyrighted by E. W. Holsinger, Charlottesville, Virginia, November 6, 1908, courtesy Library of Congress. PAGE 236, drawing by William Waud, courtesy Library of Congress. PAGE 237, right, ambrotype, courtesy Confederate Museum, Richmond, Virginia; left, drawing by Edwin Forbes, courtesy Library of Congress. PAGE 238, left, drawing by Edwin Forbes, courtesy Library of Congress; right, etching by Adalbert John Volck, courtesy Library of Congress. PAGE 239, drawing by Alfred R. Waud, courtesy Library of Congress. PAGE 240, top, drawing by Edwin Forbes, courtesy Library of Congress; bottom, drawing by Edwin Forbes, courtesy Library of Congress. PAGE 241, photograph, courtesy National Archives. PAGE 242, top, drawing by Edwin Forbes, courtesy Library of Congress; bottom, photograph by T. H. O'Sullivan, courtesy Library of Congress. PAGE 243, photograph by James F. Gibson, courtesy Library of Congress. PAGE 244, photograph courtesy Library of Congress.

CHAPTER 14 PAGE 246, drawing by Alfred R. Waud, courtesy Library of Congress. PAGE 247, photograph courtesy Library of Congress. PAGE 248, photograph courtesy Library of Congress. PAGE 249, photograph courtesy Library of Congress. PAGE 250, photograph by George N. Barnard, courtesy Library of Congress. PAGE 251, photograph by W. N. Otman, Montreal, Canada, courtesy Library of Congress. PAGE 252, top, wood engraving courtesy Library of Congress; bottom, photograph courtesy Library of Congress. PAGE 253, photograph courtesy Confederate Museum, Richmond, Virginia. PAGE 255, photograph by Mathew B. Brady, courtesy National Archives.

Index

(Underlined numbers denote
 illustrations)

Abolitionists, 7
Adair, G. W., 207
Adams, Charles Francis, 250
Adams, John, 68
Adams, Stephen Clinton, *72*
Adams Express Company, 137
"Address to the People of the Con-
 federate States" (pamphlet),
 33
Age, The (magazine), 214
Akin, Warren, 198
Akin, Mrs. Warren, 179, 198
Alabama, 2, *20*, 26, 27, 29, *32*, 32,
 41, 45, 64, 106, 107 ff, 123,
 150, *154*, 154, *155*, 155
 Capitol (Montgomery), 26
 Inauguration of Jefferson Davis
 (Feb., 1861), *18*
 secession convention, 3
Alabama, C.S.S., 146, 147, *155*
Alabama Legislature, 105
Albemarle (ship), 159–60
Alexander, Edward Porter, 66, *103*,
 143
Alexander, P. W., 206
Alexandria, Va., *195*
Allen, William, *189*
American Telegraph Company, 138
Anderson, G. B., 66
Anderson, Joseph Reid, *106*, 106
Anderson, R. H., 44
Annapolis (United States Naval
 Academy), 146
Antietam Campaign, 26, 61
Antisecessionists. *See* Secession, op-
 position to
Appomattox, Va., 22, 36, 50
Archer (schooner), 152
Arizona, 27
Arkansas, 23, 27, 34, 65
 and 15th Arkansas Infantry Regi-
 ment, 65, *86*
 and 1st Arkansas Infantry, *94*
 railroads, 128 ff
 secedes from Union (May 6,
 1861), 12, 65
Arkansas (ship), 144, 159
Arkansas State Telegraph Company,
 138
Arkansas Telegraph, 212
Arkansas *Weekly Gazette*, 29
Armistead, Lewis, 66
Armstrongs, 3-inch, *102*, 103
Army of Mississippi, 135
Army of Northern Virginia, 50, 54,
 56, 61, 63, *95*, *104*
Army of Tennessee, 53, 56, 57
Army of the Potomac. *See* Army of
 Northern Virginia

Ashe, William S., 133
Atlanta, Ga., 32, 56, 71, 84, 111,
 122, *132*, *139*, 205
 fall of, 66, 225, 245
Atlanta, C.S.S., *153*
Atlanta *Daily Intelligencer*, 200,
 203, 206
Atlanta *Southern Confederacy*, 201,
 207
Augusta, Ga., *108*, 108–9, 197
Augusta *Constitutionalist*, 207
Augusta Female Seminary, 226

Bagby, George W., 213, 217
Baird, Washington, 229
Baltic (steamer), 150
Bancroft, George, 145–46
Banks, Mrs. John, 183
Bannon, John, 193
Baptist Banner (Augusta), 197
Baptists, 185 ff
Barksdale, William, 7–8, 66
Barnard, F. A. P., 220
Barnwell, Mary, 181
Barnwell, Robert, 31, 33
Baylor, George W., 45
Beal pistol, 98
Beall, Lloyd J., 149
Beaufort College, *222*
Beaufort, S.C., *233*
Beaufort (steamer), 147
Beauregard, Pierre Gustave Toutant,
 43, *52*, 52–53, 55, 74, 98, 164,
 246–47
Beechenbrook: A Rhyme of the War
 (poem), 215
Beers, Fannie, 169
Benjamin, Judah P., 18, *19*, 19 ff,
 24, 37, 241
 and anti-Semitism, 20
 becomes first Adjutant General of
 the Confederacy, 19
 becomes Secretary of State (Con-
 federacy), 20
 becomes Secretary of War (Con-
 federacy), 19–20
 death (May 6, 1884), 21
 goes to England, 20
Benning, Henry Lewis, 66, 210
Beulah (Evans), 216
Beverly Fort, Va., *142*
Bingham, William, 229
Bingham School (N.C.), 226
Blackford, W. W., 50
Black Hawk War, 57
Blakely, Andrew, *101*
Blalock, Mrs. L. M., 163
Bledsoe, A. T., 24
Blimeal, J. Emerson, 189
Bocock, Thomas S., 32
Bohemian (magazine), 214
Botts, John Minor, *178*

Boudinot, Elias C., *27*, 27
Bouldin, Wood, *13*
Bowling Green, Ky., 65
Boyd, Belle, *165*, 165
Brady, Mathew B., *255*
Bragg, Braxton, 34, 43, 44, *52*, 53–
 54, 58, 59, 66, 206, 208, 212,
 246 ff
 denounced by Forrest, 64
Bragg, Thomas, 18, *20*
Branch, A. M., 143
Bratton, John, 71, 72, 74
Breckinridge, John C., 18, *25*, 25
Brilliant, C.S.S., *154*
Brooke, John M., *102*, 103, 107, 156
Brooke rifles, *102*, 103, 107
Brown, Isaac, 159
Brown, John (abolitionist), 6
Brown, John C., 68
Brown, Joseph Emerson, 17, *35*, 35–
 36, 37, 38, 111
Brown, William Caleb, *72*
Buchanan, Franklin, 145, *156*, 209
Buchanan, James, 27
Buckner, Simon B., 44
Buena Vista, battle of, 53
Bulloch, James D., 145, 153
Bullock, Rufus B., *133*
Bull Run. *See* Manassas
Bureau of Conscription, Confederate,
 38
Burr, J. H., 111
Burton, James, 110

Calhoun, John C., 32
Canton, Ga., 35
Capen's *Sunday Evening Bulletin*,
 204
Caperton, W. T., 13
Carter, John C., 68
Cary, Constance, 171
Cary, Hetty, 67
Catholics, 185 ff
 and nuns, 169
Centenary College, 220
Chambers, Henry C., 29
Chancellorsville, battle of, 50, 61,
 92, *183*, 189
Chapman, R. T., *152*
Charleston, S.C., 1, *7*, 18, 22, 30, 53,
 85, *107*, *145*, 156, *247*
 Arsenal, *102*
 Circular Church, *124*
 St. Michael's Church, *124*
 S.C. Club House, *124*
Charleston (ship), 150
Charleston College, 221
Charleston *Courier*, 1, 39, 206, 211
Charleston *Mercury*, 11, 206, 208–9,
 211
Charleston, Va., *76*
Chattanooga, Tenn., 79, *121*

Chattanooga *Rebel*, 205
Chaudron, Mrs. A. D., 229
Cherokee Indians, 27, 77
Cherokee Mounted Rifles, *27*
Chesnut, James, Jr., *7*, 7
Chesnut, Mary Boykin, *7*, *171*, 171, 181, 193–94
Chickamauga, battle of, 54, 58, 63, 64, 93
Chickasaw Indians, 77
Chicora (steamer), 150
Chimborazo Hospital (Richmond), *168*, 168–69
Choctaw Indians, 77
Christian, George, 221–22
Christian, Joseph, *13*
Christian Observer, 194
City Point, Va., *241*
Civil War, 1, 26, 34, 36, 37, 40, 59, 191, 200 ff, 245 ff
  Antietam Campaign, 26, 61
  Appomattox, 22, 36, 50
  Bull Run. *See* Manassas
  Chancellorsville, battle of, 50, 61, 66, 92, *183*, 189
  Chickamauga, battle of, 54, 58, 63, 64, 93
  Cold Harbor Campaign, 140
    second battle of, 50
  and Confederate military leadership, 43–68 *passim;* 69–77 *passim;* 146 ff
  and Confederate women, 163 ff
  early campaigns of, 23
  and education, 220 ff
  and fall of Confederacy, 245 ff
  and first national conscription act, 28, 30, 35, 36
  Five Forks (Va.), battle of, 63
  Fort Donelson, (Tenn.), 20, 41, 57, 64, 135, 254
  Fort Fisher (N.C.), *102*, 149
  Fort Henry (Tenn.), 20
  Fort McAllister (Ga.), *102*
  Fort Moultrie (S.C.), *10–11*
  Fort Sumter (S.C.), 1, 12, 27, 30, 31, 36, 52, *80*, 147, 220, *236*
  Franklin (Tenn.), battle of, 59, 66, 68, *83*
  Fredericksburg, battle of, 8, 50
  Gaines Mill, battle of, 58
  Georgia Campaign (1864), 56 ff, 66
  Gettysburg Campaign, 7, 28, 45, 47, 50, 51, 58, 63, 66, *75*, 80, *103*, 210, 212, 254
  Harpers Ferry (Va.), 61
  Hatcher's Run, battle of, 46, 67
  and impressment of slaves, 28, 30, 35, 38
  Jonesboro (Ga.), battle of, 70, 189
  and journalism, 200 ff
  Kelly's Ford, battle of, *71*
  and literature, 200 ff
  Malvern Hill, battle of, 44, 71, 74
  Manassas:
    first battle of, 47, 48, 52, 55, 90, 168
    second battle of, 26, 48, 50, 58, 61, 63
  Missionary Ridge, battle of, 54, 66, *101*
  Mobile Bay, battle of, 149

  Murfreesboro, battle of, 54, 65
  and Negroes, 191–92, 231 ff
  Perryville, battle of, 65
  rank and file, 77–95 *passim;* 97 ff
  and religion, 185 ff
  Saylor's Creek, battle of, 149
  Seven Day's Campaign (1862), 50, 61
  Seven Pines, battle of, 50, 56, 63
  Sharpsburg Campaign, 50, 58, 63, *79*, 80, 84, 235
  Shenandoah Valley Campaign, 48, 61
  Shiloh, battle of, 53, 65, *94*, 212
  Spotsylvania. *See* Wilderness-Spotsylvania Campaign
  Tennessee Campaign (1865), 57 ff
  and Union military leadership, 43–68 *passim;* 69–77 *passim*
  Vicksburg Campaign, 4, 28, 59, 80, 143, 150, 159, *182*, 210, 212, 254
  and volunteer troops, *10–11*
  Wilderness Campaign, 50, 63
  Wilderness-Spotsylvania Campaign (1864), 68
  See also Atlanta, Ga.; Confederate Army; Confederate Navy; Union; War Department, Confederate
Clarence (destroyer), 152–53
Clark, W. G., 207
Clarke, Amy, 163
Clarksburg, Va., 61
Clayton, Milly Ann, 177
Cleburne, Patrick Ronayne, *65*, 65–66, 68
Clemson University, 42
Clinton Central Female Institute, 223
Clisby, Joseph, 207
Cobb, Howell, 3, *4*, 26–27, 35, 212, 241
  considered for Presidency of Confederacy (1861), 27
Cobb, Mrs. Howell, 170
Cockrell, F. M., 68
Cold Harbor Campaign, 140
  second battle of, 50
College of Charleston, 221
Colt six-shooters, 98
  Navy model 1851, *99*
Columbia, S.C., *6*, *249–50*
  Baptist Church, *6*
Columbia *South Carolinian*, 125, 203, 206, 207
Columbia Theological Seminary, 187–88
Columbiad guns, *99*, *100*
Columbus, Ga., 192
"Committee of Thirteen," 9
"Committee of Thirty-three," 9
Communication and transportation. *See under* Confederacy
Concert Hall, Willard's Hotel (Wash., D.C.), *8–9*
Cone, William H., 189
Confederacy, 12, 22, 35 ff
  Army of, 3, *4*, *10–11*, 20, 25, 27–28, 30, 32, 35, 38
  aversion to taxes, 22
  communication and transportation, 128 ff

  country and town life, 112 ff
  creation of, 1 ff
  currency, 120 ff, *126*, *127*, 192; reduction, 35
  economic weaknesses, 22, 34, 105 ff, 112 ff
  education, 220 ff
  fall of, 245 ff
  government, 13 ff, 19 ff, 26 ff, 34, 38
    and governors in exile, 34 ff
    and legislative functions, 26 ff, 39 ff
  inflation, 22, 112 ff
  journalism, 200 ff
  literature, 200 ff
  military affairs, 30 ff
  military leadership, 43–68 *passim;* 69–77 *passim;* 107 ff, 146 ff
  and Negroes, 191–92, 231 ff
  and picket posts, *85*
  rank and file soldiers, 77–95 *passim;* 97 ff
  and religion, 185 ff
  states rights for, 17, 32, 38
  and tax laws, 29, 40
  and White House, *16*
  and women, 163 ff
  See also Civil War; Congress, Confederate; Davis, Jefferson; Secession; Slavery; South
Confederacy's Falstaff. *See* Toombs, Robert
Confederate Army, 3, *4*, *10–11*, 20, 25, 27–28, 30, 32, 33, 35, 38, 43 ff, 56
  Indians in service, 77
  military leadership, 43–68 *passim;* 69–77 *passim*
  rank and file, 77–95 *passim;* 97 ff
  and volunteer slave soldiers, 20
Confederate Bureau of Conscription, 38
Confederate City, Augusta, Georgia, 1860–1865 (Corley), 198
Confederate Congress. *See* Congress, Confederate
Confederate Constitution. *See* Constitution, Confederate
Confederate House of Representatives. *See* Congress, Confederate
Confederate Mirabeau. *See* Wigfall, Louis T.
Confederate Navy, 22, 107 ff, 144 ff
Confederate Navy Department. *See* Navy Department, Confederate
Confederate Ordnance Bureau, *110*, 110
Confederate Senate. *See* Congress, Confederate
Confederate State Almanac, 202
Confederate States Marine Corps, 148, *149*, 149
Confederate States Medical and Surgical Journal, 214
Confederate States Powder Works (Augusta, Ga.), 108, *109*, 109
Confederate States Treasury Notes, 120, *126*, *127*
Confederate Torpedo Bureau, *108*, 108

284

Confederate War Department. *See* War Department, Confederate

Confederate White House (Richmond, Va.), *16*, 19

Congress, Confederate, 3, *4*, 6, *8*, 20, 22, 24, 26–42 *passim;* 87, 120, 143, 159, 200 ff, 227
  abuse and violence in sessions, 29
  choosing senators, 26
  and Confederate Constitution, 27, 141
  First Congress sessions, 26, *27*
  and exclusion of journalists, 29
  and first national conscription act, 28, 30, 35, 36, *88*
  and impressment of slaves, 28, 30, 35, 38
  and legislative functions, 26 ff
  and military affairs, 30 ff
  and Provisional Congress sessions, 26
  and Second Congress sessions, 26, *27*, 28
  and secrecy, 29
  and states rights, 32
  and suspension of writ of habeas corpus, 28–29, 32
  and tax laws, 29, 40

Congress of the United States, 7 ff, 26, 30 ff, 66, 135, 138

Congress, Provisional. *See* Congress, Confederate

Connecticut, 18

"Conquered Banner, The" (poem), 216

Conrad, C. M., 156

Conscription act, first national, 28, 30, 35, 36, 38, *88*

Conservative party (N.C.), 36

Constitution, Confederate, 27

Constitution of the United States, 2, 7, *10*

Constitutional Union party, 2

Cook, Mrs. Enoch Hooper, 182

Cooke, James W., 160

Cooke, John Esten, 216

Cooke, John R., 66

Cooper, Samuel, *43*, 43, 48, 55, 56

Corbell, LaSalle, 45

Corinth, Tenn., 57

Corley, Florence Fleming, 198

Corvettes Cumberland, U.S.S., *151*

Cotton industry, 8, 9, 13, 26, 36–37, 231, *232*

Countryman (magazine), 213

Creek Indians, 77

Crisp, W. H., 123

Crittenden, John J., *9*, 11

Culpeper, Va., *116*, *117*, *119*, 235
  Court House, *240*, *242*

Cumberland Landing, Va., *243*

Cumberland Presbyterians, 185

Cumberland University, 221

Cumming, Kate, 169

Curry, Jabez L. M., *32*, 32–33

Cushing, William B., 160

Dabney, Robert L., *188*, 188, 190

Dahlgren smoothbore naval gun, *100*

Daily Southern Crisis (Jackson, Miss.), 137

Dalton, E. R., 122

Daniel, John M., 37, 190, 201

Daniel, Junius, *66*, 66, 68

Daniel, R. T., *13*

Dargan, E. S., 29

Davenport, George D., 177

Davidson College, 221–22, 223

Davis, C. H., 161

Davis, Jefferson, *3*, *13*, *15*, 19 ff, 27, 31–32, 33, 34, 35, 36, 38–39, 47, 50, 53 ff, 66, 86, 133, 134, 138, 147, 168, 190, 195, 201, 208 ff, 218, 241, 243, 246 ff, *251*, *252*, *253*
  and Benjamin, 19 ff
  cabinet members, 16 ff
  and children, *251*
  criticism by Beauregard, 53
  criticism by Lee, 51
  early political career, 13–14, 19
  denounced by Toombs, 26
  disagreements with Wigfall, 30
  elected President of Confederacy (Nov. 1861), 13
  first national conscription act, 28, 30, 35, 36, *88*
  Foote's hatred of, 29
  illness, 14
  imprisonment, 16
  inauguration (1861), *18*
  opposed by Stephens, 17
  and suspension of writ of habeas corpus, 28–29, 32, 36

Davis, Mrs. Jefferson, *253*

Davis, Varina Howell, 171

Deane pistol, 98

DeBow, J. D. B., 199

DeBow's Review, 105–6, 213

Democratic party, 32, 36, 65

Dennison, S. M., *88*

Dent, Julia, 63

Department of North Carolina, 54

Department of South Carolina, Georgia, and Florida, 53

Department of the West, 56, 57

Department of Western Virginia, *76*

Devil's Den (Gettysburg), 66

Diana (steamer), 151

Different Valor, A (Govan, Livingood), 54

Dixie Speller, The, 230

Doles, George, 68

Donelson, Fort. *See* Fort Donelson

Douglas, H. K., *189*

Dover Baptist Association (Va.), 194

Dowdey, Clifford, 54

Duffey, Edward S., *103*

Duke, T. L., 189

Duncan, Ivy W., *74*

Dyke, James H., *155*

Eakin, John R., 211

Early, Jubal Anderson, 44, 47, *48*, 48, *75*

Edgefield, S.C., 63

Edisto Island, S.C., *234*

Edmunds, John R., *13*

Edmundson, H. A., *13*

Education, 220 ff

Elder, John, 214

Ellet, Charles, 161

Ellet, Henry T., 21

Elliott, Stephen, 188

Ellison, B. F., 189

Ellsworth, George, 140

Emory College, 221

Enfield rifle (caliber .577), *97*, 97

England, 20, 107, 145, *150*

Enrica (ship), 154

Episcopalians, 185 ff

Etowah Iron Works (Ga.), 161

Evans, Jane, 216

Evans, W. E., *152*

Ewell, Richard Stoddert, 44, *46*, 47, 48, 60–61
  and Ewell's Corps, *246*

Extremists, Northern, 11
  Southern, 11

Fanny (steamer), 151

Fayetteville Arsenal, N.C., *98*

Federal Congress. *See* Congress of the United States

Federal government, 1, 12, 17, 26, *80*
  See also Congress of the United States

Federal Navy, 146, *148*, 148–62 *passim*

Federal Union. *See* Union

Fillmore, Millard, 32

Fire-eaters. *See under* Secession

First Congress. *See* Congress, Confederate

First Manassas. *See* Manassas

First national conscription act, 28, 30, 35, 36, 38, *88*

First Texas Rifles, 57

Fisher, Fort. *See* Fort Fisher

Fisher, H. J., *13*

Fitzhugh, E. H., *13*

Fitzhugh, Loring H., *76*, *127*

Five Forks (Va.), battle of, 63

Flags, various, 78

Florida, 18, 37–38, 39, 59, 61, *99*, *100*
  Department of, 53
  railroads, 128 ff
  3rd Florida Regiment, *78*

Florida, C.S.S., 152, 154, *155*, 155, 161

Florida Sentinel, 39, 42, 211

Folmsbee, S. J., *228*

Fontaine, Felix G., 206

Foote, Henry S., 29–30, 33
  hatred for Davis, 29
  leaves Confederacy, 29–30

Forbes, Edwin, *240*

Ford, Antonia, 165

Forrest, Douglas F., *150*

Forrest, French, *145*, 145–46

Forrest, Jeffrey, 64

Forrest, Nathan Bedford, 43, 44, 45, *64*, 64–65, 164

Forrest, William, 64

Fort Donelson (Tenn.), 20, 41, 57, 64, 135, 254

Fort Donelson, U.S.S. (ship), *148*

Fort Fisher (N.C.), *102*, 149

Fort Henry (Tenn.), 20

Fort McAllister (Ga.), *102*

Fort Moultrie (S.C.), *10-11*

Fort Sumter (S.C.), 1, 12, 27, 30, *31*, 36, 52, *80*, 138, 147, 220, *236*

Foster, John, 76
Four Years on the Firing Line (Nisbet), 71
Franklin College. *See* University of Georgia
Franklin (Tenn.), battle of, 59, 66, 68, *83*
Franklinton, N.C., *134*
Fredericksburg, Va., *113*, *124*
  battle of, 48, 50
Freeman, Douglas Southall, 51
Freeman, M. J., *152*
Fremantle, Arthur J. L., *218*, 232

Gaines (gunboat), 107
Gaines' Mill, battle of, 58, 71
Gainesville, Ga., 63
Gallego Flour Mill (Richmond, Va.), *115*
Gannaway, W. T., 221
Gardner, James, 207
Garlington, Henry W., *12*
Garnett, Richard B., 67
Gaston, C. A., 140
Generals in Gray (Warner), 44
Georgia, *2*, 2 ff, 17, 26, 27, 29, 31–32, 34, 35–36, 38, 42, 45, 56, 70 ff, 80, *101*, *108*, 109, 161, *252*
  Department of, 53
  railroads, 128 ff
  secession convention, 2–3
  3rd Georgia Regiment, 151
  12th Georgia Infantry, *79*
Georgia (ship), 150
Georgia Campaign (1864), 56 ff, 66 ff
Georgia Methodist Conference, 196
Georgiana (ship), 154–55
Georgia Supreme Court, 36
Germantown (sloop), 152
Gettysburg Campaign, 7, 28, 45, 47, 50, 51, 58, 63, 66, *75*, 80, *103*, 210, 212, 254
Gibbes, R. W., 207
Gill, Robert M., 70, 71, 72–73, 74
Gist, States Rights, 67–68
Goggin, W. L., *13*
Gordon, George W., 68
Gordon, James B., 68
Gordon, John Brown, 44, 47, *68*, 75
Gorgas, Josiah, *107*, 107, 108
Gould, A. W., 45
Govan, Daniel C., 67
Govan, Gilbert E., 54
Governors in exile, 34 ff
Gracie, Archibald, 67
Graham, William A., 32–33
Granbury, H. B., 68
"Grand Creole." *See* Beauregard, Pierre Gustave Toutant
Grant, Ulysses S., 43, 50, 53, 58, 63, 135, 140, 254
Green, Tom, *73*
Greenhow, Rose O'Neal, *164*
Gregg, John, 66
Grimes, Bryan, 67

Habana (steamer), 153
Habeas corpus writ, suspension of (1862–64), 28–29, 32, 36
Hall, W. B., 149

Hambleton, James P., 201
Hammond, James H., 7–8, 62, 252, 254
Hampton, Preston (son of Wade), 46
Hampton, Wade, 43, 44, *46*, 46
  and Hampton's Legion, 46
Hampton, Wade, Jr. (son of Wade), 46
Haralson, Jonathan, 108
Hardee, William J., 44, 190
Hardee's Tactics, 73
Hardings, Sam Wylde, 165
Harland, Elizabeth, 165
Harpers Ferry, Va., 61
Harpers Ferry rifle (model 1855, caliber .58), *97*, 97
Harriet Lane (steamer), 151
Harris, Isham Green, *34*, 34
Harris, Joel Chandler, 213
Hart, Nancy, 164
Harvard Law School, 32
Harwell, Richard B., 218
Hatcher's Run, battle of, 46, 67
Hawks, Francis, *149*
Hawks, William J., *189*
Hayne, Paul Hamilton, 213, 215
Helena, Ark., 65
Henry, Fort. *See* Fort Henry
Henry, George C., 41
Hewitt, John Hill, *94*
Hill, Ambrose Powell, 44, *46*, 46, 68, *189*
Hill, Benjamin, 1, *2*, 2, 3, 29, 31–32
Hill, Daniel Harvey, 44, 46, *47*, 47, 72, 80
H.L. Hunley (submarine), 22, 144, *145*
Hoke, R. F., 66, 160
Holden, W. W., 36, 210
Holmes, Theophilus H., 23, *44*, 44, 59
Holmes, W. C., 221, 222
Hood, John Bell, 43, 56–57, *58*, 58–59, 66, 80, 84, 190
Hooker, Joseph ("Fighting Joe"), 50, *240*
Hooper, Johnson Jones, 216
Hopkins, Mrs. Arthur Francis, 168
Hopkinson, James, *234*
Hospital Life in the Confederate Army of Tennessee (Cumming), 169
Hotze, Henry, 215
Housatonic, U.S.S. (ship), 22, 144
House Military Affairs Committee, Confederate, 30, *31*
House of Representatives, Confederate. *See* Congress, Confederate
House of Representatives, United States. *See* Congress of the United States
Houston, Samuel, 1, *2*
Houston, Tex., 45
Howard College, 33, 190
Howell, B., *152*
Howitzers, 12-pounder, *101*, 101
Hubbell, Jay, 215
Hudson (steamer), *148*
Hunter, Robert M. T., 18, *20*

Huntress, The (steamer), 150
Huntsville (ship), 160
Hurt, Robert B., Jr., *83*

Impressment of slaves, 28, 30, 35, 38
Independent Blues, *78*
Indianola, Tex., 150
Indians in Confederate Army, 77
Inez (Evans), 216
Ingomar (steamer), 158
Ingraham, Duncan, 145
Institution Hall (Charleston, S.C.), *4–5*
Interstate Commerce Act of 1887, 21
Iredell, James, *153*
Ironclad, C.S., *160*

Jackson, Andrew, 14
Jackson, Thomas J. (Stonewall), 37, 44, 46, 47, 48, 58, 59, *60*, 60 ff, *99*, *188*, *189*, 217, *235*, *242*
  death of, 68
  and Shenandoah Valley Campaign, 61
  with Virginia militia, 61
Jackson, W. H., 66
James Gray (tug), 149
James River (Va.), 53, *91*, *100*, 146, 149, *153*
Jamestown (steamer), *151*
Jefferson, Thomas, 23
Jemison, Robert, 1
Jenkins, Micah, 68
Jews, 185 ff
Johnny Rebs. *See* Rank and file, Confederate
Johns, Annie, 169
Johnson, Herschel V., 1, *2*, 2–3, 33
Johnson, L. M., 229
Johnston, Albert Sidney, 34, 43, 55, 56, *57*, 57 ff, 65, 68
Johnston, Joseph E., *13*, 30, 33, 34, 43, 50, 54, *55*, 55 ff, 190, 210
Jones, Custis, 114
Jones, Flora, 182
Jones, John Beauchamp, 114
Jones, John M., 68
Jones, J. W., 90
Jonesboro (Ga.), battle of, 70, 189
Joslyn pistol, 98
Journalism, 200 ff
Joyner, Mary, 169
Justice, Anne Gorman, 170

Kasey, James P., *104*
Kean, Robert G. H., 24–25
Kearsage, U.S.S., *155*, 155
Keeble, Walter, 122
Kell, J. M., *152*
Kelly, John H., 66
Kelly's Ford, battle of, *71*, *238*
Kennedy, John Pendleton, 216
Kenner, Duncan F., 20, 26
Kennesaw Mountain (Ga.), 140
Kentucky, 11, 27, 34, 45, 46, 54, 58, 59, 65
  and Kentucky Infantry, *78*
Keokuk (ship), 161
Kerr pistol, 98
Kershaw, Joseph Brevard, *66*, 66

Key West, Fla., *18*
Kitchen. Thomas, *90*
Knoxville, Tenn., 84
Ku Klux Klan, 65

Lady Davis (tug), 149
Lamar, L. Q. C., 220
Lander. S., 229
Land They Fought For, The (Dowdey), 54
Lanier, Sidney, *216*, 216
Lapwing (destroyer), 152
Law, Evander M., 66
Law, Sally, 169
Lawton, A. R., 134
Lee, Ann Carter (wife of Henry), 48
Lee, Charles Robert, 26
Lee, Henry ("Light-Horse Harry"), 48
Lee, Mary (wife of Robert Edward), 51
Lee, Robert (son of Robert Edward), 51
Lee, Robert Edward, 36, 37, 43, 47, 48, *49*, 49 ff, 55, 56, 57, 58, 62, 63, 64, 65, 84, 90, 212, *214*, 243, 245, *255*
    appointed Lt. Col. of 2nd Cavalry (1855), 48
    criticizes Davis, 51
    and family, 50–51, 194
    indorses recruiting of slaves, 243
    made military advisor to Davis, 50
    as president of Washington College, 52
    surrender of, 45, 50
Lee, Samuel P., 160
Lee, S. D., 44
Leech and Rigdon Confederate Colt, *99*
LeMat, Jean, 98
LeMat pistol, 98, *99*
Leroy, Abner Perrin, 68
Letcher, John, *37*, 37–38, 182
Leverett, Charles E., 229
Lewis, Joseph H., *252*
Limber, Jim, *237*
Lincecum, Gideon, 41
Lincoln, Abraham, 2, 3, 12, 14, 41, 210, 239–40
    elected to Presidency (1860), 1
    inaugural address, 11
Literature, 200 ff
Little, Lewis, 66
Livingood, James W., 54
Lomax, Anne, 165
Lomax, Julia, 165
Longstreet, A. B., 220
Longstreet, James, 26, 44, 45, *62*, 63–64, 84, *91*, 208
Longstreet's Corps, *103*, 135
Lookout Mountain, Tenn., *176*
Louisiana, 19, 30, 31, 34, 64, 80, 120
    cartridge box plate, 77
    7th Louisiana Volunteers, *82*
    See also New Orleans
Louisiana (ship), 158
Louisiana Lottery, 53
Louisiana State Seminary, 221, 223
Louisiana Tigers, *71*

Louisiana Zouaves, 71, *90*
Louisville, Ky., 138
Louisville *Daily Courier*, 203
Lovell, Mansfield, 144, 161
Lowry, M. P., 66
Lutherans, 185
Lynch, Patrick Niesen, 193, *195*
Lynchburg, Va., 59

McAllister, Fort. *See* Fort McAllister
McCabe, James D., 213
McCartney, Norah, 165
McClanahan, John R., 205
McClellan, George B., 42
McCollum, Duncan, 220
McCord, Louisa, 169
McGill, John, *194*
McGowan, Samuel, 66
McGuire, Hunter, *189*
McGuire, Judith, 174
McKee, John T., *89*
McLeish-Vulcan Iron Works (Charleston. S.C.), 107
McReid, Samuel, *13*
Macaria: or, Altars of Sacrifice (Evans), 216
Macarthy. Harry. 122
Mackall, William W., 54
Mackey, James S., *89*
Macon, Ga., *101*, 109–10
Macon *Telegraph*, 201, 207
MacWillie, Malcolm H., 27
Magnolia (magazine), 213
Magrath, A. G., 39
Magruder, John B., 142
Mallet, John W., 109–10
Malvern Hill (Va.), battle of, 44, 71, 74
Manassas, Va., *92*, 164
    first battle of, 47, 48, 52, 55, 90, 168
    second battle of, 26, 48, 50, 58, 61, 63
Manassas (ship), 160
Manigault, A. M., 68
Marginalia (Fontaine), 206
Marietta, Ga., 71
Marmaduke, John S., 45
"Marse Robert." *See* Lee, Robert Edward
Marshall, Humphrey, *46*, 46
Martin, James, *82*
Martin, William H., *82*
Mary Baldwin College, 226
Maryland 1st Cavalry, *83*
Mary Sharpe College, *228*
Mason, Emily, *169*, 169
Maury, Matthew Fontaine, 107
Meekins, Mrs. A. M., 165
Memminger, Christopher G., 18, *22*, 22, 211
    and Confederate financial problems, 22
Memphis, Tenn., 144, 159
Memphis *Appeal*, 201, 205, 206
Memphis City Hospital, 168
Memphis *Daily Argus*, 203
Mercer University, 221

Meridian *Clarion*, 202
Merrimack (steamer), 22, 152, 156, *157*
Methodists, 185 ff
Mexican War, 13, 48, 51, 53, 55, 59, 61, 63, *100*, 146
    and capture of Mexico City, 48
Meyer, Gustave, 206
Michelbacher, Maximilian J., 193, *195*
Miles, William Porcher, 30, *31*
Military Division of the West, 53
Milledgeville, Ga., 42
Miller, William C., 155
Mills, Roger Q., 92–93
Mills, Susan P., 195
Milton, John, 37, 38
Minnegrode, Charles, *190*, 190, 193
Minor, George, 107, 145
Missionary Ridge, battle of, 54, 66, *101*
Mississippi, 13, 18, 23, 34, 39, 64
    and 19th Regiment, 189
    and 7th Mississippi Infantry, *78*
Mississippi (ship), 158
Mississippi, Army of, 135
Mississippi Central Railroad, 137
Mississippi rifle (caliber .54), 97
Mississippi Valley, 7
Mississippian (newspaper), 7
Missouri, 27, 34
Missouri (steamer), 160
Missouri Compromise, 11
Mitchell, E. L., *228*
Mobile, Ala., 41, 53, 108
Mobile *Advertiser and Register*, 206–7
Mobile and Ohio Railroad, 128
Mobile Bay, battle of, 149
Moderates, 10–11
Moffit, James Newland, *161*
Monitor (ship), 22, 144, *157*
Montgomery, Ala., *18*, 26, 108, 123
Montgomery *Advertiser*, 202, 210
Montgomery *Daily Mail*, 123, 208, 211
Montgomery Theater (Montgomery, Ala.), 23
Moore, A. B., 38, 105
Moore, Marinda B., 229
Moore, Thomas O., 158
Moorman, Marcellus N., *105*
Morgan (gunboat), 107
Morgan, John Hunt, *45*, 45, *99*
Morman war, 57
Morris, William S., 138–39
Morse Confederate Breech-Loading carbine, *98*
Morton, Charles, 122
Moultrie, Fort. *See* Fort Moultrie
Murfreesboro (Tenn.), battle of, 54, 65
Muscogee (steamer), 160
Myers, A. C., 30

Napoleons, 12-pounder, 101
Nashville, Tenn., 30, 34, 41, 57, 59, 80, 84, *140*
    and manufacture of war materials, 107, 109
Nashville (steamer), 160
Nashville *Christian Advocate*, 194

National conscription act, first, 28, 30, 35, 36, *88*
Naval leaders, Confederate, 144 ff
Navy, Confederate. *See* Confederate Navy
Navy Department, Confederate, 21, *145*, 145, 152, 160
Neely, John, 229
Negroes, Confederate, 191–92, 231 ff
   See also Slavery
Neuse (steamer), 160
New Orleans, La., 19, 52, 59, 98, 138, 144, 157, 158, 161, *187*
   fall of, 158–59
New Orleans *Bee*, 203, 212
New Orleans *Crescent*, 203, 212
New Orleans *Daily True Delta*, 203, 209, 212
New Orleans *Picayune*, 206
Newport News, Va., *151*
Newton, Cincinnatus, *13*
Newton, Ella King, 168
Nisbet, James C., 71, 73 ff
Niter and Mining Bureau, 108
North, 7, 17, 33
   See also Union
North Anna river (Va.), *118*
North Carolina, 18, *20*, 27, 32, 36–37, 44, 77, *180*
   Department of, 54
   and 43rd North Carolina Regiment, 234
   and Rough and Ready Guards (14th North Carolina Regiment), *72*
   secedes from Union (May 20, 1861), 12
North Carolina (steamer), 160
North Carolina Standard, 36, 210
Northeastern Railroad, *247*
Northern Extremists, 11
Northern superiority, 7
Northern Virginia, Army of, 50, 54, 56, 61, 63
Northrop, L. B., 80

O'Bannon, Lawrence W., 194
Ochiltree, Thomas P., *73*
O'Farrel, John, *104*
Ogden, D'Orsay, 122
Oglethorpe University, 221
Old Dominion (ship), *150*
Oldham, W. S., 33, 138
Ordnance Manual (1863), *110*
Oreto (destroyer), 152, 155
"Our National Confederate Anthem," 217
Oury, Granville H., 27
Owsley, Frank, 37

Palmer, Benjamin M., *187*, 187–88, 193
Palmer, John Williamson, 216
Palmer, Mrs. Oran, 183
Palmerston, Lord, 250
Palmetto Guards (S.C.), *80*
Palmetto State (steamer), 160
"Palmetto State Song, The," *217*
Parker, William H., 146, 147
Parrington, Mary, 122
Parrott, Robert P., 103
Parrotts, 10-pounder, 101, *102*, 103

Patellus house (Va.), *172*
Patrick Henry (steamer), 146
Paxton, Elisha Franklin, 67
Peabody Normal College, *224*
Peace Convention (Wash., Feb. 4, 1861), *8–9*, 10–11
Pea Ridge, battle of, 77–78
Peck, William R., *117*
Pegram, John, *67*, 67
Pelham, John, *71*
Pember, Phoebe Yates, 94–95, 169, 171
Pemberton, John C., 44
Pender, Dorsey, 66
Pendleton, A. J., *189*
Pendleton, Sandie, 47
Pendleton, William N., 190
Pensacola Bay, Fla., 53, *99*, *100*
Perry, Benjamin F., 1, 2, 3
Perryville, battle of, 65
Petersburg, Va., *114*, 161
   and Blandford Church, *186*
   and Grace Episcopal Church, *198*
Pettigrew, Caroline, 170
Pettigrew, James Johnston, 44
Phoenix (ship), 160
Pickens, Francis Wilkinson, *10–11*, 149
Pickens, Mrs. Francis W., *10–11*
Pickett, George Edward, *45*, 45, 51, 63
Pickle, John Scott, *173*
Pickle, Mrs. John Scott, *173*
Pierce, Franklin, 13
Piggott, Emmeline, 165
Pistol, carbine, *98*
Plymouth (sloop), 152
Poindexter, Mrs. S.A., 229
Polk, Leonidas, 44, *67*, 68, 144, 183, *189*, 189–90
Pollard, Edward A., 209, 218
Pope, John, 50
Porcher, Francis P., 120
Porter, John L., 145, 156
Port Gibson Female College, 223
Port Hudson, La., 80, 212
Post, John Eagen Howard, *83*
Powell, Charles Stevens, *98*
Powell, Jennie, 122
Presbyterians, 185 ff
President Davis and His Administration (St. Clair-Abrams), 218
Press Association of the Confederate States of America, 207–8
Preston, John, 246
Preston, Sally, 58
Protestant Episcopal Theological Seminary (Alexandria, Va.), *195*
Provisional Congress. *See* Congress, Confederate
"Provisional Navy of the United States," 147
Pryor, Sara Agnes, 171

Quakers, 185
Quarles, William A., 68
Quarles mill (No. Anna River, Va.), *118*
Queen of the West (steamer), 151
Quinn, Charles W., *155*
Quintard, Charles T., *188*, 188–89

Railroads, 128 ff, *130*, *131*
Rains, George Washington, 108
Rains, James Gabriel, *108*, 108–9
Raleigh, N.C., 36
Raleigh (steamer), 160
Raleigh and Gaston Railroad, *134*
Ramseur, Stephen, 66
Randall, James Ryder, 215
Randolph, B. F., *13*
Randolph, George W., 20, 23, *24*, 24, 25
Randolph, Victor, 145
Randolph-Macon College, 221
Rank and file, Confederate, 77–95
   passim; 97 ff
   clothing shortages, 83–85
   courage, 92–93
   drinking and gambling, 90–91
   favorite songs, 89
   food shortages, 80–82
   illiteracy, 78–80
   sports, 90
   types of arms, 97 ff
Rappahannock, C.S.S., *150*
Rappahannock River (Va.), *240*, *242*
Rappahannock Station, Va., *181*
Ray, Mrs. Polly, 183
Reagan, John H., 18, *21*, 21, 22, 133, 138–39, 141
Rebel War Clerk's Diary, A (Jones), 114
Rebs. *See* Rank and file, Confederate
Reid, Samuel C., Jr., 206
Religion, 185 ff
Remington pistol, 98
Republican party, 1, 6–7, 36, 200
Resaca, Ga., 72
Resources of Southern Fields and Forests (Porcher), 120
Rhett, Robert Barnwell, Jr., 208, *209*, 209
Rhett, Robert Barnwell, Sr., *3*, 3, 208–9
   home of, *123*
Richmond, Va., *16*, 19–20, 27, 28, 30, 42, 53, 54, 57, 58, 65, 73, 80, 113, *168*, *194*, 209, *248*, *255*
   Beth Ahabah, *195*
   Capitol Building, *23*
   capture of, *135*
   First African Church, *244*
   Governor's Mansion, *40*
   industrial activity of, 106 ff
   Monumental Church, *191*
   St. Paul's Church, *190*
   State Armory and Arsenal, *106*, 107
Richmond (ship), 160
Richmond *Dispatch*, 206, 209
Richmond *Enquirer*, 201, 202, 210
Richmond *Examiner*, 37, 201, 209
Richmond *Musketoon*, *98*
Richmond *Whig*, 32, 209, *210*, 210, 211
Rifles, 3-inch, 101
Ringold, May S., 42
Rise and Fall of the Confederate Government (Davis), 66
Rivers, R. H., 229
Roanoke Island (N. C.), 20, 151

Roanoke River, 159
Robert E. Lee (ship), *148*
Roberts, Albert, 205
Roberts, William P., 44
Robinson, George O., *217*
Rockwell, William Harrison, *93*
Rodman smoothbore guns, *100*
Rogers, Asa, *13*
Roland, Charles P., 57
Rome *Confederation*, 217
Roosevelt, Theodore, Sr., 146
Rose, A. S., 143
Rough and Ready Guards, *72*
Rowland, Kate Mason, 169
Royston, G. D., 143
Ruffin, Edmund, *80*
Rushin, Thomas Jefferson, *79*
Russell, William H. ("Bull Run"), *218*
Rutledge, Francis H., 188
Ryan, Abram Joseph, *216*, 216

Sabot Hill (Seddon home), 24, 25
St. Augustine, Fla., 59
St. Clair-Abrams, Alexander, 218
St. Elmo (Evans), 216
St. John, Isaac M., 108
St. Philip (ship), 150
Sanger, Donald B., 63
Sansom, Emma, 164
Savage pistol, 98
Savannah (steamer), 160
Savannah *Morning News*, 202
Savannah *Republican*, 121, 134, 206–7
Saylor's Creek, battle of, 149
Scales, Cordelia, 171
Scharf, J. Thomas, 156–57
Scott, T. M., 68
Scott, Winfield, 43, 48, 59
Secession, 1–12 *passim;* 32, 146, 191
    Alabama convention, 3
    fire-eaters, 3, 6, 7, 9
    first convention, *6*
    Georgia convention, 2–3
    leaders, 3, 8, 38
    legality of, 3
    and Lincoln's election to Presidency, 1 ff
    newspapers' influence on, 3, 7
    opposition to, 1, 7, *9*, 37
    Ordnance for South Carolina, *10*, 11–12, 31, *217*
    See also Confederacy
Secession Hall (Charleston, S.C.), *7*
Second Cherokee Mounted Rifles. *See* Cherokee Mounted Rifles
Second Cold Harbor. *See* Cold Harbor, second battle of
Second Congress. *See* Congress, Confederate
Second Manassas. *See* Manassas, second battle of
Seddon, James A., *24*, 24–25, 211
Seddon, Sally Bruce (Mrs. James A.), 24
Selma, Ala., 64, 106, 107 ff
Selma (gunboat), 107
Seminole Indians, 77
Semmes, Paul J., 66
Semmes, Raphael, 145–46, *152*, 153, *155*

Semple, James A., 145
Senate, Confederate. *See* Congress, Confederate
Senate Finance Committee, Confederate, 31
Senate Military Affairs Committee, Confederate, 30
Senate, United States. *See* Congress of the United States
Seven Days' Campaign (1862), 50, 61, 141
Seven Pines, battle of, 50, 56, 63
Sharkey, William L., 1
Sharpsburg Campaign, 50, 58, 63, *79*, 80, 84, 235
Sheffey, J. W., *13*
Shenandoah, C.S.S., *153*, *154*
Shenandoah Valley Campaign, 48, 61, 245
Shepperson, W. G., 206
Sheridan, Philip H., 48, 245
Sherman, William T., 42, 53, 56, 57, 58, 140, 205, 245
Shields, Jeff, *235*
Shiloh, battle of, 53, 65, *95*, 212
Shirley, John T., 159
Shores, William, *94*
Shreveport *News*, 120, 142, 202
Sibley, Henry H., *73*
Simms, William Gilmore, 216, 252
Simons, Thomas Y., 211
Simpson, Lucy F., 182
Sims, Frederick W., 134
Sinclair, Arthur, 158
Sinclair, George T., 155
Sinclair, William H., *155*
Sisters of Charity of Nazareth, 169
Sisters of Our Lady of Mercy, 169
Sisters of St. Dominic, 169
Slavery, 1, 5 ff, 11, 16, 20, 117, 231 ff
    and contrabands, *243*
    and impressment of slaves, 28, 30, 35, 38
    and projected insurrections, 238 ff
    support of, 37, 38
    and volunteers for Confederate Army, 20
Slidell, Mrs. John, *165*
Smith, Charles Henry, 217
Smith, C. Shaler, 109
Smith, Edmund Kirby, 43, 44, *59*, 59, 120
Smith, Gustavus Woodson, *23*
Smith, J. J., *189*, *233*
Smith, Preston, 66
Smith, Richard, 229
Smith, W. B., *152*
Smith, William R., 1, *2*, 3
Smith and Wesson pistol, 98
Smythe, Charles W., 229
Sneed, J. R., 207
Some Adventures of Captain Simon Suggs (Hooper), 216
Sorrel, G. Maxley, 45
South, 11, 32, 33
    aversion to taxes, 22
    and beginning of secession, 1 ff
    and diminishing power in Congress, 8
    and Extremists, 11
    industrial potential, 7, 40

and Moderates, 10–11
    and slavery, 1, 5 ff, 11, 16, 20, 28, 37, 38, 117, 231 ff
    and Southern rights, 3, 19
    See also Civil War; Confederacy; Negroes
South Carolina, 1 ff, 18, 22, 30, 31, 34, 39, 41, 46, 48, 63, 150, 177, 191
    Department of, 53
    and Palmetto Guards, *80*
    secedes from Union (Dec. 20, 1860), 1 ff, *10*, *12*, 31
    See also Charleston
South Carolina College, 188, 220; University, 31
South Carolina General Assembly, *10*
Southern Army. *See* Confederate Army
Southern Education Board, 33
Southern Express Company, 111, *133*, 137, 138
Southern Field and Fireside (magazine), 213
Southern History of the War (Pollard), 218
Southern Illustrated News, 213, *214*, 215, 217
Southern Literary Companion, 213
Southern Literary Messenger, 213
Southern Monthly (magazine), 213
Southern Punch (magazine), 214, 219
Southern Recorder, 203
Southern Telegraph Company, 138 ff
Southern Union, 203
Southern Woman's Story, A (Pember), 169
Southfield, U.S.S., 160
Southwestern Army, 59
South-Western Telegraph Company, 138 ff, 207–8
Sparrow, Edward, 26, 30
Spiller, E. N., 111
Spotswood, W. A., 145
Spotsylvania-Cold Harbor Campaign, 140
Spotsylvania Court House (Va.), *237*
Springfield musket (caliber .58), *97*, 97
Spring Hill, Tenn., 45
Stafford, A., 68
Star of the West (ship), 150
Starr pistol, 98
States rights, 3, 17, 32, 38
Steele, John H., 200
Stephens, Alexander H., 1, 3, *13*, 16, *17*, 17
Stephens, Linton, 17
Sterling, Richard, 229
Stevens, Walter H., *104*
Stewart, A. P., 44
Stiles, R. R., *160*
Stone, Kate, 126–27, 179, 198
Stonewall Brigade, 67, *89*
    See also Jackson, Thomas J.
Stonewall, C.S.S., *150*
Strahl, O. F., 66, 68
Streight, A. D., 164
Stribbing, V. M., *152*

Stuart, James Ewell Brown ("Jeb"), *45*, 45, 46, 50, 68, 98
Stuart's Horse Artillery, *71*
Sturgis, Samuel D., 64
Sumter, C.S.S., *152*, 153, 155
Sumter, Fort. *See* Fort Sumter
Sumter Light Guard, 76
Supreme Court of the United States, 6
Surry of Eagle's Nest (Cooke), 217

Tattnall, Josiah, 145–46
Tatum, Mrs. Olive, 183
Taylor, Richard, 43, *44*, 44, 71, *73*, 151
Taylor, Zachary, 53, 59
Tax laws, Confederate, 29, 40
Teaser (gunboat), *149*
Telegraph, *133*, 138 ff
Tennessee, 18, 27, 29, 30, 34, 41, 45, 54, 57, 59, 64, 77, 79, 108, *121*, 144, 159, *176*
    1st Infantry, *188*, 189
    55th Tennessee Infantry Regiment, *83*
    railroads, 127 ff
    secedes from Union (May 7, 1861), 12, 64
Tennessee (ram), 107, 144, 159
Tennessee, Army of, 53, 56, 57
Tennessee Campaign (1865), 57 ff
Tennessee River, 58
Texas, 2, 18, 30, 39, 41, 57, *78*, 91, 170
    1st Texas Rifles, 57
    railroads, 128 ff
    secession ordnance, 12
    10th Texas Regiment, 92
Texas (ship), 160
Texas Brigade, 58
Thompson, John, 213, 215
Thompson, W. F., *13*
Thornwell, James H., 187–88
Thrasher, J. S., 207–8
Tift, Asa, 158–59
Tift, Nelson, 158–59
Tigers. *See* Louisiana Tigers
Timrod, Henry, 213, 215
Tompkins, Sally L., 168
Toombs, Robert, *3*, 3, 17, 25–26
    challenges Hill to duel, 44
    denounces Davis, 26
    resigns position as Secretary of State, 25
Trader, D. C., 65
Trains. *See* Railroads
Trans-Mississippi Department, 59, 77, 141
Transylvania University, 57
Tranter pistol, 98
Treatise on the Law of Sale of Personal Property (Benjamin), 20
Tredegar Iron Works (Richmond, Va.), *105*, *106*, 106, 107, 109, 113, 158
Trenholm, George A., 18, *22*, 22
Trescot, William H., 41, *48*
Trezevant, Louis, *31*
Trinity College, 221–22
Turner, J. A., 213
Tuscaloosa (destroyer), 152, 160
Tuskegee Women's College, 223

Twenty-sixth N. C. Regiment, 36
Twiggs, David E., 44
Tyler, John, *8*, 10–11, 27

Union, 3, 7, 11–12, 17, 32, 41, 56, *135*, 200 ff
    and military leadership, 43–68 *passim*; 69–77 *passim*
    and secession, 1 ff
    and Unionists, 3
    See also Civil War; Congress of the United States; Federal government; Secession
Union Navy. *See* Federal Navy
United States Military Academy. *See* West Point
United States Naval Academy. *See* Annapolis
University of Alabama, 221
University of Georgia, 32, 221
University of Mississippi, 220
University of Nashville, *224*
University of North Carolina, 32, 44, 221
University of South Carolina, 31, 188
University of Virginia, 221–22, 223

Vance, Zebulon B., 32, *36*, 36–37, 38, 237
    elected governor of North Carolina, 36
Van Dorn, Earl, 45, 150
Van Dorn Guard of Texas, *78*
Van Horn, John, 138
Vernon, Ida, 122
Verot, Augustine, 188
Vicksburg Campaign, 4, 28, 59, 80, 143, 150, 159, 182, 210, 212, 254
Vicksburg *Citizen*, 202
Virginia, 19–20, 22, *23*, 24, 25, 27, 28, 30, 37, 42, 45, 50, 53, 55, 59, 61, 80, *100*, *113*, *125*
    and Department of Western Virginia, *76*
    and 8th Virginia Cavalry, *78*
    electoral ticket, *13*
    and 4th Infantry, Stonewall Brigade, *89*
    legislature, 11
    militia, 61
    railroads, 128 ff
    secedes from Union (April 17, 1861), 12
    and 6th Virginia Cavalry, *72*
    and state coat of arms, *88*
    and 13th Virginia Infantry, *78*
    and Virginia Artillery, *104*, *105*
    See also Richmond
Virginia (ship), 22, 107, 144, 145, 152, 156 ff
Virginia No. 2 (ship), 160
Virginia Military Institute, 61, *105*
Virginia, Northern, Army of. *See* Army of Northern Virginia
Volunteer troops, *10–11*

Waddell, James I., 153–54
Wadley, William R., 133, 134
Wailes, B. L. C., 1
Walker, James W., *13*
Walker, Leroy P., *19*, 19
Walker, Lucius M., 45

War Department, Confederate, 13, 19, 20, 107, 108, 113, 114, 133, 161, 206
Warner, Ezra J., 44
Warner, J. H., 161
Warren, Kittrell J., 217
Warrenton, Va., *120*
Washington, Booker T., 239
Washington, Ark., *Telegraph*, 211
Washington College (Va.), 52
Washington, D.C., *8–9*, 10, 19, 44, *150*, *164*, 209
Washington, Ky., 57
Watterson, Henry, 205
Watts, Thomas H., *20*
Wearing of the Gray (Cooke), 217
Weber, Margaret, 169
Weehawken (ship), 153
Wesleyan University, 223–24, 229
West, Department of the, 56, 57
Western and Atlantic Railroad, 128, *141*
Western Department. *See* Department of the West
West, Military Division of the, 53
West Point (United States Military Academy), 13, 43, 48, 52, 53 ff, 106, 108
Wharton, John A., 45
Wheeler, Joseph, 33, 44, *45*, 45
Whig party, 1, 2, 3, 18, 19, 26, 28, 32, 36, 186, 211
White House, Confederate. *See* Confederate White House
Whitney pistol, 98
Whitworths, 12-pounder, *102*, 103
Wigfall, Louis T., 20, 30, 33, 56
Wilcox, Cadmus Marcellus, *67*, 67
Wilderness Campaign, 50, 63
Wilderness-Spotsylvania Campaign (1864), 68
Wiley, Calvin H., 226
Willards Hotel (Wash., D.C.), *8–9*
Williams, Kenneth P., 63
Williams, Samuel C., *13*
Williams, T. Harry, 53
Williamson, Adolphus P., *104*
Williamson, William P., 145, 156
Willington, Aaron S., 211
Wills, George Whitaker, 234–35
Wilmington and Weldon Railroad, 129, 133
Wilson's Creek, battle of, 77
Winder, Charles S., 67, *173*
Winn, David R. E., 69–70, 72, 74, 75–76
Wise, Henry A., 201
Wise, Obadiah J., 201
Woodstock, Va., *70*
Wren, Ella, 122
Wright, A. R., 66, 151

Yale University, 19
    Law School, 35
Yancey, William L., 3, 19, *29*, 29
Yandell, D. W., 58
Yarborough, John B., 222
York, Pa., *75*
Yorktown, Va., 80, *100*
    Baptist Church, *115*

Zionists, 190 ff
Zouaves. *See* Louisiana Zouaves